P9-EAI-519

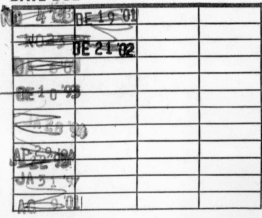

William L. Deegan
Dale Tillery
and Associates

❁❁❁❁❁❁❁❁❁❁❁❁❁❁❁❁❁❁❁❁❁❁❁❁❁❁❁

Foreword by Clark Kerr

Renewing the American Community College

❈❈❈❈❈❈❈❈❈❈❈❈❈❈❈❈❈❈❈❈❈❈❈❈

Priorities and Strategies for Effective Leadership

Jossey-Bass Publishers
San Francisco • London • 1985

RENEWING THE AMERICAN COMMUNITY COLLEGE
Priorities and Strategies for Effective Leadership
by William L. Deegan, Dale Tillery, and Associates

Copyright © 1985 by: Jossey-Bass Inc., Publishers
433 California Street
San Francisco, California 94104

&

Limited
Street
C1Y 8QE

Library of Congress Cataloging-in-Publication Data

Deegan, William L.
  Renewing the American community college.

  (The Jossey-Bass higher education series)
  Includes bibliographies and index.
  1. Community colleges—United States. 2. Leadership.
I. Tillery, Dale. II. Title. III. Series.
LB2328.D37   1985   378'.052   85-45052
ISBN 0-87589-664-2

Manufactured in the United States of America

The paper in this book meets the guidelines for
permanence and durability of the Committee on
Production Guidelines for Book Longevity of the
Council on Library Resources.

JACKET DESIGN BY WILLI BAUM

Published in cooperation with
ERIC Clearinghouse
for Junior Colleges

EDUCATIONAL RESOURCES INFORMATION CENTER

ERIC Clearinghouse For Junior Colleges

UNIVERSITY OF CALIFORNIA, LOS ANGELES

FIRST EDITION

Code 8530

The Jossey-Bass
Higher Education Series

Consulting Editor
Community and Junior Colleges

Arthur M. Cohen
University of California, Los Angeles

Foreword

The two great innovations in higher education in the United States have been the land-grant movement of the nineteenth century and the community college movement of the twentieth. The land-grant colleges introduced training for the productive segments of economic life, initially agriculture and engineering, and the research and services associated with them. It became national policy for higher education to be open to able young persons from all segments of the population. The United States became the most productive nation on earth. The community college movement began the great transformation into a learning society in which each person who wishes to do so can study almost any subject in almost any geographical community. The United States is becoming the nation with the best educated citizens in the world and was the first to offer universal access to postsecondary education.

This new book on the future of the American community college is by any reckoning the best available review of this second great movement, of where it has come from and to where it may be going. The emphasis of the volume is on the word *toward*—on the continuing evolution of the movement as it, once again, confronts a future full of uncertainties. As the authors write about the fifth generation of community colleges, they present a series of possibilities among which selections can and will be made, not a blueprint that must be followed. *Renewing the American Community College* portrays the possible interaction between inexorable constraints and pressures, on the one hand, and the free choices of the many individual actors, on the other, in the unfolding drama whose next act is a secret. What will the constraints and pressures, and even fate, ordain? What will free choice seize upon as most desired within the bounds that confine it? Nobody fully knows—including the authors of this volume. Yet there are all those blank pages of The Future to be written upon. Anyone who wants to help fill in those pages will do well to read and ponder these essays.

These thirteen essays have a remarkable unity about them in their format and line of argument. They actually flow along in a consistent narrative form. Each looks at the past, the present, and the future in an organized way. They even use many of the same basic concepts. Sixteen authors have actually followed a consistent plan! This is a commentary both on the persuasiveness of the editors, Dale Tillery and William L. Deegan, and the common sense and self-discipline of the authors. The readers are the great beneficiaries. The whole clearly adds up to more than the sum of its constituent parts.

I first came to know the community college movement in its third period of great growth—1950 to 1970—and I worked with many of the "builders" of those days. Recently, I have once again had the opportunity, in connection with a study of leadership in American higher education under the auspices of the Association of Governing Boards, to visit a significant number of community colleges, now entering their fifth period. The changes between the two periods are dramatic, even traumatic. The builders are almost all gone; the managers have taken over. Most of them are highly efficient. But a few of the presidents have become primarily survivors; and in the process of surviving, some have become servants to any group or person with power. The clear visions are almost gone. What remains are questions and speculations about new directions on top of the strong base of past accomplishments. The "movement" has fractionated into many differentiated parts. I have even come to think that there is no such thing any longer as *the* community college, but rather a series of groupings of institutions with those at one end of the spectrum having little resemblance to those at the other end. The one thing I wish this volume did to a greater degree is to paint the movement today in its great diversity and to portray the many different paths taken along the way.

These essays have stimulated me to think about some of the elements that may come to help define the fifth generation of community colleges. Each reader will have his or her own list. My list includes the following reflections:

- Several paths are laid out in these essays as alternatives to each other. They may *all* be taken but, to varying degrees and in varying ways by different institutions. *The* movement may become *several* movements. My reaction to the question of which of several directions will be taken is this: all in one place or another, but not everywhere the same.

- Individual institutions may also fractionate within themselves, with one segment going one way and another segment another way. For example, in some places there may come to be (and there is, in fact, already) a *stabilized* section with a unionized, full-time faculty teaching transfer, vocational, remedial, and liberal education courses to a more or less steady clientele and a *catch-as-catch-can* segment following changing demands for advanced technical or life-enhancement or problem-oriented courses with a shifting clientele, a shifting faculty, and a shifting series of locations. The first segment will emphasize guild rules; the second will concentrate on market demands. The first will form its own pressure group; the second will respond to the pressure groups of the surrounding community. I once wrote of the multiversity with its diverse internal communities; and now the same may be said of the multicollege. The Acropolis and the Agora will come to be accommodated within the same city-state—opposite though they are. The tragedy will be if one sector tries to kill off the other, as has already happened occasionally.

• The problems of executive responsibility will intensify— unionized faculty, more heavy handed state controls, more interventions by the courts, more fractionated boards, more pressures from more community groups are the order of today and tomorrow; and on top of that add an institution going in two or more directions at the same time.

• The greatest attribute of the community colleges is their quick adaptability to what the public wants. What will the public want? Higher quality certainly, and particularly in transfer and technical training areas; this is the great theme set forth in this volume for the fifth generation, along with higher productivity. But I suggest these additional themes: more "coping" courses as the process of coping becomes more complex for individuals—coping with health, with finances, with advancing age, and with so much else; more developmental programs to help people (including youth, despite the strictures of K. Patricia Cross to the contrary, for youth sometimes will be given "A Better Chance") with counseling and other supportive services; more cultural and other leisure-time offerings. We have undergone, over the past two decades, the greatest explosion of "rights" in our modern history. One of these rights is education wherever education is felt to be needed. The great demographic depression of the next fifteen years for higher education as a whole will be offset for the community colleges by the continuing explosion of this right.

• Perhaps scholarly research can make a greater contribution to the future of the community college than it has in the past, but the record is a very spotty one. I would count more on what the people want and on what society needs to shape the future than on what the scholars find. The researchers have historically come too late with too little.

• Beyond the fifth generation (1995 is suggested in this volume as its duration) will be a sixth generation as the second great reform movement in American higher education keeps on adapting more quickly and more precisely than any other segment to the requirements of a learning society. That sixth generation may come to justify an identification as "The Learning Society Community College," where attention is given not only to what people individually want but also to what should be offered to them as a matter of carefully thought-out educational policy—what skills are most worth having and what knowledge is most worth knowing.

Berkeley, California   Clark Kerr
August 1985

Preface

American public community colleges are currently in the middle of a period in their evolution when a number of forces are competing to influence their future. Publications such as K. Patricia Cross' "Community Colleges on the Plateau," Cohen and Brawer's *The American Community College,* or Vaughan and Associates' *Issues for Community College Leaders in a New Era* have served to emphasize the importance of this period.* Metaphorically speaking, we might view community colleges as currently occupying a space between two parentheses. The first parenthesis represents the evolution of these institutions through what we call in this book the first four generations of community colleges.

The second parenthesis is yet to be determined, and it is a major purpose of this book to provide both a framework for examining the development of the community college and specific policy and program proposals that can help focus the debate as

*K. Patricia Cross, "Community Colleges on the Plateau," *Journal of Higher Education,* 1981, 52 (2), 113–123; A. M. Cohen and F. B. Brawer, *The American Community College,* San Francisco: Jossey-Bass, 1982; G. B. Vaughan and Associates, *Issues for Community College Leaders in a New Era,* San Francisco: Jossey-Bass, 1983.

community college educators enter the "fifth generation"—a period from the mid 1980s to the mid 1990s.

A number of issues make this a time of great uncertainty, a time when decisions will be made that may have a profound impact on the character and functions of community colleges in the decade ahead. Some issues have been building over time as the community colleges evolved into the fully comprehensive institutions they are today. Other issues have only recently emerged. The issue of the mission and contribution of the community college is clearly a priority concern that has generated much controversy over the past few years. Whether to maintain a comprehensive mission or to eliminate some dimensions is a fundamental question that community college leaders must answer. The problems involved in meeting the growing need for developmental education while continuing to provide quality education for an increasingly diverse student population present other serious challenges. New patterns of student attendance, an aging and "tenured-in" faculty, the need for curriculum reform, and the development of new delivery systems for education are all pressing issues that demand effective responses.

Community college service programs are also in a period of rapid change. Community service programs and the opportunities for linking with other learning environments have led to significant and often spectacular growth. Along with growth has come a whole new set of problems that must be more effectively analyzed for their impact on the fundamental character of the college. In contrast, as student needs, interests, and attendance patterns have changed, student service programs have had to search for a more effective operating rationale.

In addition to these issues of teaching, learning, and service, questions of governance, finance, and the need for more effective and realistic planning present fundamental challenges to community college leaders. The shift in power and authority from local districts to state agencies was a profound change that occurred in the past decade. The impact of this shift on the ability of community college leaders to finance, plan, and govern their own programs is still being assessed, but it is an issue of great consequence for the future of community colleges.

In response to these challenges, their importance, and the immediacy of the need to confront them, this book offers both analyses of the issues and concepts and proposals for action to assist community college leaders in making decisions that will be in the best long-term interests of the colleges.

Plan of This Book

Renewing the American Community College is organized into four parts: The Community College in Perspective; Improving Teaching and Learning; Assessing Programs and Services; and Strengthening Governance, Finance, and Planning. Each part is preceded by a brief introduction.

The two chapters in Part One provide both a framework for examining the growth in community colleges and a context for the rest of the book. Chapter One, by Dale Tillery and William L. Deegan, offers an analysis of the development of community colleges through four generations and of the evolution of significant issues, functions, and problems. In Chapter Two, K. Patricia Cross acknowledges the changes in the mission of the community college and questions whether, as we enter the fifth generation, community colleges can be institutions of both equality and excellence. Together these two chapters provide an analysis of both the past and the present, an analysis that is crucial for making informed judgments about the future.

The three chapters in Part Two cover major aspects of teaching and learning in the community college setting. In Chapter Three, Jonathan Warren draws on current data to examine the characteristics of community college students—their backgrounds, abilities, needs, and aspirations. He sees community college students as primary participants in a major change in American higher education—the extension of higher education to all segments of American society. Chapter Four, by Chester H. Case, examines the role of the community college faculty member from the perspective of four central issues: the work of teaching, the career of teaching, rewards and incentives, and the teacher's involvement in the community college as an organization. He concludes the chapter with an examination of alternative futures for the professional life of the community college faculty member. Richard A. Donovan deals with the complex issue of developmental education in Chapter Five. Donovan reviews the prominent trends that have emerged in developmental education and concludes with an exploration of the effects of technology, new patterns of collaboration, staff development, and other new developments.

The changes and developments in the service programs of community colleges are the focus of Part Three. In Chapter Six, Jane E. Matson and William L. Deegan review the evolution of student service programs and the theoretical foundation and basic assumptions that have guided these services through four generations. They also discuss a number of alternative strategies for community college administrators to consider as they analyze the future of student service programs. In Chapter Seven, Joseph N. Hankin and Philip A. Fey review the emergence of community services and the philosophy that has contributed to the growing emphasis given to community services in community colleges across the country. While citing the tremendous opportunities ahead, they warn that a careful examination of community service programs must take account of the harsh realities of institutional mission and resource allocation. Chapter Eight, by Marvin J. Feldman, follows with an analysis of the increasing connections between community colleges and other educational providers. He sees both promise and peril in these increased linkages and cautions that the question of whether these connections will lead to more effective education or to a loss of values may become the central issue in the fifth generation.

The issues of governance, relations with government at all levels, financial control, and planning are the focus of Part Four. In Chapter Nine, Richard L. Alfred and David F. Smydra analyze the evolution of community college governance and the changing roles of key participants in the governance process. They conclude with a summary of six key issues that must be confronted in the coming decade, and they offer proposals for confronting these issues. S. V. Martorana and Eileen Kuhns trace the development of relations between community colleges and federal, state, and local government in Chapter Ten. The final section of this chapter proposes a new framework for viewing the relationship between government and the community college—a framework that places community colleges within the context of a "communiversity." In Chapter Eleven, James L. Wattenbarger discusses the changes that have occurred in community college finance in the first four generations. He concludes his analysis by proposing a set of guidelines for community college leaders and government representatives to consider as they develop plans for financing community colleges in the future. In Chapter Twelve, Richard C. Richardson, Jr., and William R. Rhodes discuss the need for more effective planning in the face of the challenging demands for both increased quality and fiscal constraint. They conclude by presenting an analysis of the differences between the management and leadership needs of community colleges and offer a conceptual framework and criteria to guide strategic planning in the decade ahead. In Chapter Thirteen, William L. Deegan, Dale Tillery, and Rudy J. Melone propose an agenda for action that we hope will serve as a catalyst for funding agencies and policymakers as they consider priorities for the fifth generation.

Although no single model can be appropriate for all public community colleges in America, we hope the perspectives on the evolution of the community college, the analyses, proposals, and scenarios presented by each contributing author, and the agenda for action will provide federal, state, and campus policy makers with a broad conceptualization of what community colleges have been and are and with specific proposals to facilitate the important choices that must be made in determining what community colleges will become.

Acknowledgments

We would like to thank a number of people who contributed to the completion of the book. The willingness of the contributing authors to conform to guidelines and to make revisions through several drafts is deeply appreciated.

In addition, Mary Versteck and Dorothy Miller of the Center for Community Colleges at Teachers College, Columbia University, and Donna Santo of the Borough of Manhattan Community

College contributed significantly to the revisions and production of the final manuscript.

Finally, the staff of the Word Processing Center and Nita Camp and Hope White-Davis of the Department of Higher and Adult Education at Teachers College, Columbia University, served beyond the call of duty to help us through the many changes on the way to the completed manuscript.

August 1985   William L. Deegan
                                                   Tallahassee, Florida

                                                   Dale Tillery
                                                   Berkeley, California

Contents

✥✥✥✥✥✥✥✥✥✥✥✥✥✥✥✥✥✥✥✥✥✥✥✥✥✥✥

xix

Contents

The Authors

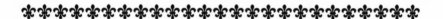

William L. Deegan received his B.S. degree in business administration from the University of Buffalo (1965), his M.A. degree in educational psychology from Ohio State University (1966), and his Ed.D. degree in higher education from the University of California, Berkeley (1969). He is the author of a number of journal articles and monographs dealing with management issues in higher education, and he has been a guest lecturer and consultant at colleges and universities in the United States and England.

Deegan's recent publications include *Ensuring Effective Governance* (1985), *Translating Theory into Practice: Implications of Japanese Management Theory for Student Personnel Administration* (1985), and *The Management of Student Affairs Programs in Community Colleges: Revamping Processes and Structures* (1982). His most recent project is a study of the management of contract training programs in community colleges. Deegan has served on the research staff of the Center for the Study of Higher Education at the University of California, Berkeley; as a faculty member at Teachers College, Columbia University in New York City; and as a consultant to a number of task forces and commissions. He is currently associate professor of higher education and director of the Community College Instructors Program at Florida State University in Tallahassee, Florida.

Dale Tillery, professor emeritus at the University of California, Berkeley, was educated at the University of Chicago with an A.B. degree in economics (1941) and at the University of California where he received an M.A. degree in psychology (1949) and the Ph.D. degree in higher education (1964). Following his undergraduate study, he served as a naval aviator before returning for graduate work. While at the University of California, Tillery served as dean of the School of Education, director of the Center for Research and Development in Higher Education, and director of several programs to prepare leaders for higher education.

Tillery has written extensively on the community college and student decisions about education and career. For the Carnegie Commission on Higher Education he authored *Breaking the Access Barriers* (with Leland L. Medsker, 1971), and he was the primary author of the Commission's policy statement on community colleges, *The Open Door College* (1971). During the mid 1960s he directed a massive longitudinal study of student decisions and outcomes from grade nine through the first year of college or other postsecondary experiences. In addition to annual reports to schools and colleges, he authored *Distribution and Differentiation of Youth* (1973) and *Educational Goals, Attitudes and Behaviors* (with Ted Kildegaard, 1973).

Tillery has served as a consultant on higher education to many institutions, state bodies, and industries in the United States and other countries. In 1973 he served as an American delegate to the Conference on the Future Structures of Postsecondary Education sponsored by the Organization for Economic Cooperation and Development. In 1983 he was honored by his peers with the Distinguished Service Award from the Council of Universities and Colleges for contributions to community college development. He now serves as chief consultant to a four-year project to improve planning and learner outcome evaluation in California and Hawaii, funded primarily by the Fund for the Improvement of Postsecondary Education.

Richard L. Alfred is associate professor of higher education and program chairman for higher and adult education at the University of Michigan in Ann Arbor.

Chester H. Case is president of Los Medanos College in Pittsburgh, California.

K. Patricia Cross is chairperson for administration, planning, and social policy at the Graduate School of Education, Harvard University.

Richard A. Donovan is professor of English and director of networks at Bronx Community College in New York.

Marvin J. Feldman is president of the Fashion Institute of Technology in New York City and president of the Association of Presidents of Public Community Colleges.

Philip A. Fey is director of the Office of Continuing Professional Education and an associate professor (adjunct) in the Department of Higher and Adult Education, Teachers College, Columbia University.

Joseph N. Hankin is president of Westchester Community College in Valhalla, New York, and an associate professor (adjunct) in the Department of Higher and Adult Education, Teachers College, Columbia University.

Eileen Kuhns is an associate professor and director of administration programs, School of Education, Catholic University of America.

S. V. Martorana is a professor in the College of Education and a research associate at the Center for the Study of Higher Education, Pennsylvania State University.

Jane E. Matson is professor emeritus at California State University in Los Angeles.

Rudy J. Melone is president of Gavilan College in Gilroy, California.

William R. Rhodes is a postdoctoral associate with the Department of Higher and Adult Education at Arizona State University in Tempe.

Richard C. Richardson, Jr., is professor of higher education at Arizona State University in Tempe.

David F. Smydra is vice-president of New Detroit Incorporated in Detroit, Michigan.

Jonathan Warren is a private consultant in Berkeley, California.

James L. Wattenbarger is a professor and director of the Institute of Higher Education, University of Florida.

Renewing
the American
Community College

❖❖❖❖❖❖❖❖❖❖❖❖❖❖❖❖❖❖❖❖❖❖❖❖

Part One

The Community College
in Perspective

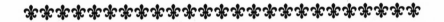

Community colleges have experienced tremendous growth in their first four generations. This growth has occurred not only in the numbers of students and colleges but also in the missions and the role of community colleges in American society. The two chapters in Part One provide a framework for examining that growth and a context for the rest of the book. Chapter One offers a conceptualization and analysis of how community colleges have developed through four generations and how significant issues, functions, and problems have changed within and between generations. The concept of community college generations is used not as an absolute but rather as a way to denote periods or stages during which major events occurred that helped shape and propel the community college movement. Too often community colleges have been subject to misunderstanding about how they developed and about their mission, structure, clientele, and programs. Chapter One presents a comprehensive analysis of the evolution of these issues—an analysis that should be of great use to readers as they consider the concepts and proposals presented in other chapters.

In Chapter Two, K. Patricia Cross acknowledges the evolution of the community college mission and questions whether community colleges can be institutions of both equality and excellence in the fifth generation. Cross first offers an analysis of the mission debate, which currently is the focus of much attention, and then proposes major choices for community college educators to consider as a broad background for the more specific functions and issues discussed in succeeding chapters of the book. Together, these two chapters in Part One constitute an analysis of both the past and the present—an analysis that is crucial for making informed judgments about the future.

Dale Tillery
William L. Deegan

1

The Evolution of Two-Year Colleges Through Four Generations

This chapter offers a brief historical framework to assist readers in interpreting what has happened to the public two-year college since its beginning and in making projections about its near-term future. Making predictions about the future of educational institutions without understanding changes in their character over time is particularly hazardous; thus, some historical insight is essential to the discussion at hand.

The beginnings of this uniquely American institution were humble. There were even doubts about its survival. However, there were three influences that vouchsafed its development, if not its transformation into something quite different from the early junior college. First was the rapid industrialization of the United States and the mechanization of its agriculture, both leading to increasing demands for trained men and women. A second influence was the democratization of public school education, which led to increasing completion rates from high schools. At the same time, federal policies encouraged the growth of postsecondary education that was pragmatic, affordable, and in proximity to the people. Finally, there was the emergence of the American research universities. Several great university presidents encouraged the creation of the first junior colleges.

A Framework of Four Generations

The institution's four developmental periods, or generations, as we prefer to call them, were:

Generation 1: Extension of High School (1900–1930)
Generation 2: Junior College (1930–1950)
Generation 3: Community College (1950–1970)
Generation 4: Comprehensive Community College (1970–mid 1980s)

In fundamental ways, the four generations differed markedly. Thus, we of the fifth generation view the community college as a still emerging institution. The logic of social adaptation helps explain some of the changes that occurred in the first four generations and suggests directions for the fifth generation. Less deterministic influences were also factors in the transformation of the colleges from a few scattered extensions of the public schools into a national movement of postsecondary opportunity for youth and mature adults. Today, nearly 1,000 public community colleges serve the world's widest diversity of students and account for over one-third of the enrollments in contemporary American higher education. Each of the generations was influenced by state and national leaders who interpreted or advocated roles and missions for the institution and who guided the development of new colleges. They are part of the story of the four generations.

Contemporary community colleges are something quite different from the unfolding or fulfilling of the first high school prototypes. There was metamorphosis: Changes were rapid and were influenced by other models and ideologies of education. Propensity for change in the community college resulted primarily from: (1) a lack of certain academic traditions during its formative years; (2) the diversity of local communities that nurtured the colleges; and (3) the effectiveness of local, state, and national advocates in shaping a new institution. Over the generations, the philosophy and mission of many community colleges became increasingly equalitarian and utopian, guiding newly established colleges to respond quickly to the economic and social trends of society. In doing so, the colleges cut themselves free from many of the traditions and constraints of other segments of education. The outcomes of this independence are now widely debated. Aspects of these developments have been analyzed by Breneman and Nelson (1981) in their economic perspective on the community college. In our section on Generation 4, we will take issue with some of the strategic choices these authors propose for the coming generation of community colleges.

Generation 1: Extension of High School (1900 to 1930)

William Rainey Harper is credited with the first recorded use of the name, when he called the lower division of the new University of Chicago a junior college. More importantly, he and other leading university presidents in Michigan, Minnesota, and California urged high schools to offer more than a few postgraduate courses. They envisioned the formation of junior colleges not only to free the universities for advanced study but also to encourage broader postsecondary education for the people. These ideas fell on very fertile ground created by social demands and by federal policies for more and "useful" education beyond high school. The most dramatic development of the time was the collaboration between the federal government and the states in the land grant movement, which greatly expanded higher education and influenced what was to be taught in its institutions. Although his words were cast in what is now viewed as elitist language, Harper anticipated the large number of students who would neither seek nor be encouraged to pursue the B.A. degree: "students not really fitted by nature could stop naturally and honorably at the end of the sophomore year" (1900, p. 37).

The primary factor in the increased demand for and expansion of higher education was the increase in completion rates from the secondary schools. So as early as the late 1880s, the increasing attendance at and graduation from American high schools resulted in new demands for higher education that could not, or would not, be met by existing colleges and universities. Slowly, the high schools began to offer postsecondary courses. At first, these courses were offered to remediate gaps in academic preparation or to raise grade point averages that were too low for college matriculation. Soon, additional lower-division courses were added to the curriculum. It is often forgotten, however, that the first state legislation authorizing local high schools to provide college work, the Caminetti Act of 1907 in California, permitted them to offer certain postsecondary vocational courses as well.

The first continuously operating junior college was established in Joliet, Illinois in 1901. A decade later, the school board of Fresno, California, established a two-year college program. For the state that became the model for junior college development, it was another seven years before even a score of school districts followed the Fresno example. It is likely that this slow beginning, particularly outside the West, was related to the expansion of land-grant universities and private liberal arts colleges.

Organization. The colleges of this early period were clearly extensions of high schools. Existing school facilities were used, and teachers continued to teach in very much the same way that they taught high school courses. Local school boards had residual authority under various state patterns of legislative and administrative law. In most communities, the same board served both high school and college. As with the public schools, state boards of education had a great deal of control over junior college mission, teacher certification, and curriculum. Internally, management and supervision were the responsibility of administrators who carried on the traditions of school principals. Thus, there was little role for teachers in decision making, and they shared few of the traditions and prerogatives of higher education. Finally, funding formulas were generally similar to those of the high schools, but in some states oil revenues from the public domain were allocated to the junior colleges.

Purposes, Programs, and Students. Access for students who were neither fully prepared nor, perhaps, ready or able to leave home was clearly part of the mission of the early junior colleges. Although the idea became fashionable in Generation 3, there was early awareness that the high school extension colleges were serving new students to higher education. Remediation was as much a function of the early colleges as it was during later periods of great growth in postsecondary education. Many of those who stayed in school as postgraduates did so to make up deficiencies or to improve skills in writing and mathematics. Increasingly, however, junior college student bodies became representative of high school graduates. Thus, there were many students who needed vocational instruction, as well as those who planned to transfer to senior colleges and universities. At the time, the mean age was still in the early twenties, but this was to rise sharply over the next generations.

Early legislation reflected state interest in the role of the emerging colleges. Furthermore, the groundwork was laid for the comprehensive college when legislatures authorized civic, liberal arts, scientific, and technical courses of instruction (Callan, 1983).

We have already noted the influence of the universities in founding the junior colleges, but they also had direct influences on courses of study, teaching, and grading. The idea that courses for university transfer should be parallel in content, teaching, and texts died slowly in the colleges. At the time, universities had powerful controls in their acceptance of transfer credit; in some cases they actually served as accrediting bodies.

Counseling and student support services, which gained near parity in importance with instruction in the third generation, was a very modest function in the beginning. Little attention was given to career guidance and financial aid, and educational counseling essentially consisted of relaying information about transfer requirements. It should be noted, however, that high schools, at the time, were small and rather intimate places. Some students had close and helpful relations with teachers as they made choices about education. The days of concerns about affirmative action, psychological counseling, and financial aid were yet to come.

Relations with Others. The junior colleges' relations with other institutions were much less complex and coordinated than in later generations. The colleges were part of the schools, so articulation downward was not a major issue. As we have noted, school boards made policy for both school and college, and both were managed by a common cadre of administrators. Tensions did begin to rise, however, as the colleges sought to establish their own identities and to gain recognition in higher education. Only slowly did state legislatures and departments of education recognize differences between schools and junior colleges in matters of finance, governance, and facilities. Finally, very little was done to nurture relations with business and labor in order to better serve those students who were preparing for early employment or to take some education to the workplace.

Generation 1 was a period of modest and hesitant development for the public two-year colleges. However, crucial foundations for the future were established. The idea of the intermediate college was conceived by some of America's greatest educators; communities and states recognized the growing demand for access to higher education; and community services, so dear to the fourth generation, found their roots in the traditions of the community schools. Leonard V. Koos not only told the story of these beginnings in *The Junior College Movement* (1925) but was one of the most influential builders of the next generation.

Generation 2: The Junior College (1930 to 1950)

The Great Depression affected the junior colleges in several ways. Perhaps the most important consequence was the reduction of state funding, even though enrollments continued to grow. California was still the state to watch, but there were major junior college developments in Michigan, Illinois, and Texas. In the first decade of this period, enrollments in California almost doubled, and by 1936 the state had forty-two junior colleges. Wherever the opportunities were available, youth and adults took advantage of occupational retraining at local junior colleges, while others prepared for new careers as the nation slowly began to recover. Nevertheless, the Depression and war years resulted in a near moratorium on the founding of new colleges. Those that were established, however, continued to grow both in enrollments and in importance. Generation 2 began with 259 public two-year colleges and closed with 299.

Walter C. Eells' 1931 book, *The Junior College,* was useful in establishing an institutional paradigm that could be used by states and local communities for establishing new colleges with instant missions and myths. Equally important in shaping a national movement were the professional and lobbying services of the American Association of Junior Colleges in the nation's capital. The junior colleges, like the rest of higher education, responded to increasing demands for education beyond high school by graduates and mature adults, particularly the thousands of returning veterans. The resulting expansion and competition in postsecondary education led, among other things, to state higher education commissions, which influenced the development of junior colleges in relation to other segments of education. They often clarified state interests in the junior college mission. One of these commissions (Strayer, 1948) gave particular attention to the goals and objectives of junior colleges. The goals Eells had advocated were now stated as social policy in California. Perhaps for the first time, the goal of equal opportunity for postsecondary education for mature adults as well as for younger students was affirmed. Now the mission, which became doctrine for the public two-year colleges, was defined as: (1) terminal education, (2) general education, (3) transfer and career orientation and guidance, (4) lower-division preparation for university transfer, (5) adult education, and (6) removal of matriculation deficiencies. It must be noted, however, that not only did the language and definition of these objectives change over time, but so did their relative priority in institutional mission and practice.

Organization. Although the junior colleges moved toward the collegiate model of governance, they emerged as something unique, primarily as a result of their fervor for local control. Junior college boards of trustees were established in one of several patterns. Most commonly, these boards were elected by citizens in legally defined communities (districts). In a few states, the trustees were appointed by local or state governments. And in New York, for example, the junior colleges were the responsibility of other locally elected governing agencies. The common—but not universal—authority of these boards to levy local taxes and the high proportion of funding under their control gave considerable authority to many boards of trustees. Under state laws and generally benign supervision by state education departments, the trustees could build colleges, employ and dismiss faculty and other personnel, approve programs, and set standards and policies to promote access and quality of instruction. Local control became the cornerstone of junior/community college governance, even when compromised by increasing state authority.

The majority of faculty members during this period were still former high school teachers, but there is evidence that their university peers were becoming their primary reference group (Medsker, 1960). Many characteristics of junior college teachers did not fit the university model. In particular, they were more inclined to be members of unions; they did not take part in or advocate peer review; and they had little opportunity for professional development. These differences were not greatly modified in later generations, even when the colleges were defined as a major segment of higher education.

Near the close of Generation 2, junior college budgets are estimated to have reached $30 million. Although other financial arrangements were in place in several states, California still had considerable influence on junior college funding legislation. That state's 1947 budget for junior colleges totalled $16 million: "Of this amount, 23 percent was from State funding, 30 percent from the federal government, and 47 percent from local tax sources. In the same year the Legislature established the foundation program as the basis for financing junior colleges. This mechanism provided a guaranteed state-funded base, established computation tax rates as guidelines for local governing boards taxing authority, and provided State equalization funding to remove differences in district assessed valuations" (Callan, 1983, p. 3).

These and similar arrangements lasted well into Generation 4, providing a relative stability of financing, which is no longer characteristic of finance in any segment of public education in the United States. It should be noted that federal financial support has been inconstant over the generations but did become very important in the next period of community college development.

As Generation 2 ended, modern new junior college facilities were being built and whole new campuses designed. For the first time, faculty members were involved substantially in setting the educational specifications for classrooms, laboratories, and shops.

Purposes, Programs, and Students. General education took on new importance as a function of the junior colleges, as did student services and guidance. Other cornerstones of the future were set as the colleges competed with the high schools for the education of adults and began to take over much vocational education. In some parts of the country, these developments were negotiated with the secondary schools, which were becoming increasingly academic in mission. This broadening of junior college programs and services was stimulated by faith in a second chance for youth and adults. With increased numbers of first-in-the-family sons and daughters to participate in higher education, junior college student bodies became more representative of the eighteen-to-twenty-one-year-old populations of their communities.

The colleges were responsive to these new college goers, but in some junior colleges the fit between students and program priorities was questionable. Whereas at least two-thirds of the faculty workload was in transfer education, a much lower proportion of entering students transferred to senior institutions. A 1937 study of students entering junior colleges shows that 75 percent did not continue beyond the sophomore year (Eells, 1941). These students were referred to as terminal in Generation 2. However, Eells' and subsequent studies of transfer rates must be read as minimal estimates in view of the "stop-out" patterns of college going, which began early in the junior colleges (Tillery, 1970). The increasing access to higher education affected both the nature of two-year college programs and transfer rates. These trends continue in the 1980s and contribute to increasing misunderstanding of the role and mission of the community colleges.

Relations with Others. Although junior colleges improved their articulation with the senior institutions in order to facilitate student transfer, liaison with the high schools weakened as the colleges broke away from the public schools. Tensions and neglect in school-college relations were not universal, but they were widespread enough to cause problems for both institutions. Some high school teachers and counselors had reservations about the open door and a second chance for previously unsuccessful students. Perhaps more serious were the rare efforts to coordinate school and college courses of study, particularly for occupational students. Later generations of educators came to regret this mutual neglect and made efforts to improve relations.

Junior colleges received increasing support from the federal government and from the several states during this period. The colleges were seen as good investments and safeguards against overexpansion of universities. The colleges' professional associations were very successful in making the case for preparing people in their own communities for gainful employment and for opening up new opportunities for working and underprivileged youth and mature adults. We have already noted that these healthy relations with government were reflected in stable and adequate funding patterns in many states.

Both business and labor were increasingly conscious of the junior colleges, and new linkages began to emerge. One of the most important developments of this period was the establishment of labor-management advisory committees for many occupational and technical programs. These groups remained a lasting bridge to the private sector over the years. With industry, early efforts were made to define appropriate levels of paraprofessional/technical education for junior colleges. These overtures did not bear fruit until the next generation. However, there was growth in business courses and programs, and much more attention was given to career guidance and placement.

Generation 3: The Community College (1950 to 1970)

"The most striking recent structural development in higher education has been the phenomenal growth of the community college" (Carnegie Commission on Higher Education, 1970, p. 3). This assessment at the close of the third generation indicates the scope and importance of twenty years of growth and transformation of the American two-year college. The leap from one-half million to two million students was unparalleled, as was the spread of colleges across the country.

Organization. During this third period, as today, most community colleges were governed by trustees of local districts, which in many places were expanded into multi-unit institutions. In a few states, such as Hawaii, the community colleges were established as segments of the state university. Another pattern, notably in Florida, was a much more centralized state system with appointed boards. In most states, the community colleges were redefined as a part of higher education, and they became essential segments of state systems of postsecondary education.

Governance of community colleges in Generation 3 became more complex: Many districts became multi-unit, faculty made increased demands for formal roles in decision making, and state agencies exerted new influences in legislative and coordination affairs. The political model of governance was, and remains, dominant; and organized constituency groups engaged in vigorous lobbying of legislatures and state agencies. Faculty groups were particularly successful in such activities, and many states established some form of "meet and confer" legislation to bring faculty viewpoints to bear on trustee deliberations. In addition, faculty senates began to play important roles in academic affairs.

Although faculty members generally identified themselves with colleagues in the universities, they increasingly committed themselves to the open-door mission of the community college. They designed new courses and programs in technical, paraprofessional, cooperative, and remedial education. They sought ways of responding to the special needs of mature adults and minority students.

Funding patterns during this period remained stable, with adjustments for growth and inflation. By now, the several state patterns of financing community colleges were well established, and there was increased federal support, primarily in the form of student financial aid and capital funding. It is not an overstatement to say that Generation 3 was the golden age of financial support for community colleges. Financial well-being was visible in colleges that were the pride of local communities. Although the building of new colleges continued into the next generation, it did so at a more modest pace.

Purposes, Programs, and Students. So much attention has been given to the growth of the community college that the meaning of its transformation from the junior college has not been well understood. Rarely is a community college an overgrown junior college. The community colleges look different; they have different personnel and students; their leaders play different roles; and their mission, while cast in the language of the late junior college, takes on different priorities. Both community college and university leaders studied the public two-year colleges. However, most studies laid the groundwork for advocating expansion or broader missions for community colleges. The influence of spokespersons for the public two-year college became particularly significant during the third generation. Cross (1971) observed that no other educational institution has been so shaped and promoted by so few leaders as has the community college. But other voices were also heard that questioned and were critical. They anticipated the current decade of criticism by practioners and scholars alike. This change in the literature is apparent in Vaughan's *Questioning the Community College Role* (1980).

A few writers made notable contributions to understanding the evolving community college and to proposals for its reform. Two men, in particular, brought to their research and teaching at major universities years of distinguished experience in junior colleges. The writings of Leland L. Medsker (1960) and B. Lamar Johnson (1952) were remarkably influential during this period of expansion. However, they were not without concern for the institution they were helping to build. In his conclusion to *The Junior College: Progress And Prospects,* Medsker wrote: "It will soon be a hundred years since the two-year college was conceived. There were realistic expectations that have been fulfilled, and there were also overexpectations. The next ten years will sharpen and identify whatever role it is to have in the future" (1960, p. 319). These leaders did not anticipate the identity crisis of the next generation of community colleges.

Clark Kerr, as chairman of the Carnegie Commission for Higher Education, gave special attention to issues related to the future of community colleges. One of the most widely used policy statements of the commission was *The Open Door Colleges* (1970). It recognized the important role of community colleges in articulated state systems of higher education, the need for increased federal support, and the call for expansion of community colleges in order to ensure equal access to higher education for all. The model of state systems that gave such new importance to community colleges in higher education, *A General Pattern for American Higher Education,* was the work of T. R. McConnell, 1962.

Relations With Others. During the third generation, community colleges were finally separated from the public schools, sometimes by mandatory state legislation. Now, with their own campuses and governance structures, they identified even more strongly with higher education. This contributed to further loss of liaison with the public schools. However, coordination with the other segments of higher education was at its best. Noteworthy achievements were articulation agreements, interfaculty communication, and assured openings in senior institutions for community college transfer students. It was a period of breaking barriers to access for a majority of Americans (Medsker and Tillery, 1971).

In spite of the belief that coordinated systems of postsecondary education contributed to greater equity in educational opportunity, there were early warnings of possible counteroutcomes as a result of channelling "high-risk" students into community colleges. Many of these students were from ethnic minority and other underrepresented groups. In particular, the "cooling out function" and the practice of tracking students with different abilities into state systems of higher education were viewed by some sociologists as contributing to social stratification rather than to the reduction of barriers to equal opportunity. In *The Open Door College,* Burton Clark succinctly describes the cooling out process: "The latent terminal student is allowed into transfer curriculum but encounters counseling and testing that invite him to consider alternatives, subtle pressures to hedge his bet by taking courses that serve a terminal destiny, tough talk in orientation classes about realistic occupational choices, probationary status, perhaps, and finally grades that will not allow transferring" (1960, p. 163).

This was, indeed, common practice in the community colleges of Generation 3. Few community college leaders viewed occupational and technical careers as "terminal destinies"; they did, however, believe that unrealistic student aspiration was a major factor in the low persistence of students with unsuccessful academic preparation from high school. Thus, while trying to help students find programs of study that would lead to achievement of their educational and career goals, community colleges sought to protect the standards and quality of their own courses, programs, and instruction. At the time Clark was doing his case study, most of the colleges affirmed that they were open institutions but that specific courses and programs were not open to unprepared students. This view of the open door began to break down under social pressure for equality of opportunity. In contrast to Karabel (1972) and other social critics, we view the major threat to equality of opportunity in higher education to be flaws in articulation within state systems. For many students, full educational development requires opportunities to move within coordinated systems of institutions over time, place, and purpose.

The year 1970 was one of great confidence in the community colleges. Their campuses were among the best in the land, and as community centers they served a large segment of the public. The faculty and administrators were well educated, and many of their leaders were graduates of major university leadership programs. Federal policies and groups, such as the Carnegie Commission for Higher Education, encouraged continued but disciplined expansion. There are those who believe, however, that the claims and public rhetoric of the community colleges of this period exceeded their achievements.

Generation 4: The Comprehensive Community College (1970 to the mid 1980s)

There were trends in community college affairs during this generation that (1) were never fully realized, (2) added to confusion about the mission of the colleges, and finally (3) led to reform as the colleges entered their fifth generation. Thus, an ideology about the role of the community college is emerging in the 1980s that arouses state and university leaders to charge the community colleges with neglect of their traditional responsibilities in favor of what might best be called community education. It is not just national advocates who seek to shape the new ideology. In fact, certain policies and practices of many community colleges have contributed to the identity crisis. However, as in all periods, individual colleges are not as much alike as the literature, including this book, might suggest. Some leaders and colleges, for example, responded enthusiastically to the call by the president of the American Association of Community Colleges to define the role of the institution as the shaping of society (Gleazer, 1969), but others did not.

It was difficult to adopt an appropriate name for a period that ended with confusion about the community college's mission. We considered using Gleazer's phrase, the "community's college" or our "community learning center" to designate the institutions of this period. However, we believe a less expansive designation is more realistic, thus the "comprehensive community college."

Organization. Governance of colleges and their state systems, their funding, and their structure were preeminent domains of change in this period. Community colleges not only continued to grow in number and size, but they were organized into larger districts and subsystems. This was particularly true in urban areas, which had the majority of enrollments. By the late 1970s, over 75 percent of total community college enrollments were in colleges with 4,000 or fewer students, and almost a third had fewer than 1,000 students. One of the objectives of multi-unit districts was to keep the size of individual campuses relatively small. There was, however, great diversity in institutional size, with most large colleges concentrated in California, Florida, Michigan, Texas, and New York. Small colleges were found predominantly in those states with the lowest percentage of total undergraduates in the public two-year colleges. Although the pace of building new colleges slowed down, the number exceeded that recommended by the Carnegie Commission in 1970. Enrollments doubled during this generation.

Collective bargaining laws were passed in many states, and a majority of faculties in those states elected to organize. Over time, the contract became an acceptable way of responding to faculty interests in the welfare of their institutions and participation in their governance. In spite of pressures to broaden the scope of bargaining, unions have not seriously encroached on the role of faculty senates in academic affairs; contrary to earlier predictions, the senates appear to be more influential today than they were at the beginning of Generation 4. While concerns about the encroachment of unions on prerogatives of trustees and management have diminished, tensions remain. We do not yet know whether collective bargaining has compromised the leadership role of chief executive officers. There are those who believe that their options have been reduced, while others believe that they now have greater freedom to influence the external environments that interface with their colleges. Like their university peers, they are much less involved in internal academic affairs than were their predecessors (Kerr, 1984). Finally, many campus presidents of multi-unit districts report that they are free from some problems that are now resolved at the district bargaining table.

The context of system governance in the several states has changed as community college constituency groups have become formally organized. Lobbying by faculty groups has proven to be particularly effective as, like trustees and administrators, they have sought to influence legislatures and state governing agencies. Such activities resulted, in part, from funding instability near the close of the fourth generation as a consequence of tax reforms and economic stringency. These factors also exacerbated dilemmas about governance of state systems. In those states with long traditions of local control, conflicts about how systems of community colleges are to be governed were most severe (Tillery and Wattenbarger, 1985). Tensions mounted "in most states between those who [sought] to maintain local control over pay scales, course offerings, and enrollment guidelines and those who advocate[d] growing regulation of these matters by the state" (Breneman and Nelson, 1981, p. 38).

These and related topics will be carefully analyzed in later chapters, but it is germane to note here that governance and finance involve fundamental issues of social policy: equity, efficiency, and educational mission. "The tension between the mission and finance of community colleges reflects many of the fundamental problems of today's economy: the facts of scarcity, the need for trade-off, the limits of government, the costs of inefficiencies, and the conflicts between the haves and have-nots when the economic pie is not growing" (Breneman and Nelson, 1981, p. 39). We conclude that there is no ideal model for financing community colleges because of the dissimilarities among the states and perhaps among colleges within states. However, study of this diversity should help us understand how the several state patterns "impact on governance, incentives, performance, costs, and responsiveness to local needs" (Breneman and Nelson, 1981, p. 37). These issues are legitimate concerns of both state governments and local governing boards. Primary challenges for Generation 5 will include delineating roles in resolving the mission dilemma of community colleges, evaluating the quality and outcomes of their programs, and planning for the future. It is unlikely that public accountability can be achieved without such coordination.

Generation 4 opened with generally stable financing of the comprehensive community colleges and with new state and federal financial aid programs for students. It ended amid taxpayer revolts in the several states and reductions in federal support. As a result, all but a few colleges have suffered enrollment losses or have reached plateaus in growth. Economic stringency, changing demography, and competition from other suppliers of education have stimulated new approaches to strategic planning by many community colleges (McIntyre, Swenson, and Tillery, 1983).

Purposes, Programs, and Students. Challenges to contemporary public two-year colleges are directed at their fundamental beliefs and practices: open access, the scope (comprehensiveness) of their programs, and recurring education for adults.

The open-door concept has always been illusive, but until the late 1960s and 1970s it meant: "To be successful the colleges should maintain a balance between their efforts to attract new students and their capacity for placement, instruction, and curriculum development" (Cohen and Associates, 1975, p. 160). Open access was transformed in the fourth generation as a result of "efforts to seek, recruit, enroll, and retain every possible student in the community" (Roueche, Baker, and Brownell, 1971, p. 11). Soon it was influenced by a major shift in social values—the belief that students had the right to fail. Thus, the doors were open not just to colleges as opportunities for achievement but also to courses and programs for which students might not yet be qualified. In its most radical manifestation, "opportunity" often meant first come, first served. In practice, unprepared students might have access to courses, but some students who were prepared might not.

Fortunately, there was no universality in this shift in values, although these practices were widespread. As the period closed, the colleges were in hasty retreat from such heresy. Substantial efforts were being made to (1) assess student readiness to learn; (2) guide students in course and program selection; and (3) measure learning outcomes.

Comprehensiveness of community college programs has also been misunderstood, and its relevance to state interests has been debated in state legislatures and governing agencies. So much has been written about the generally accepted purposes of the community college that we hesitate to get caught in the litany again. Suffice it to say that comprehensiveness of program and services means more than the sum of the parts and certainly more than a potpourri of courses and services. The comprehensive program must be rationally planned, coordinated, and renewed. This is essential if students are to make sound decisions about educational and career goals through classroom and guidance experiences. The essential concept is that students are able to change objectives—if they choose and are so prepared—without having to drop out of one institution and then seek admission to another. Comprehensive program and services make it possible to design individual programs for the diverse students in contemporary community colleges.

During the fourth generation, community colleges did expand their markets with courses and programs that were viewed as nontraditional in reference to clientele, location, and delivery of instruction. The scope and style of these developments were quite individualistic and were greatly influenced by the special characteristics of the communities being served. The new markets were essentially defined by special groups: handicapped persons, recent immigrants, reentry women, and other underrepresented groups. Colleges also differed in designating such courses as credit or noncredit and as to fees charged, if any. Courses for these new students helped maintain enrollments in a period of declining numbers of college-aged youth. We view many of these activities as extensions of earlier community service rather than as responses to the call for a new mission for community colleges.

Community development has not, in fact, become a new mission for the comprehensive community colleges. Few colleges have made serious efforts in community development, and some that have tried have failed. In suggesting that this goal may be an "impossible dream," Cohen makes the following observation: "Except for a few isolated cases, the community dimension of the community college is narrow, inchoate, and removed from the mainstream of college operations. And it enjoys the dubious distinction of being the function least coherently defined, least amenable to assessment" (Cohen and Associates, 1975, pp. 82–83). Although community services fall under various administrative units, few colleges in 1970 were even organized to do much about it. At that time, 70 percent of the community colleges had less than one full-time-equivalent administrator in community services, and only 12 percent had three or more (Tillery, 1970). Even at the close of the fourth generation, community development had not made great strides; in 1980, Edmund J. Gleazer wrote that: "It is time for us . . . with those whose influences join ours, to shape the community environment which sets before us tasks and new learning ventures" (p. 38). However noble, the challenge is widely viewed as unrealistic for an already overburdened college. Nevertheless, contributing to the cultural and intellectual life of communities is an important function of community colleges.

As the colleges move farther into the next generation, there is still widespread ambiguity about the mission of the comprehensive community college. Perhaps more important are uncertainties about priorities and program balance within the mission. The issue is serious enough to cast doubt on the accountability of some institutions. In some states, there has been reduced funding and demands for increased state supervision. Two major assumptions are central to criticism of the contemporary community colleges: (1) the preparation of students for transfer is being neglected; and (2) the colleges are doing things that should be left to other social agencies. These assumptions raise important policy issues that involve both state and local interests. They cannot be resolved by withdrawal of state funding for certain programs or by arbitrary efforts to limit the scope of community college education. Rather, they require cooperative efforts to clarify the mission of an institution that has been encouraged throughout its history to be more than a stepping stone to the university or the workplace.

The need for valid information is central to concerns about the transfer function of community colleges. Studies of transfer rates are often based on imprecise definitions of students who should rightly be counted as preparing for transfer to senior institutions. It is our view that no precise definitions of the pool of pretransfer students now exist. Thus, transfer rates as now reported are misleading. Furthermore, only a portion of public two-year college students has ever been expected to transfer. That proportion in Generation 4 declined for several reasons: (1) there was a significant drop in the number of high school graduates, who make up the largest pool of potential transfers; (2) senior institutions were recruiting students who, in earlier periods, would have first entered junior colleges; (3) the proportion of older students, many of whom were not interested in transfer, greatly increased; and (4) students in all types of institutions moved from academic to pragmatic education. This latter trend has led to increasing numbers of reverse transfer students (from universities to community colleges). State systems of higher education are in jeopardy if the transfer function breaks down. However, the major breakdown in this generation was in articulation among the segments of higher education. Responsibility for such neglect is so widespread that problems with the transfer function should not be placed solely at the door of the community colleges.

Many who question the mission of the contemporary community colleges are primarily concerned, we believe, about apparent imbalances in the programs offered. This criticism comes down ultimately to questions about who should be educated and who should pay for such education. This is so because program balance and the characteristics of student bodies are inexorably linked. The mix of students in community colleges sets Generation 4 apart from earlier periods. Participation rates of many underrepresented groups (reentry women, ethnic groups, the disabled, displaced workers) increased sharply in this generation. Student mix varied from region to region and from college to college, as did ways of using the comprehensive program in serving diverse students.

Breneman and Nelson (1981), in presenting strategic choices facing the fifth-generation community colleges, define comprehensiveness to mean giving equal priority to academic, vocational-technical, and community service programs. That is not the way most community colleges use the comprehensive program. Again, the colleges seek, however imperfectly, to fit their programs to the needs of their students. The other segments of public and private higher education may rightly tailor their programs to more traditional academic definitions of mission. In a sense, students are expected to fit themselves to these programs, rather than the other way around. Neither history nor contemporary social policy would suggest this as appropriate for community colleges.

As the generation ended, institutions were not emphasizing community over college; nor were they prepared to abandon educational services to their communities. This dilemma of mission or program balance still is a serious one. In 1985, we find major efforts in all parts of the country to clarify institutional role in relationship to available resources, changing demography, and the capabilities of other providers of education.

Student support services also underwent great change during this period. By 1970, there was talk of near parity of importance, if not workload, between instruction and support services. The colleges had almost equivalent numbers of administrators for each of the two functions. However, along with the expansion of student services there was a splintering of personnel and functions. New programs were developed, but many of them were on the fringes of institutions. They lacked proper status, rewards for staff, and professional development. Although the need for support services was widely affirmed, this function of the comprehensive college was being compromised by loss of personnel under retrenchment and by dysfunctions in the way student services were organized. Not only is a cafeteria approach to providing services inefficient, but it fails to recognize the holistic needs of students as they make education and career decisions.

Relations with Others. On balance, the community college, during this fourth generation, gained new status with the public, enhanced its linkages with the private sector, and improved its articulation with the secondary schools. We have already noted two sets of relations that deteriorated during this short span of time: (1) Community colleges in some states were charged with neglect of their academic role and faced new competition from senior institutions for mature adult students and for the reduced pool of high school graduates; (2) State governments reduced financial support, called for higher student fees, and exerted greater authority in community college affairs. Continuing scarcity of public resources and concerns for college mission appeared to drive these trends toward centralization in governance. The trauma seemed to be greatest among colleges in states that made recent shifts from local funding sources to predominantly state financing. The linkage between finance and governance has been noted. Thus, the states with long traditions of local authority experienced the most severe conflicts in system governance. It is unlikely that economic recovery, alone, will heal these wounds. Rather, fiscal and educational policies in most states reinforce the need for substantial clarification of the role and mission of the community colleges. The generation closed with improved strategic planning at both college and state levels to achieve these objectives in balanced and rational ways.

In the 1970s, considerable improvements were made in nongovernmental accreditation, with the use of new standards for evaluation and the training of accrediting teams. Because the regional associations are committed to the improvement of all aspects of institutions, they have important roles to play in the clarification of mission. This gain has been somewhat offset by duplicate and often fragmented efforts by state agencies to evaluate institutional effort. In matters of institutional review and evaluation, there are tensions between the profession and the states; but progress is being made toward delineation of responsibilities to achieve public accountability while protecting the vitality of nongovernmental accreditation (McIntyre, Swenson, and Tillery, 1982).

The private sector and community colleges hit it off very well in this period. There were new efforts to establish cooperative programs with business and industry, although some of them were little more than uncoordinated work and study. As the generation ended, urban colleges, in particular, were developing new relationships through contract learning and the sharing of high-technology facilities and equipment in the workplace. The American Association of Community and Junior Colleges provides leadership for these new models of cooperation. Shifts in student interest from academic to career-oriented education has stimulated these and other trends in occupational education. Because such shifts in student demand have frequently been at the expense of general, liberal education, there are calls for curriculum reforms in order to provide conceptual learning, which is likely to be essential for survival and mobility in careers of the future.

The Fifth Generation (the mid 1980s to the mid 1990s)

We have sketched the nature and scope of the transformations of the public two-year colleges over four generations. Attention has been given to their achievements, as well as to unfulfilled dreams, to conflicts in ideology, and to the challenges for reform. The comprehensive community colleges of today are very different from the junior colleges that preceded them. They, in turn, will be different from those that follow. It is the purpose of this chapter to provide a special lens through which to view the colleges in transition. This perspective invites the reader to understand the remarkable vitality and flexibility of the community colleges. It should now be useful to put the several dimensions of the public two-year colleges in juxtaposition across the four generations. Table 1 presents aspects of organization. Table 2 provides highlights of purpose, program, and students. Finally, Table 3 shows the key trends in relations with others. A vertical scan of the tables quickly shows how the four generations have changed over time. The thirteen dimensions for each generation convey that period's special identity and its directions of change.

The chapters that follow were written by leaders of community colleges and universities from all regions of the country. Each of them challenges us to think in new ways about the future of the colleges; their role, programs, and services; their students and faculties; and the ways colleges may be organized, financed, and managed. Each chapter focuses on the community colleges in transition to their fifth generation. We coauthors share

Table 1. Organization Across the Four Generations.

Period	Governance	Role of Executive	Role of Faculty	Finance	Facilities
1900–1930 1 High School Extension	Local school boards and state departments of education. Codes of legislative and administrative law. Residual authority with school boards; management by school administrators. Decentralized.	School administrator. Little status in higher education. Minor efforts to build "college" identity. Deference to state board in legislative affairs.	Little distinction from high school role. Close supervision by administrators; rules and regulations. Little professional development or faculty organization.	Extension of K–14 funding formulae based on ADE/FTE students. Local taxes and state foundation funds. Use of oil revenues from public domain. Underfunded.	Use of high school facilities. Slow trend toward JC campus identity. Conversion of some high schools as first generation ended.
1930–1950 2 Junior College	Emergence of local JC trustee boards and special state monitoring agencies. Beginning of multicampus districts. Primacy of local control under school model.	Leaders for college identity and comprehensive programs. Developers: community support and capital funding. Shift away from school style of administration.	University became the model for faculty with demands for more role in welfare and academic matters. Some unionization. Little interest in peer evaluation and little professional development.	Funding: 40–50 percent local, 25–30 percent state foundation, 25–30 percent federal. No tuition or low fees. Still school funding patterns. Local bonds for construction.	Trend toward separate JC campuses. West: modern college facilities. Educational specification with faculty participation. Use of business and military sites in some communities.
1950–1970 3 Community College	Separate local CC boards or local agency control. CCs part of university in few states. State governing boards and state systems of higher education. More attention to system governance.	Builders. New systems and colleges. University preparation for role. Much attention to state legislation and resource development. Leadership and management styles more like university.	Faculty senates, often established under law. States move toward collective bargaining. Initiatives in curriculum and instruction. Organized state faculty groups with political influence.	Separate CC funding using ADA/FTE formulae. Diverse state models. New federal support and categorical state funds. Rise in fees and tuition. Stable funding.	State-of-art planning for facilities. Great growth in many states with increased federal support. World-class campuses used as community centers; new facilities for vocational and technical programs.
1970–mid 1980s 4 Comprehensive Community College	Governance conflict. Increased state authority; contract negotiations with faculty and staff. Move toward political model of governance. Efforts to delineate state-local responsibilities.	Managers of scarce resources. Political negotiators. Role conflicts: faculty and trustees. Use of cosmopolitan leaders. Use of strategic planning.	Collective bargaining. Organized and politically sophisticated. Seek primacy in academic and professional development affairs. Senates survive collective bargaining.	State models: (a) 1/3 tuition, 1/3 local taxes, 1/3 state; (b) state support and 1/3 tuition; (c) no tuition with state and local funding. Tax rebellion. Retrenchment.	Slowdown in growth of new colleges. Outreach facilities developed; use of community sites. New learning centers. Beginning of deferred maintenance.

Table 2. Purpose, Programs, and Students Across the Four Generations.

Period	Mission	Students	Curriculum	Support Services
1900–1930 1 High School Extension	Extension of the public high school: lower-division courses and some vocational courses; remediation for matriculation standards. New students: access for students unprepared or unable to leave home.	High school graduates not yet ready for university: • low GPA • course deficiency • family resources • personal needs Working students and those preparing for employment.	Regular school courses to make up deficiencies. "Parallel" university lower-division courses, civic, liberal arts, limited vocational work, remediation. Few noncredit or community service courses.	Limited counseling and advising. Vice-principal locus of student services. Focus: student activities, athletics, and discipline. Student decision making about education and career much less important than instruction. Little financial aid or job placement.
1930–1950 2 Junior College	Influence of national spokespersons. Peoples' colleges. Beginning of a more comprehensive program. Importance of student services. Some takeover of high school vocational courses and programs.	Near normative group of high school graduates. Second chance for young and mature adults. First generation students to higher education. Most students declare objective to transfer; less than 1/3 do.	Increasing vocational preparation with development of technical and paraprofessional programs. More organized approach to remediation. Curriculum makes second chance possible for underprepared students.	Student personnel concept: career and program guidance, personal counseling, and activity program viewed as co-curricula. Attention to student programming and placement in courses. Counseling veterans, close of generation. Attention to financial aid.
1950–1970 3 Community College	Open door. New emphasis on extended day and on technical education. Community college key to opportunity for those groups underrepresented in higher education. Expansion of community services and counseling.	"New students." Outreach to disadvantaged and mature adults. Career orientation. Marked increase in ethnic and part-time students. Increased transfer rates with good outcomes. High percentage first admission of university eligibles.	Four functions of CC now national pattern: transfer preparation, vocation/technical education, remediation, and guidance. Some increase in community services.	Professionalization of student services and counseling. New concerns for university articulation and equality of access. Cocurriculum more myth than reality. Better staff for extended day programs. End of period: less attention to student assessment and course placement. "Right to fail."
1970–mid 1980s 4 Comprehensive Community College	Mission ambiguity. Tilt toward noncredit programs and community service. Nontraditional delivery; electronic learning centers, TV, "store front" sites, cooperative education. Ideological conflicts about CC role.	Something for all: • Mature adults • Reentry women • Underrepresented • Career renewers • Reverse transfers • On-job trainees • Joint high school enrollees Apparent decline: transfer and completion rates.	Growth of noncredit and community service programs, but transfer and occupational programs dominate. Dropping enrollments in liberal arts/humanities. Search for sharper definition of remediation. New concern for learner outcomes.	Expansion and fragmentation of student services. Federal funding for affirmative action and financial aid. Decline in holistic counseling. Under retrenchment, competition for funds. Move toward categorical state fund for counseling. Renewal with increased attention to assessment, placement, and learner outcomes.

Table 3. Relations with Others Across the Four Generations.

Period	With Schools	With University	With Government	With Private Sector
1900–1930 1 High School Extension	K–14. Common boards, teachers and facilities with the schools. Use of school courses to make up matriculation standards. New tensions as JC seeks college identity. Local control derived from school heritage.	Major university presidents conceive JC. Bifurcated university. JC protects university from unqualified students. University influences on instruction and course of study; has control over student transfer. Support from university.	Modest recognition and funding. Early permissive legislation but no capital funding. Some use of oil revenues from public domain. First legislation enacted in California. Benign neglect of state system governance.	Little assessment of needs of business and labor. Modest placement activities but few efforts to articulate education with the workplace.
1930–1950 2 Junior College	Breaking away from the schools. Fewer high school teachers employed. Tensions with schools about open door and second chance. Some reluctance in schools to advise students to use JC for first admission.	Improved articulation for transfer students. Some independence gained in lower-division program. Good transfer outcomes. Beginning of state master planning for higher education and system coordination.	Junior college viewed as good social investment; alternative to over-expansion of the university sector. Federal support for education of veterans and some for manpower retraining.	Development of labor/management advisory committees. Better placement programs and community need assessment studies. Joint efforts to define level of technical programs for community colleges. About 25 percent of students with business majors.
1950–1970 3 Community College	Legislation for separate community college districts. Take over of many adult and vocational programs from schools. Neglect or breakdown of school-college liaison.	State master plans: CCs part of state systems of higher education. New articulation agreements and provisions for transfer of students who have earned eligibility. High point in community college-university relations.	Vast support. Community college seen as way to solve social and economic problems. Growth encouraged on a national scale. Federal student financial aid. Many state funding formulae are enrollment driven.	Active labor/management advisory committees for vocational programs. CC-level technical programs defined. Difficulties with apprenticeship programs in matters of standards and equal access. Improvements in career guidance and placement. Joint efforts to reform general education for career students.
1970–mid 1980s 4 Comprehensive Community College	Competition for adults. Improved articulation for vocational education under legislation. Some joint enrollments of select students. The colleges join in efforts to improve the preparation of high school students.	Increased misunderstanding of contemporary CCs by university officials. Both institutions neglect articulation. New competition for scarce state resources and for high school graduates. Questions about community college transfer programs.	Fear of overexpansion and concerns about the comprehensive community college mission. Trends toward increased state authority and loss of local tax funds. New attention to system governance and accountability and planning.	Expansion in vocation and technical education. Period begins with development of cooperative education programs, ends with expansion of contract learning with business and industry. Relations with private sector primary focus of national community college leadership in the 1980s.

the belief that the future holds options for policies and actions that can renew the mission of the colleges and enhance both the quality and productivity of their programs and services. Management and faculty leaders, trustees, state governing agencies, and legislators are seeking solutions to the problems we have identified. Our book, then, can be viewed as a resource for those in the colleges and in government who will shape community colleges for a society in transition.

Shaping the future community colleges will not be easy. No end is in sight for fiscal stringency in any domain of public affairs. Institutions, if they are to survive, will have to be highly productive and publicly accountable. The pace and scope of social and technological change is so rapid and profound that we do not yet know how, where, or what people ought to learn. Finally, the colleges will be competing and/or linking with both new and traditional providers of education who may have or think they have answers to these questions. In the course of writing this book, we have done future studies of demographics, economics, life-styles, technology and work, and education. With help from futurists and leaders from several community college constituency groups, we have attempted to draw implications from future trends for the remainder of the fifth generation of community colleges (McIntyre, 1984). Six major trends emerge, with implications that will influence institutional planning and management, education policies and practices, and legislation.

Trend One: Adults will have increasing needs for recurring education. Among the implications for community colleges is that most suppliers of education will respond to such adults' needs for occupational retraining, academic remediation, and lifelong learning. This competition will require the colleges to offer cost-effective programs falling within their mission and with verifiable learner outcomes.

Trend Two: Regional and community variations in demography, economics, and occupational characteristics will become even more pronounced. Consequently, community colleges, whether in state systems or with primary local control, will need to offer programs and services that fit the needs of their local communities.

Trend Three: New information and learning technologies will change why, how, and where people learn. As a result, much more formal learning will take place in the periphery (industry, the military, community agencies, and the media) of traditional educational institutions. Community colleges, therefore, will need to redesign their curricula and methods of instruction. They must be much more effective in assessing the prior preparation of entering students, placing them in appropriate courses of study, and measuring learning outcomes. Faculty training in the new technologies of learning and instruction will be essential.

Trend Four: The American economy, in spite of fluctuations, will be strong enough to provide resources for the improvement and expansion of education. However, competition from other social institutions does not ensure increased funds from either federal or state governments. This means that competition for both public and private resources will demand greater public accountability as a result of good institutional planning, efficient management, and clear evidence of achieving college objectives.

Trend Five: Aging facilities and equipment will become an increasing problem in providing education of high quality. This trend will be exacerbated by needs for new technologies for management and instruction. Regional cooperation among the colleges and with high-technology industries will be essential for access to state-of-the-art equipment and facilities in some areas of instruction and management. Furthermore, state appropriations for maintaining the infrastructure of the colleges will be based on evidence of efficient management and public accountability.

Trend Six: The mean age of college personnel will continue to rise. As a result, modest opportunities to employ younger and differently educated faculty and managers may hinder reforms in both educational programs and management. There will be greater need for staff development and employment practices that will bring needed special talent to the community colleges.

Harold Hodgkinson captures an essential characteristic of the American public two-year colleges over their four-score history as he, too, looks toward their future. "The community college mission depends, in large part, on the character of changes that are occurring in our society" (McIntyre, 1984, p. 5). He concurs with the view that: "It is a future which will involve a transformation of world society at all kinds of levels, and while taking place slowly at first, will gather pace with sudden force" (Evans, 1982, p. vii). The community colleges will be particularly affected by such change because of their closeness to communities. Our analysis of the past and sense of the future leads us to believe that the colleges will cope successfully with the resulting challenges. Their physical plants are essentially in place; their faculties and managers are flexible and responsive to social change; their leaders have political sensibilities and skills in building consensus; and governance tensions are more a manifestation of vitality than of instability. Finally, the dominant value of the community colleges is right for the future: The doors are open for those who want to learn.

References

Breneman, D. W., and Nelson, S. C. *Financing Community Colleges: An Economic Perspective*. Washington, D.C.: Brookings Institution, 1981.

Callan, P. *Director's Report, October–November 1983*. Sacramento: California Postsecondary Education Commission, 1983.

Carnegie Commission on Higher Education. *The Open Door Colleges*. New York: McGraw-Hill, 1970.

Clark, B. *The Open Door College*. New York: McGraw-Hill, 1960.

Cohen, A. M., and Associates. *College Responses to Community Demands: The Community College in Challenging Times*. San Francisco: Jossey-Bass, 1975.

Cross, K. P. *Beyond The Open Door: New Students to Higher Education*. San Francisco: Jossey-Bass, 1971.

Eells, W. C. *The Junior College*. Boston: Houghton Mifflin, 1931.

Eells, W. C. *Present Status of Terminal Education*. Washington, D.C.: American Association of Junior Colleges, 1941.

Evans, C. *The Micro Millenium*. New York: Washington Square Press, 1982.

Gleazer, E. J., Jr. *This Is the Community College*. Boston: Houghton Mifflin, 1969.

Gleazer, E. J., Jr. *Call to the 1981 Convention*. Washington, D.C.: American Association of Community and Junior Colleges, 1980.

Harper, W. R. *The Prospects of the Small Colleges.* Chicago: University of Chicago Press, 1900.

Johnson, B. L. *General Education in Action.* Washington, D.C.: American Council on Education, 1952.

Karabel, J. "Community Colleges and Social Stratification." *Harvard Educational Review,* 1972, *42* (4), 521–562.

Kerr, C. *Presidents Make a Difference.* Washington, D.C.: American Association of Governing Boards of Colleges and Universities, 1984.

Koos, L. V. *The Junior College Movement.* Boston: Ginn, 1925.

McConnell, T. R. *A General Pattern for American Public Higher Education.* New York: McGraw-Hill, 1962.

McIntyre, C. *Planning and Future Studies.* Sacramento: Office of the Chancellor, California Community Colleges, 1984.

McIntyre, C., Swenson, R., and Tillery, D. *Delineation of State Agency, Accreditation, and Institutional Responsibilities.* Sacramento: Office of the Chancellor, California Community Colleges, 1982.

McIntyre, C., Swenson, R., and Tillery, D. *Models of Strategic Planning.* Sacramento: Office of the Chancellor, California Community Colleges, 1983.

Medsker, L. L. *The Junior College: Progress and Prospects.* New York: McGraw-Hill, 1960.

Medsker, L. L., and Tillery, D. *Breaking the Access Barriers.* New York: McGraw-Hill, 1971.

Roueche, J. E., Baker, G. A., and Brownell, R. L. *Accountability and the Community College: Directions for the 70s.* Washington, D.C.: American Association of Junior Colleges, 1971.

Strayer, G. D. *Survey of the Needs of California in Higher Education.* Sacramento: California State Department of Education, 1948.

Tillery, D. *Changes in Community College Organizations.* Berkeley: Center for Research and Development in Higher Education, University of California, 1970.

Tillery, D., and Wattenbarger, J. "State Power in a New Era: Threats to Local Authority." In W. L. Deegan and J. F. Gollattscheck (eds.), *Ensuring Effective Governance.* New

Directions for Community Colleges, no. 49. San Francisco: Jossey-Bass, 1985.

Vaughan, G. B. (ed.). *Questioning the Community College Role.* New Directions for Community Colleges, no. 32. San Francisco: Jossey-Bass, 1980.

2

K. Patricia Cross

Determining Missions and Priorities for the Fifth Generation

As we consider the issues of quality and mission in the fifth generation of the community college, we face a fundamental question: Can we be equal and excellent too? John Gardner (1961) asked that question twenty years ago, and we are still searching for the answer. It is not easy to define the purpose and mission of community colleges today—not nearly as easy as it was in the third generation, when community colleges were in high agreement on a common purpose and a national mission to open the doors of higher education to previously unserved segments of the population. Once the doors have been opened, however, and those previously unserved students are in attendance, what is the goal? Is it, for example, to retain students until they have completed some defined set of learning experiences that constitutes a "program" of study? Or is it to provide them with whatever educational experiences seem to serve their needs at the time? How important is retention, and what constitutes "reasonable progress" in a community college? Are community colleges failing in their task when up to 40 percent of the students in California community colleges complete fewer than two courses in two years (Hunter and

34

Sheldon, 1981)? How important is the transfer function? Should community colleges be distressed that studies have shown that "not more than one in twenty enrollees completes a two-year program and transfers in the succeeding term" (Cohen and Brawer, 1982, p. 54)? Community colleges are being judged on these traditional criteria. How appropriate are they?

The answers to these questions depend heavily on what community colleges are trying to do. The easy way out of the goals problem is a strategy that was used with reasonable success by most community colleges in the 1970s and 1980s—embrace comprehensiveness. The problem with the comprehensive mission is that carrying it out with *excellence* suggests that all of the basic functions that constitute the comprehensive community college must be done well: The transfer program must prepare students just as well as the university does for upper-division work. Vocational programs must prepare students for entry-level jobs, as well as for advancement in their chosen occupations. Remedial programs must actually ameliorate past educational inequities and prepare students for citizenship, family life, cultural and esthetic appreciations, and lifelong learning. Community education must respond appropriately to the educational needs of a wide range of people and organizations.

Can any college perform all of those functions with excellence—or even adequately in today's climate of scarce resources and heavy competition for students? Some people think not, and friends as well as critics of the community colleges are wondering out loud if the community colleges can be all things to all people. Are there some functions that should not be provided and some people who should not be served—at least not by a given community college?

The difficulty of the questions and the rising confusion about institutional purpose has college presidents worried. In one survey (Duea, 1981), college presidents were asked to name the most critical issues facing their colleges at the time of the survey and over the next decade. Out of some twenty critical issues listed, the changing mission and purpose of their institutions was ranked fifth in current importance but second in importance among those issues that presidents of public colleges and universities thought their institutions would be facing in the next ten years. Only inflation and financial concerns ranked higher.

Fortunately, the question of mission for community colleges has stimulated a growing number of thoughtful articles in the literature. While none will answer the questions for any given college, they should spark discussion and illuminate the options available. Basically, five major themes or foci run through the current commuity college mission debate. I shall identify them as follows: (1) the comprehensive focus, (2) the vertical focus, (3) the horizontal focus, (4) the integrated focus, and (5) the remedial focus.

The Comprehensive Focus

The comprehensive mission includes the five traditional programs of community colleges. These are well known to community college educators, and some of the chapter titles used by Cohen and Brawer (1982) in their book, *The American Community College,* offer widely accepted and succinct definitions: (1) "Career Education: Preparing Students for Occupations," (2) "Compensatory Education: Enhancing Literacy Through Remedial Studies," (3) "Community Education: Reaching Out with Extended Services," (4) "Collegiate Function: New Directions for the Liberal Arts," and (5) "General Education: Developing an Integrated Curriculum."

Among community college educators, the comprehensive mission is far and away the favorite, and at the present time many of the other foci are proposed not as alternatives to the comprehensive mission but rather as priorities of or improvements needed in a given area within the comprehensive mission. So strong is the commitment to the comprehensive mission that those who have been either bold or foolish enough to suggest the elimination or deemphasis of one of the five original program functions of community colleges have found themselves almost immediately in the midst of heated controversy. Consider, for example, the reaction to the recommendation of the Brookings report (Breneman and Nelson, 1981) that community colleges should deemphasize the transfer function and leave the education of baccalaureate-bound students to four-year institutions. Or consider the critical and often defensive reactions to Edmund J. Gleazer's (1980) suggestion that it is time for community colleges to deemphasize their association with higher education in favor of building stronger associations with the nonacademic community. Community colleges, like any other organization, nation, or person, are hesitant to give up anything once gained, even if doing so might refocus resources in an area of greater potential strength.

Whether community colleges are going to have to give up the comprehensive mission remains in doubt, but there is little doubt that priorities will have to be set and observed over the next decade. It is going to be difficult, if not impossible, to pursue excellence simultaneously in all five of the traditional programs making up the comprehensive community college. Most of today's analysts question the continuation of the comprehensive mission on the grounds that it spreads community colleges' resources too thin. Breneman and Nelson (1981) think the decision regarding mission will ultimately be settled on the basis of financial support, and they don't see enough financial support forthcoming to support the comprehensive mission. They label the comprehensive mission a gamble, observing that "the greatest risk of an unflinching commitment to the comprehensive mission is that sufficient financial support will not materialize, and the college will suffer across the board, becoming less competitive and less distinctive in all program areas" (p. 213). The California Postsecondary Commission sounded pretty much the same warning, saying that "unless the colleges make programmatic choices and set budget priorities they will probably do many things less well and some things unsatisfactorily in the future" (California Postsecondary Education Commission, 1981, Preface).

Despite such warnings, most colleges resist strongly any talk of abandoning the comprehensive mission, as it does have some notable strengths. In the first place, the comprehensive mission has strong roots in the historical arguments for equal access to educational opportunity—namely, that all potential students should be within commuting distance of the type of education that serves their needs. Furthermore, despite its complexity, it is easy to administer. Faculty will grumble but understand a leader who allocates scarce resources with an even hand as long as every department is equally deprived. What they are less likely to understand is an out-and-out statement embracing vocational education or community education or transfer programs as the wave of the future for the college. Some community colleges have enunciated clear priorities quite successfully, but the battle is never easy if it means giving up some function that already has incumbents. The comprehensive mission is enormously powerful. It is attractive to most community college educators, it avoids the controversy of setting priorities, and it has become part of the community college tradition. It is mostly outside researchers and analysts who are warning that in the long run community colleges will have to set priorities in order to use scarce resources where they will do the most good.

The Vertical Focus

The vertical focus can be roughly equated to emphasizing the transfer function of the comprehensive mission. Basically, the vertical focus calls for establishing relationships with high schools to ensure that recent high school graduates are prepared for college-level work and for articulating with four-year institutions their requirements for transfer. The goal of the vertical mission is to push or pull students through the traditional system—from high school through community college to a baccalaureate degree. Colleges electing this option would offer the liberal arts courses needed for transfer to four-year institutions, stress student retention, offer transfer counseling services, conduct follow-up studies of students transferring to four-year colleges to see how well they performed, accept performance on standardized academic achievement tests as a critical dimension of quality, and develop opportunities for faculty members to articulate course content with their departmental peers in four-year colleges.

The vertical focus is generally conceded to be the most prestigious and most easily understood model. Firmly anchored in traditional concepts of what a college should be, it places the community college between the high school and four-year college as an essential part of the formal educational system.

There is now considerable activity, both within and outside the community colleges, focused toward strengthening the vertical focus. Indeed, some of the most powerful voices in higher education are more supportive of the vertical focus than of any other. For example, the prestigious Carnegie Foundation deplores the discontinuity of American education and calls for "an effective progression from elementary school through high school through college" (Hechinger, 1981, p. 128). Derek Bok (1982), president of Harvard, came down heavily on the side of continuity in education by suggesting that financial aid should be based on the likelihood of the student's completing college. The University of California task group studying retention and transfer urges more articulation and communication with community colleges in the hope of greater continuity through the system (Kissler, 1980). Dozens of examples could be cited of concern in high places for the breakdown in the vertical transition of students through the formal school system. The widespread conclusion is that better articulation between high schools and colleges is a high priority and that community colleges have a major obligation to establish smooth connections to enhance the flow of more students through the system.

The most effective implementation of the vertical function is underway at Miami-Dade Community College; what has become known as the "Miami-Dade system" is influencing thinking throughout the country. Miami-Dade has many arrows to its bow and is without question a comprehensive community college. Nevertheless, the current priorities of Miami-Dade are clearly cast in the direction of traditional values and standards while preserving the concept of the open door (McCabe, 1981). The gems in its computerized crown involve an individualized monitoring system for making sure that students are making satisfactory progress in their courses of study (Anandam, 1981; Kelly, 1981), a system for articulating transfer requirements with each of the four-year institutions in Florida (Harper, Herrig, Kelly, and Schinoff, 1981), a special program for academically superior students (Robertson and Thomas, 1981), and, most recently, a program of research and communication with Dade County high schools to improve student preparation prior to their entry into postsecondary education (Losak, Schwartz, and Morris, 1982).

I doubt if in the history of the community college movement there has ever been as much attention given to traditional academic standards as there has been in the last four or five years. Attention, of course, almost always goes to areas perceived as neglected, and there is widespread agreement throughout the nation that traditional academic values have been neglected. The point is that the vertical position of the community colleges between the high schools and four-year institutions is being vigorously reasserted, and it constitutes one major focus for the community college of the 1980s.

The Horizontal Focus

The horizontal focus has strong roots in the community college movement, particularly in Generation 4. It reaches out to develop linkages with the community rather than build linkages within the formal educational establishment. In the horizontal scheme, for example, industry would become a full partner in the educational mission, with the community college offering employee training programs on campus or at the worksite; employer advisory boards would have a strong influence on the curriculum; and job placement would be emphasized. While relationships with employers are one important part of a community-oriented college, the horizontal focus is far broader than a career-orientation: Senior citizens' centers, the local library system, the chamber of commerce, and local theaters and museums are all potential partners in the education of the people of the community.

A special building for community events—from sports to theater to meetings of community groups—might be used to attract people to the campus. Faculty would be rewarded for their participation and leadership in community affairs. The community college electing the horizontal focus would become a major force for the improvement of the local community through education.

The horizontal focus has been most vigorously articulated by the American Association of Community and Junior Colleges. Although Edmund J. Gleazer, former president, and Dale Parnell, the current president, would establish their linkages in somewhat different places, the leadership of both men is concerned with reaching out to embrace new partners in education. Gleazer (1980) has the most sweeping vision of the community college of the future. He sees community colleges as the hub of all education going on in the community, serving people of all ages throughout their lifetimes and helping the community solve problems and build a better community through education. He urges community colleges to provide the leadership for assessing community needs and for convening and coordinating educational services for the community.

Gleazer upset many in the community college movement by making a choice between horizontal and vertical emphases. In his book, *The Community College: Values, Vision, and Vitality* (1980), he raised the question of whether it might not be time for the community colleges to deemphasize their identification with higher education and even to reconsider their use of the term *college.* "It may get in the way of what really needs to be done in the community" (p. 5), he said.

Although many regard Gleazer's horizontal focus as idealistic and too radical for implementation in the late 1980s, I suggest that it should not be dismissed too quickly. As soon as the current crisis in academic quality is resolved—which will be within the next five years or so—community colleges will be faced with even harder decisions with respect to the viability of the comprehensive mission and will be asking whether their future lies more in the concept of the "junior" or transfer college or in some other direction. I predict that the horizontal focus will challenge the vertical for predominance before the end of the decade. That seems to me a likely scenario for two reasons: First, as every educator knows only too well, the pool of traditional college students has just started its downward slide, and traditional students will become increasingly scarce for the rest of the decade. This means that traditional four-year colleges, which once were content to leave low-achieving students to the community colleges, are going to reassert their "right" to go after any student who is able to be in residence full time on the campuses that many four-year colleges must maintain. Unless community colleges can establish a competitive transfer program and can keep costs significantly below those of four-year institutions, they will probably ultimately lose the fight for the baccalaureate-bound market.

The second reason the horizontal focus will emerge stronger than ever after 1985 is that community colleges are far ahead of traditional four-year colleges in capitalizing on the rich and only partially tapped adult part-time market. Community colleges are ideally suited, philosophically and geographically, to serve lifelong learners with jobs, families, and roots in the local communities. Furthermore, the less cumbersome faculty committee system of community colleges makes them able to respond quickly and appropriately to cooperative educational ventures with other providers of education. The rising interest of business and industry in human resource development makes corporate education the most actively growing educational activity in the nation. Community colleges appear to have the inside track on alliances with business, and Dale Parnell and the current American Association of Community and Junior Colleges (AACJC) board are pushing hard for national legislation to strengthen this particular form of horizontal extension (Parnell, 1982).

The evidence is just beginning to pile up that students are using community colleges in a strikingly different manner than most traditionalists think, and most of the current student usage patterns are creating pressures toward the horizontal focus. Almost two-thirds of all community college students are studying part time, and the typical load is one course per semester. Most of today's community college students do not fit the vertical focus very well; they do not come directly from high school, nor do most plan to go on to a four-year college. In fact, the authors of the Statewide Longitudinal Study of California Community Colleges found that very few students enrolled in or even identified with any "program" of study. They concluded that "it is obvious that California community colleges are neither 'two-year transfer institutions' nor 'two-year vocational education institutions,' but something very different" (Hunter and Sheldon, 1981, pp. 3–11).

The Integrated Focus

The term *integrated focus* may be used to contrast Arthur Cohen's proposal for a general education focus with the horizontal and vertical foci already discussed. Cohen proposes giving major attention to linkages within the college rather than to external linkages either vertically or horizontally. The college emphasizing the integrated focus would emphasize multidisciplinary courses, team teaching, and curriculum development across departmental lines and in general would follow many of the current proposals being generated for the improvement of general education in higher education. Cohen's intent is to make liberal arts and the humanities an important part of the learning experience of all learners, be they transfer, career, compensatory, or community education students. The trend that distresses Cohen most in community college education is the collapse of the sequential curriculum. He believes that a community college education should contain a "sequence of intended learnings" in which "sequence" is defined as "a pattern of progression that has some rationale, order, and deliberate arrangement" and "intended learnings" have outcomes that are defined in advance (Cohen, 1980, p. 35). He takes a dim view of the community college that "purports to serve up anything that anyone in the community wants" (p. 36).

Cohen's proposal is not unlike the vertical focus with respect to curriculum development. The difference lies in the goal. Whereas the vertical focus requires laying a solid liberal arts foundation acceptable for transfer to a four-year college, the integrated focus would provide a continuing liberal arts education for lifelong learners—from college graduates to local blue-collar workers to grandmothers.

Cohen's focus advocates a program of studies that calls for a reconceptualization of all five of the traditional functions of the community college. His integrated focus would place liberal education for the informed citizen at the hub of career, compensatory, collegiate, and community education. Community colleges would not only guarantee the availability of liberal education to all students at any time in their lives but would *require* it, lest, as Cohen says, "the gulf between social classes in America be accentuated as members of the elite group learn to control their environment, while the lower classes are given career education and training in the basic skills" (Cohen and Brawer, 1982, p. 327).

The Remedial Focus

Finally, a proposed focus for community colleges recommended by the Carnegie Council in 1979 has received little discussion and has generally been met with little enthusiasm by community colleges. I don't find it especially surprising that community colleges failed to respond to the Carnegie proposal that community colleges assume "residual responsibility for youth." Clark Kerr and the members of his council tried to address the real and growing youth problem in the United States by suggesting that community colleges develop a comprehensive set of "youth service functions," which would include guidance, job preparation, job placement, referral to other community agencies for help with legal and medical advice, apprenticeships, and almost any other type of service needed by young people to help them become responsible and productive citizens. In this remedial focus, the community colleges would be identified as "full service institutions for the young."

There are two major problems with the proposal, first and foremost of which is the fact that community colleges have not been rewarded in the past for their social concern. Indeed, they are quite likely to have been the targets of sometimes vicious criticism for enrolling disproportionate numbers of minorities, for recruiting students with poor academic skills, for poor retention of students, for failure to provide upper-division transfers to four-year institutions, for preserving the social class structure, and a host of other charges related to their present remedial role of taking on the "youth problem." Having been burned in the past for their handling of a problem that no one yet knows how to deal with, it is unlikely that they are going to move more heavily into remedial functions in the future unless some sorts of rewards are forthcoming—special funding, feelings of accomplishment, recognition by others, and the self-satisfaction of having served individuals and society well.

A second major flaw in the Carnegie proposal is that almost no college wants to be identified these days as the "institution for youth," which is a declining population and quite opposite from the direction in which most community colleges are currently moving. Community colleges, more than any other type of institution, are becoming institutions for adults. What seems more likely is that community colleges, which have borne most of the remedial functions, will now be joined in those efforts by the high schools, under vigorous public pressure to improve academic programs, and by the four-year colleges, under severe demographic pressures to recruit and retain students.

Conclusion

Generation 5 presents difficult choices for community colleges. The comprehensive mission that has served as the flag around which community colleges could rally and derive strength and identity is not as strong or as clear today as it was ten to twenty years ago. While current criticism regarding lack of quality is directly largely at slippage on the vertical dimension, fidelity to the comprehensive mission will require new efforts to establish standards and quality across all programs. That, as many people have pointed out, will be a gamble as long as resources remain limited. Shoring up one program necessarily results in at least temporary neglect of some other function. The yo-yo syndrome can be the result. For example, the transfer function may receive attention until criticism becomes strong over failures in the community education program. Resources diverted to that program for a few years then may permit criticism to arise over the failure of vocational programs to keep up with the changing times. And so it goes. The result is that community colleges are perpetually defending themselves against criticism, constantly putting out fires instead of getting on with establishing their own identity and moving toward quality in the goals they have set for themselves. The institutions that have the best chance of maintaining the comprehensive mission are large colleges, especially those in multicampus districts in which individual colleges can diversify their "specialties."

The vertical focus has the advantage of having legitimacy in the eyes of most people—legislators, educators (especially those in four-year colleges and universities), and the general public. But that more stereotyped version of a "real college" can also be a disadvantage when community colleges must compete with four-year colleges on their terms. When community colleges were established, and especially during the great growth decade of the 1960s, four-year institutions were delighted to leave the new populations, who were generally less well-prepared academically, to the community colleges. That situation is changing dramatically, however, and four-year institutions will be tough competitors in the late 1980s and 1990s for full-time students. Colleges that appear to have the best chance of succeeding in the vertical focus are those located in states with growing populations of youth and low competition among four-year institutions and those in areas with relatively high income and education levels.

The horizontal focus has the advantage of tapping into the most rapidly growing population of learners, namely part-time adult learners. That population will continue to expand throughout the late 1980s and 1990s, not only in numbers but also in demand for education services. Most adults are location-bound, and four-year residential campuses have difficulty competing in this market. The problems in the horizontal focus are (1) that it may come close to the comprehensive focus in spreading resources too thin, (2) that there is a great deal of work to be done in selling the concept to the general public—and to many community colleges' faculties, and (3) that the current move *away* from local control and funding is counterproductive to establishing the community relationships that are essential for success. Nevertheless, for small to moderate-sized community colleges dedicated to establishing the necessary relationships in the community and selling the concept to students, taxpayers, and local business and community agencies, the horizontal focus seems a viable focus for the late 1980s.

The integrated focus also has a lot of "selling" to do in order to gain understanding and acceptance. It may, however, be a "sleeper" with more potential for the future than is apparent now. Job skills are changing so rapidly and many are of such a specific nature that some industries are saying that what they want colleges to do is to provide a general educational background and to develop the capacity in workers to continue to learn new job demands as they come along. Such industries are convinced that they will have to teach the specifics on the job, and many industrial programs are growing at a rate that far exceeds even the golden age of growth for higher education in the 1960s. Consolidated Edison's training budget, for example, ballooned from $400,000 in 1970 to 5.5 million in 1980, and the Bell System is still investing heavily in education and training (Craig and Evers, 1981). There are at present many calls for greater cooperation between community colleges and industry. If that cooperation should take the form of greater differentiation between the education offered by colleges and the training offered by industry, then the integrated focus would be an appropriate role for community colleges. If, on the other hand, cooperation takes the form of jointly developed and taught programs, then the viability of the horizontal focus is strengthened.

Job-related education is not, however, the major argument used by advocates of the integrated focus. There was once considerable hope among underemployed humanities faculties that more mature adult learners would have a greater appreciation of liberal education than would traditional college students. That hope has not yet been turned into college enrollments; adults appear just as interested in career education as younger students. There is, however, the argument that there would be an adult market for general education if colleges taught it as a truly integrated educational experience rather than as preparation for academic majors.

Finally, the remedial focus will probably continue to be a part of the program of every open-door college but the major focus of very few. Although there is brave talk about improving the high schools to the point that remediation is no longer needed, most community college students are not coming directly from high school; and, even if high schools improve their teaching of the basic skills greatly over the next decade, there will still be a great deal of "catching up" to do. So far, remediation is a well-accepted part of the community college mission and funding has been protected reasonably well in most places for that critically important social function.

These, then, are the choices: (1) to remain with the comprehensive mission and gamble that it can be done well—less of a gamble for large institutions than for smaller ones, (2) to work hard on improving the vertical focus and gamble that community colleges can compete with four-year institutions for the baccalaureate-bound student, (3) to define a community-based horizontal mission and gamble that constituents and the community can be convinced to support and lobby for that function, (4) to tackle the integrated focus and gamble that industry and students really do want liberally educated workers and citizens, or (5) to give renewed effort to remedial programs and to demonstrate effectiveness and gamble that confidence can be won and the community college will continue to receive the major portion of funds marked for remedial services.

No mission definition is guaranteed success in the late 1980s and 1990s, but by making a careful analysis of the strengths of the college and the market available to it, the risk can be reduced considerably. It seems clear that no college will "succeed" by settling for mediocrity across the board or by letting some of the five traditional programs of the comprehensive mission slide into disrepute through neglect and lack of attention to standards of performance for both faculty and students.

Quality of education is the central challenge to community colleges in their fifth generation. This can only be achieved if there is central agreement on mission.

References

Anandam, K. "Promises to Keep. . . . Academic Alert and Advisement." Unpublished manuscript, Miami-Dade Community College, 1981.

Bok, D. *The President's Report, 1980-81.* Cambridge, Mass.: Harvard University, 1982.

Breneman, D. W., and Nelson, S. C. *Financing Community Colleges: An Economic Perspective.* Washington, D.C.: Brookings Institution, 1981.

California Postsecondary Education Commission. *Missions and Functions of the California Community Colleges*. Commission Report 81-14. Sacramento: California Postsecondary Education Commission, 1981.

Cohen, A. M. "Dateline '79 Revisited." In G. Vaughan, (ed.), *Questioning the Community College Role*. New Directions for Community Colleges, no. 32. San Francisco: Jossey-Bass, 1980.

Cohen, A. M., and Brawer, F. B. *The American Community College*. San Francisco: Jossey-Bass, 1982.

Craig, R., and Evers, C. "Employers as Educators: The Shadow Education System." In G. G. Gold, (ed.), *Business and Higher Education: Toward New Alliances*. New Directions for Experiential Learning, no. 13. San Francisco: Jossey-Bass, 1981.

Duea, J. "Presidents' Views on Current and Future Issues in Higher Education." *Phi Delta Kappan*, 1981, *62* (8), 586–588.

Gardner, J. *Excellence: Can We Be Equal and Excellent Too?* New York: Harper & Row, 1961.

Gleazer, E. J., Jr. *The Community College: Values, Vision, and Vitality*. Washington, D.C.: American Association of Community and Junior Colleges, 1980.

Harper, H., Herrig, J., Kelly, T. J., and Schinoff, B. R. "Advisement and Graduate Information System." Unpublished manuscript. Miami-Dade Community College, 1981.

Hechinger, F. "The High School–College Connection." In Carnegie Foundation for the Advancement of Teaching, *Common Learning: A Carnegie Colloquium on General Education*. Washington, D.C.: Carnegie Foundation for the Advancement of Teaching, 1981.

Hunter, R., and Sheldon, M. S. *Statewide Longitudinal Study. Report on Academic Year 1979–80*. Part 4: *Spring 1980 Results*. Sacramento: Office of the Chancellor, California Community Colleges, 1981.

Kelly, T. J. "Restructuring the Academic Program: A Systems Approach to Educational Reform at Miami-Dade Community College." Unpublished manuscript, Miami-Dade Community College, 1981.

Kissler, G. R. (chairman). *Report of the Task Group on Retention and Transfer.* Berkeley: Office of the Academic Vice-President, University of California, 1980.

Losak, J., Schwartz, M. I., and Morris, C. *High School Preparation as Viewed by Academically Underprepared Students.* Miami, Fla.: Office of Institutional Research, Miami-Dade Community College, 1982.

McCabe, R. H. "Why Miami-Dade Community College Is Reforming the Educational Program." Unpublished manuscript. Miami-Dade Community College, 1981.

Parnell, D. "Putting America Back to Work: Community, Technical Junior Colleges Ready." *Community and Junior College Journal,* 1982, *52,* 12–15.

Robertson, P. F., and Thomas, S. C. "Emphasis on Excellence." Unpublished manuscript. Miami-Dade Community College, 1981.

Part Two

Improving Teaching
and Learning

The three chapters in Part Two cover major aspects of teaching and learning in the community college setting. In Chapter Three, Jonathan Warren examines the characteristics of students as they enter community colleges and as they progress. He sees community college students as primary participants in a major change in American higher education—the extension of higher education to all segments of American society. Warren discusses the leadership role community colleges have played in opening up opportunities for participation in higher education and the changes in delivery systems, time frames, attendance patterns, and responsiveness to student needs that community colleges have pioneered. He draws on current data to analyze community college students—their backgrounds, abilities, needs, and aspirations. Warren presents and analyzes research about student college experiences, attitudes, outcomes, and the implications of those outcomes for community college education in the fifth generation. He concludes the chapter with a projection of the coming patterns of community college education for the decade ahead.

In Chapter Four, Chester H. Case examines the role of the community college faculty member and asks what that role will be like in the mid 1990s. Case wonders if the professional roles of the faculty will have moved to the center of the college's functioning or if faculty will be spun out to the periphery of the organization and bypassed by innovations made by the college as it seeks ways to fulfill its educational mission in a changing, threatening environment. Case discusses the role of the faculty member from the perspective of four major issues: the work of teaching, the career of teaching, rewards and incentives, and the involvement of the teacher in the processes of the community college as an organization. He then analyzes a number of policy and professional development issues that confront community college leaders. He concludes the chapter with an analysis of different alternative futures for the professional life of the community college faculty member in the fifth generation.

Richard A. Donovan deals with the complex issue of developmental education in Chapter Five. He traces the history of this relatively new community college function and concludes that the necessity of providing developmental education is a problem that is not going to disappear during the fifth generation. Donovan reviews the major trends that have emerged in developmental education and analyzes progress made in the areas of instruction and counseling, program administration, in-service education, educational collaborations, and assessment. He then concludes the chapter with an analysis of the future of developmental education and how it will be affected by technology, new collaborations, staff development, and trends that emerged in the fourth generation. Donovan tempers his optimism about progress in developmental education by reminding readers of the very real problems that lie ahead as the developmental education movement heads into a new era. His analysis, proposals, and cautions should provide valuable insights to college policymakers as they confront this issue in the decade ahead.

3

Jonathan Warren

The Changing Characteristics
of Community College Students

Community college students in the 1980s have been the primary participants in a major change in American higher education. They embody the extension of higher education to all segments of society. They account for the increase of women from two college students in five in 1970 to more than half in 1980. They include proportionately more minority students and older undergraduates than do their counterparts in four-year colleges and universities. They have made part-time attendance a common and accepted practice. In the 1970s, therefore, community colleges brought women, minority students, older students, and part-time students more fully into higher education, broadening the population served as well as the flexibility of service.

While educating a broader segment of the population and accommodating part-time students have been important educational developments in higher education, accepting discontinuity in college enrollment is a more significant change. Enrollment in community colleges is fluid, as "recurrent" students move in and out and back in again, perhaps changing colleges, while incorporating their educational experiences into their adult lives.

The assumption that a college education must occur in a fixed period of years after graduation from high school is being effectively challenged by community college students. Arranging for more flexible enrollment patterns may turn out to be the community colleges' contribution to higher education in the 1980s, as accommodating a more diverse student population was their contribution in the 1970s.

Removing higher education from an artificially imposed time frame can have many important implications, presenting problems as well as opportunities. Intermittent educational experiences are more difficult to integrate than are experiences that flow in an unbroken sequence. Yet movement in and out of college gives students an opportunity to mesh their educational activities with the work and growth experiences central to their lives outside college, a possibility not yet fully taken advantage of by community colleges.

Who Are the Community College Students?

In 1980, about four and a half million students were enrolled in community colleges. That was 37 percent of all college students and 49 percent of all undergraduates. Descriptions of a group of several million students, even when they are broken into subgroups of various kinds, are often interesting but not necessarily useful. Knowing the proportions of men and women in two-year colleges, for example, is interesting only incidentally unless men and women differ in ways that are educationally relevant. Do men and women enter college for different reasons? Do they respond differently to different educational programs? When questions such as these are answered affirmatively, examining the relevant student characteristics is useful.

Distribution by Sex. All the growth in college enrollments between 1970 and 1980, an increase of 40 percent, can be attributed either to growth in the college-age population or to the increased enrollment of women, predominantly in community colleges (see Table 1). If the percentage of all college students who were women in community colleges had been the same in 1980 as it was in 1970, about 1.3 million women would have been community college

Table 1. College Students in 1970 and 1980 by Type of College, Sex, and Enrollment Status.
(numbers are in thousands)

	Universities and Four-Year Colleges			Community Colleges			All Institutions		
	Men	Women	Total	Men	Women	Total	Men	Women	Total
1970									
Full time	2,760	1,877	4,637	766	458	1,224	3,526	2,335	5,861
Percent	32.0	21.7	53.7	8.9	5.3	14.2	40.8	27.0	67.8
Part time	943	745	1,688	602	487	1,089	1,545	1,231	2,776
Percent	10.1	8.6	18.7	7.0	5.6	12.6	17.9	14.3	32.2
Total	3,703	2,621	6,324	1,368	945	2,313	5,071	3,566	8,637
Percent	42.9	30.3	73.2	15.8	10.9	26.7	58.7	41.3	100.0
1980									
Full time	2,877	2,603	5,480	842	908	1,750	3,718	3,511	7,229
Percent	23.8	21.5	45.3	7.0	7.5	14.5	30.8	29.0	59.8
Expected[a]	.87	1.16	.99	.92	1.66	1.20	.88	1.26	1.03
Part time	982	1,138	2,120	1,153	1,585	2,738	2,135	2,723	4,858
Percent	8.1	9.4	17.5	9.5	13.1	22.6	17.7	22.5	40.2
Expected	.87	1.28	1.05	1.61	2.73	2.11	1.16	1.85	1.47
Total	3,859	3,741	7,600	1,994	2,494	4,488	5,853	6,234	12,087
Percent	31.9	31.0	62.9	16.5	20.6	37.1	48.4	51.6	100.0
Expected	.87	1.20	1.01	1.22	2.21	1.63	.97	1.46	1.17

Source: Data taken from Anderson, 1981.

Note: The 1970 figures were adjusted to the new method of aggregating data from enrollments in two-year branches of four-year institutions, which was instituted in 1972, putting them in the community college rather than four-year college category.

[a] Figures in the "Expected" rows show the 1980 enrollments as a proportion of the enrollments expected from growth in the college-age population alone, assuming no increase in overall attendance rates and no change in the distribution of students.

students in 1980. Instead, there were almost 2.5 million. More than a million women were enrolled in community colleges in 1980 who would not have been if the enrollment patterns of 1970 had persisted. In contrast, in 1980 community college men were barely 4 percent more numerous than their 1970 percentage would have predicted.

While women students in most respects have the same educational needs as men, they differ in their educational goals. Younger women enroll disproportionately in community college programs leading to occupations low in pay and prestige. For example, secretarial studies, nursing, education, health technology, and therapy were the planned fields of study of 33 percent of the new full-time women students in community colleges in 1982 compared with 2 percent of the men (Astin, Hemond, and Richardson, 1982). Outside the occupational programs, more women than men were interested in general learning and in the social aspects of college. Thus, a shift in the sex distribution produces a change in students' educational purposes.

As age increases, the ratio of women to men in community colleges also increases and women students show additional differences from men students. Women in their thirties and older are often looking for ways to extend their horizons after their family responsibilities have been reduced. In this age group, women more often than men are concerned with occupational training (Lenning and Hanson, 1977). They tend to be apprehensive about competition and less confident than men (Scott, 1980), needing social support groups as well as help in negotiating the administrative and educational systems of the college. Women aged fifty and older, however, have fewer problems in deciding what courses to take and in balancing family responsibilities with those required for achievement in college than do younger returning women students (Smallwood, 1980).

Distribution of Part-Time Students. Another change from 1970 to 1980 in the higher education student constituency was the increase in part-time students. That increase was almost 50 percent greater than can be accounted for by the growth in the college-age population (see Table 1). Full-time students increased their numbers only through growth in the college-age population, as did men students. Further, almost all the growth in part-time students occurred in the community colleges: More than 60 percent of community college students in 1980 were part time; fewer than half were part time in 1970.

The educational implications of that ten-year shift in characteristics of community college students are substantial. Part-time students are more frequently concerned with occupational preparation and advancement than with transfer to four-year colleges. They are more definite in what they want from college than are their full-time counterparts. Their strong commitment to occupational preparation reduces the opportunities for academic or intellectual exploration. Community colleges, in responding to the needs of a predominantly part-time student body, have taken on larger roles in providing training services for local business and industry and in serving the immediate educational needs of the local community at the expense of their role in providing general education appropriate to a bachelor's degree (Cohen and Brawer, 1982).

Distribution by Age. In 1981, fewer than half of all community college students were within two or three years of high school graduation, and more than one-quarter were twenty-five or older (U.S. Bureau of the Census, 1983). During the 1970s, women thirty and older made up an increasing percentage of college students, while the age distribution of men students changed only slightly. Thus, over a ten- or twelve-year period, three interrelated changes occurred in the composition of the college student population, all more pronounced in community than in four-year colleges—toward more women students, more part-time students, and more older students.

Between 1980 and 1990, the population in the eighteen-to-twenty-four-year-old range is expected to decline by 15 percent while the twenty-five-to-forty-four-year-old group is expected to grow by 25 percent (Dearman and Plisko, 1980). With community colleges attracting increasing proportions of older students, the average age of their students can be expected to climb. With that change will come a corresponding growth in the proportion of part-time students.

The qualities of part-time students described earlier apply equally well to older students. If educationally relevant differences exist between younger part-time and younger full-time students, or between younger part-time and older part-time students, both of which seem likely, documentation of those differences has not been found.

Students twenty-five years and older tend to enroll intermittently and to be part time (Knoell, 1976). Proportionately more are white and middle class (Zwerling, 1980). They move in and out of college, perhaps at more than one college, and they mix studies with outside commitments—to a job, family, or both.

Simply because of their age, older students more often have established life patterns involving their families and jobs, even though they may use the community college as a vehicle for changing their lives or for exploring possibilities for change. Even in exploration, though, their feeling of urgency and desire for clarity of direction contrast with the needs of younger students, who are more comfortable with less purposeful exploration (Roelfs, 1975). The desire for explicit direction does not mean that older students enter community colleges knowing what they want. They need help in planning and choosing their directions both educationally and beyond college (Morstain and Smart, 1977; Tough, 1981).

Older students more often than younger ones want specific occupational training. Younger students are more often concerned with occupational exploration and developing general skills for finding a job. Personal adjustment, family, and job are more often issues for the younger than the older students, probably because for many of the older students these issues have been settled (Lenning and Hanson, 1977).

Older students typically are not attracted to broad educational programs with general goals. General education programs do not appeal to them. They want to know where their courses are taking them and how. They want their instructors to be clear in their objectives and in their expectations for their students. Seminars and classes based largely on student discussion do not appeal to older students as much as to younger ones. The older students want practically oriented courses, including those that provide off-campus, "hands-on" experience.

Racial and Ethnic Minorities. While community colleges in 1980 enrolled 49 percent of all undergraduates, they enrolled 56 percent of the minority students (Grant and Eiden, 1982). Perhaps because of the number of predominantly black four-year colleges, only half of the black but two-thirds of the undergraduate Hispanic students were in community colleges. Asians and Native Americans had 58 and 68 percent, respectively, of their undergraduates in community colleges. This overrepresentation of minority students in community colleges is related to but not wholly accounted for by their overrepresentation in the lower division. As educational level increases, the percentages of minority students in the college population declines steadily.

The high school graduation rate of Hispanic students traditionally has been well below that of blacks, and at least until 1980 had been rising only slowly if at all (Astin, 1982). If current efforts of Hispanics to raise their educational attainment produces even a moderate increase in their rate of high school graduation, the enrollments of Hispanics in community colleges will rise dramatically.

In recent years, Southeast Asian immigrants have enrolled in community colleges in increasing numbers, often taking courses in English as a second language and occupational courses. They tend not to be interested in degrees of certificates, withdrawing when they have acquired a satisfactory level of English proficiency and employment.

Academic Ability. The American higher education system is organized so that the most capable students, in general, attend the selective colleges and universities. Somewhat less capable students attend the less selective four-year colleges and universities, and still less capable students attend community colleges. Yet the overlap is substantial. Capable students are found in all types of institutions. The intent of most community colleges to provide an opportunity for advanced education to the adult population at large without regard to prior educational achievement produces a body of students that spans a broad range of academic competence.

In 1982, about 25, 40, and 60 percent of the entering full-time students in community colleges, four-year colleges, and universities, respectively, said that they had been in the top fifth of their high school classes. In the same three groups of colleges, 12, 22, and 34 percent of the entering freshmen said that their high school grades had averaged A-minus or better (Astin, Hemond, and Richardson, 1982). Clearly, the prior academic records of community college students as a group are poorer than those of students in four-year colleges and universities. But one student in eight who entered a community college had largely A's in high school, and one in four reported having been in the top quarter of his or her class. Community colleges enroll an appreciable number of students from the most capable group, although proportionately fewer than the four-year institutions.

The academic preparation of community college students has been improving since 1970. About half the entering full-time community college students in 1970 reported that they had been in the top half of their high school classes. By 1982, that proportion had grown to three-fourths. The growing community college population is drawing many of its new recruits from among capable high school graduates who previously would not have gone to college or who in the past would have gone to four-year institutions.

Within a large, nationally representative sample of the high school graduates in 1980, 35 percent entered four-year colleges and 25 percent entered community colleges (National Center for Education Statistics, 1984). Among students in the top quarter in tested academic ability, more than three times as many entered four-year as entered two-year institutions. Yet 21 percent of that academically capable group entered community colleges.

No knowledgeable person doubts that students in community colleges, on the average, are lower in academic ability than are students in four-year colleges. That difference reflects one of the purposes of community colleges—to provide an opportunity for higher education to all adults inclined to commit themselves to it. Yet the figures cited here are only part of the picture. They refer to students entering college for the first time, having recently graduated from high school. Those students represent less than a third of the community college population. The academic ability of the other two-thirds, including those who enter a community college having already received a bachelor's degree, has not been assessed, nor has their impact on the educational climate of community colleges.

Social Class. Community college students, on the average, are from families with lower incomes and less educated parents than those of students in four-year colleges and universities, but the range in all three types of institutions is wide. In the high school graduating class of 1980, 27 percent of those who entered community colleges and 61 percent of those who entered four-year colleges were from families in the top quarter of an index of social class (National Center for Education Statistics, 1984). Students from families below the top quarter differentiated only slightly between two-year and four-year institutions.

Educational Purpose. Although community colleges enroll students at all levels of ability, income, parental education, and social class, one clear influence on enrollment is their educational purpose. And this is strongly linked to geographic accessibility. Among the 1982 freshmen entering community colleges, one third lived ten miles or less from the college and another third lived from ten to fifty miles away. In contrast, about 40 percent of the students entering four-year colleges and a quarter of those entering universities lived within fifty miles of the institution (Astin, Hemond, and Richardson, 1982). Thus, since community colleges draw students from all levels of ability and social class found within fifty miles of the college, many of the characteristics of community college students are those of the people in their surrounding communities.

The generally lower ability of community college students means that they are less likely to have access to academically demanding lower-division courses than are students in four-year colleges. The differences in social class imply generally less interest in general educational goals and more in direct occupational preparation among community college students than among students in four-year colleges. Both these differences result in community colleges providing, in general, a less rigorous academic climate than is found in four-year colleges and universities.

Student Aspirations and Expectations

The effectiveness of community colleges is often criticized on the ground that proportionately fewer students who start in community colleges attain a bachelor's degree than do those who start in a four-year college (see, for example, Eckland and Henderson, 1981; Pincus, 1980). Such comparisons neglect differences in the aspirations and educational inclinations of students who enter the two types of colleges, as well as the value of educational experiences shorter than four or even two years. Many community college students have no intention of continuing beyond a community college program and are inclined toward activities and life patterns that are not enhanced by academic study.

Student aspirations are difficult to specify precisely, perhaps because they are in fact imprecise. Of two large, well-designed studies of California community college entrants, for example, one showed slightly more than one-third planning on achieving a bachelor's degree or higher (Sheldon, 1983), while the other showed a comparable figure of two-thirds (Renkiewicz and others, 1982). A national sample put this figure at three-fourths (Astin, Hemond, and Richardson, 1982). Of course, variations in response to questions about future plans depend on which students are asked, but all three samples were large and representative. Variations as great as these suggest that sources of error other than sampling error were operating and that the question itself may be difficult to answer. Students may be uncertain about their plans, may give the answer they think most other students will give, may not understand the question, or may just check the wrong box on the questionnaire. The form of the question and the circumstances in which it is asked will also produce variations in response. Certainly, the plans of many entering students are still too poorly formed for that information to have much utility.

The distinction between academic and occupational curricula is a traditional one that has been losing its importance in recent years. In the past, occupational curricula in community colleges were intended to be completed in two years or less and were not ordinarily followed by transfer to a four-year college, while academic curricula were expected to lead to transfer. Both curricula were expected to be completed. The value of a transfer program was assumed not to be realized until students enrolled in a four-year college and perhaps not until they had completed a bachelor's degree (see, for example, Eckland and Henderson, 1981). The value of an occupational program was considered unrealized until it was completed and the student was qualified for a specified kind of employment.

The fluid character of community college enrollments, with students moving in and out of college and between types of colleges and programs, makes obsolete the assumption that failure to complete a program implies failure to benefit from it; in fact, this assumption may never have been valid. Some occupational programs, such as accounting and computer science, may lead to employment after varying periods of study, with or without a certificate or two-year degree, or into a four-year program that leads to a bachelor's degree or beyond. Nursing and some allied health fields have similar options. General academic programs designed to provide the first two years of a four-year program may be "terminal" in the sense that some students will go no farther in a degree program, and they may lead into occupational programs, such as paralegal programs, or directly to employment.

The most popular broad field of study in 1982 among first-time, full-time students was business, which a quarter of the students reported as their probable field of study. Engineering, the probable choice of 15 percent of the respondents, was the second most popular field (Astin, Hemond, and Richardson, 1982). Professional fields, primarily nursing and allied health fields, accounted for 13 percent, and technical fields (building trades, computer science, electronics, and others) for 12 percent. Compared with choices in 1970, the technical fields and engineering had doubled proportionately by 1982. The arts and humanities, social sciences, and education had all declined, with arts and humanities showing the greatest loss, proportionately and in total numbers, from 74,000 students in 1970 to 25,000 in 1982. Similar but less drastic changes occurred among students entering four-year colleges. The shift during the 1970s from liberal arts to fields with clear occupational implications occurred in higher education generally. It was extreme in the community colleges, where a 20 percent shift occurred among entering students from academic to occupational programs.

The trend toward greater student interest in occupational rather than academic fields may continue, may stop with the existing mix of programs, or may reverse direction with a return to greater interest in general education or the liberal arts. The most likely trend, however, is toward greater mixing of the two orientations, toward incorporating general learning into occupational programs with further blurring of the occupational-academic distinction.

The long-term movement in higher education toward accommodating a growing proportion of the population strengthens the economic reasons for college attendance. On the one hand, the newly attracted students are from lower socioeconomic levels and view college primarily in terms of opportunity for economic advancement. On the other hand, the growing complexity of occupational requirements and the rapidity with which they change give greater importance to general kinds of learning in college that permit occupational flexibility. Those influences do not point toward a return to the liberal arts of two or three decades ago or more. They do, however, suggest the increasing importance of college curricula that have broad applicability beyond the requirements of specific occupational fields.

Students' College Experiences

A wide variety of students—men and women, young and old, the academically competent and those needing academic help—enter community colleges for reasons that range widely in substance and clarity. Students may be starting a long-term academic program in an inexpensive college close to home where they expect the faculty to be more supportive than in a four-year institution. They may be looking for direct preparation for early entry into an occupation or for further advancement in an occupation in which they already have experience. They may hope to shift to a more satisfying or better-paying occupation or want greater knowledge or competence in a field without occupational importance. Some are not at all sure what they want but have nothing better to do with their lives at the time.

The experiences students find in community colleges reflect the diversity in their backgrounds and purposes. The students who are poorly prepared academically may improve their knowledge and skills sufficiently to continue on to bachelor's and graduate degrees, or they may find the struggle too difficult and withdraw within a few weeks of entry. The students with academic objectives will differ in their college experiences from those with occupational goals. Yet despite that variability in experiences, community college students across the country show patterns of similarity.

A questionnaire developed by Educational Testing Service (1974) has been used for about ten years to give community college students a vehicle for describing their college experiences. It asks students to look back over the past few weeks or the past semester and describe their experiences and their reactions to them. Responses between 1979 and 1982 from almost 10,000 students in twenty community colleges in which at least 200 students responded were summarized for the discussion that follows. The responses were drawn from colleges in fourteen states representing every region of the country. While those twenty colleges are not a representative sample of community colleges, they are diverse enough that student perceptions common to all twenty colleges have a strong claim to broad generalizability.

The students in all the colleges had generally favorable reactions to their instructors, describing them as being clear in their instruction and in their expectations for students, giving more in class than the students could get from reading the text, being responsive to student questions and concerns and sensitive to their students' capabilities in not pitching the instruction over their heads, avoiding busywork in their assignments, and being readily accessible for help. These views were held by from 65 to 90 percent of the students in the twenty colleges. At the same time, 30 to 45 percent of the students in different colleges reported having had at least one course that was too much like high school courses. While that implies that some courses were undemanding, about a third of the students overall, from 20 to 50 percent at individual colleges, said the instructors piled on the work as though theirs was the student's only class.

Despite their general satisfaction with instruction as a whole, the students expressed some strong preferences for particular kinds of instruction. Even though many were older than typical college students, were working at least part time, and had had prior job experience, two-thirds or more wanted their college activities to include actual job experience. Further, they wanted that experience to take place in real job situations, even at the cost of taking longer to reach their educational objectives. About the same numbers wanted class activities to include experiences in the community, away from the college, whether job oriented or not. These preferences held equally for older and younger students and for men and women. Among the third of the students who did not indicate a clear preference for class experiences on the job and in the community, most were uncertain or indifferent. Removing those students gives endorsements of six or seven to one to off-campus experiences.

A second general set of preferences appears in the students' desires for clearly structured classes. Class activities consisting primarily of informal discussions without texts or formal assignments were rejected by the students almost two to one. By about the same two-to-one margin, the students said that they wanted grades that would let them compare their performance with that of other students.

Despite their desire for structure in their classes, the students wanted differences in abilities to be accommodated. Again by a two-to-one margin, they rejected the suggestion that classes should stay on schedule even when some students get left behind. They stated an overwhelming desire, four or five to one, for class assignments that allow students to work together, which may express the apprehension felt about studies by many returning students. By a slight margin of about three to two, they expressed a preference for small classes that meet only once a week rather than large classes that meet more often. Taken together, these preferences, which were expressed consistently in all twenty of the colleges, indicate a general desire for the faculty to give clear direction to the students' learning while including extensive practical experience on the job and in the community and allowing students the opportunity for collaborative learning.

In keeping with the students' feelings of comfort with the faculty and their classes, comparatively few reported poor achievement or academic problems. No more than 10 to 30 percent of the students in different colleges reported that the class material had been over their heads, that they had gotten so far behind in a course that they couldn't recover, or that they had had trouble understanding the material they were to study. From 20 to 30 percent said that they had had too little time for the work expected of them, that they had not had enough time for the reading assigned, that studying had taken so much time that they had had little time for anything else, or that they had not been able to handle their studies in the time available. Those percentages seem acceptable. Some proportion of the students in a college will, for any of a number of reasons, find themselves overloaded or in academic difficulty. If that were not the case, the programs might justifiably be considered too undemanding.

While from 60 to 80 percent of the students reported that they knew what they wanted to do when they finished college, from half to three-quarters said that they needed more information about what the job situation would be like when they left college. This was by far the most commonly expressed student need in all twenty colleges. Yet from 30 to 60 percent of the students had never talked with a counselor about their future plans. Comparatively few (10 to 20 percent) said that they were not getting what they wanted, but 20 to 30 percent said they would like a field of study with more definite job possibilities and another 20 to 40 percent were uncertain on that issue. From 20 to 35 percent of the students reported having changed their occupational plans since enrolling.

Sizable minorities of the students, therefore—20 to 40 percent in the various colleges—were uncertain about their goals, had changed their plans, or wanted to see a closer connection between their studies and a job. Well over half wanted help with occupational information and job planning. General satisfaction with the instruction and the belief that they were getting what they wanted do not imply that the students were sure of their directions or capable of making unassisted decisions about their plans.

Compared with students in four-year colleges, community college students, particularly the older students, feel greater pressure to make immediate educational and occupational decisions and less freedom or opportunity to defer those decisions while they explore their options.

Student Outcomes

The benefits to students of enrollment in community colleges are not well documented. The percentage of entering students who transfer to a four-year college, the most commonly used indicator of institutional success, is appropriate to only a small proportion of the entering students. Many of those who enter planning to transfer may represent success when they have explored different options, clarified their own preferences, completed a short-term occupational program, and left college, at least temporarily. Others may enter because they can find no immediate alternative to college, flounder for a semester or two, and leave—but then return a year or two later with more experience and maturity and eventually complete a transfer program and bachelor's degree. The "cooling out" function does not necessarily represent a disservice to the student.

Success in occupational programs and others not directed to transfer is also difficult to define precisely and to document. New employment in a program-related field and advancement in a job already held are both seen as success for the student and the college. But either may occur independently of the college's programs, and many students may use their college experiences successfully in employment that has no apparent relationship to their programs.

The gross outcomes of community college enrollment, defined in terms of the general educational or occupational activities to which students move after their experience in the community college, do not permit ready interpretation. For example, a student who, after two semesters of part-time study, has acquired an elementary understanding of accounting or has discovered that the study of history and literature can be rewarding has benefited from college regardless of what he or she may do next. These kinds of short-term accomplishments, while probably numerous, do not get documented and acknowledged. Many direct but undocumented benefits of instruction may lead to other successes through a chain of accomplishments. Basing all the evidence of educational success on general, long-term consequences such as completion of a bachelor's degree or employment related to the field studied, with little information on the students' initial purposes and characteristics and none on the intervening processes that led to their eventual educational or occupational status, produces an incomplete picture.

Direct evidence of short-term accomplishments might be found in the English capabilities, after completion of one or two English courses, of students for whom English was not the language spoken in their homes. It might be found in the understanding of the capabilities and limitations of computers demonstrated by students who have completed two or three courses in computer science or in an appreciation of the importance of political compromise among students completing a two-course sequence in American institutions. Evidence of success might consist of the changes in students' plans—either a narrowing of focus or a broadening of scope—after a semester of enrollment. In themselves, such indicators of success and others like them are limited. But the overall success of a college consists of a multitude of such limited instances. It can best be described through aggregating the many small-scale, short-term instances of student accomplishment to which the college and its faculty contribute. That aggregation should not be simply a tallying up of thousands of small successes but the integration of those successes into general and substantial accomplishments.

Knoell (1976) attests to the fact that community colleges do not yet adequately assess their accomplishments. After studying the academic records of 32,000 students—a representative sample of the community college students in California—over seven semesters, she concluded that the colleges were unable to "measure their success in responding to the needs of successive groups of new students with nontraditional, often idiosyncratic objectives" (p. 25). They are only slightly more successful in measuring their success with traditional students.

Despite its interpretive limitations, information on degrees awarded is often all that is widely available. Nationally, from 1976 to 1980, associate degrees awarded in academic and occupational fields combined accounted for about 25 percent of the enrollment of second-year students in community colleges the preceding fall, or about 16 percent of the entering students two years earlier. Another 4 percent earned certificates of completion of an occupational program (Grant and Eiden, 1982). Although these figures are for the country as a whole and thus fluctuate from state to state and locality to locality, they indicate that about one in five of the students who enrolled in community colleges in the latter half of the 1970s eventually received an A.A. degree or an occupational certificate.

Transfer to four-year institutions is more difficult to document than is completion of a program because of the requirement for coordinated data from two independent institutions. In one study, for example, Friedlander (1980), after reviewing the available information on enrollment trends, reported that typically fewer than 10 percent of community college students actually transferred. He attributed that low transfer rate to the shift of student interests from academic to occupational emphases, the growing proportion of community college students in remedial courses, the growth of interest in "community education" having neither transfer nor occupational objectives, and the growing enrollment of older students who tend to enroll part time and to have high rates of withdrawal. In contrast, evidence from a national study of the high school graduates of 1972 suggested that more than one in four of community college entrants can be expected ultimately to transfer (Eckland and Henderson, 1981). And a New York study showed that 40 percent of the students who had entered a two-year campus of the City University of New York in 1970 had transferred within five years and that 27 percent either had completed a bachelor's degree or were still attending college (Alba and Lavin, 1981). Yet another study showed that among 6,500 students who entered fifteen California community colleges in the fall of 1978, 9.5 percent had transferred three years later (Sheldon, 1983). Yet almost 30 percent of those classified as transfer students were still enrolled in the sixth semester of the study, and any students who had transferred but had not been reached in the last follow-up would also swell the percentage of those who had transferred. A realistic estimate of the number that ultimately transferred may therefore be 10 to 12 percent.

Some sense of the nature of the community college population and the flow of students into and out of it can be found in enrollment figures for the California higher education system. The total enrollment in all California community colleges is slightly more than one million students. Each year for nine years, from 110,000 to 120,000 students nineteen years old or younger— that is, students fresh or almost fresh from high school—entered the California community colleges. During the same nine-year period (1974–1982), from 45,000 to 55,000 students per year transferred from a community college to a four-year institution in California—a branch of the University of California, a campus of the California State University system, or a private college or university (California Postsecondary Education Commission, 1982, 1983). Thus the annual flow of new students into the community colleges in California is only 11 or 12 percent of the community college enrollment, while those who move on to a four-year institution make up about 5 percent. Between 80 and 90 percent of California community college students are therefore adults several years out of high school who will probably not enter a four-year college.

In an earlier study of California community college students, it was found that 35 percent of those who entered in 1972 had in three years completed no more than one semester (Knoell, 1976). However, 14 percent had been enrolled continuously for seven semesters. These two groups, totaling half of the entering students, depart appreciably from the expectation that students attend community colleges for two years, or perhaps a little longer if they work part time, and complete an A.A. degree.

The dominant element in the California enrollment figures is the 80 to 90 percent of the student population who have come late to college and will not continue on to a four-year institution. For them, completion of a degree or certificate is not an appropriate indicator of success. The fluid nature of community college enrollments, illustrated by this overwhelming percentage of students who do not fit traditional expectations, calls for flexibility in community college programs and services and for short-term, cumulative indicators of accomplishment. It points up one of the challenges of the fifth generation of community colleges.

A third benefit students take from community colleges, in addition to preparation for further education or for employment, is illustrated by the students classified as "special interest" in Sheldon's (1983) study—slightly more than a quarter of the total sample. These students enrolled in search of some direct personal benefit—to extend their own capabilities and range of experiences, to improve their language capabilities in either English or a foreign language, or to satisfy a desire for some form of personal growth. They were rarely concerned about degrees or certificates. They often took only one course at a time, and 70 percent of them had been enrolled for no more than two semesters during the three years of the study. Because most of the special interest students are part time and enrolled only for short periods, they may be comparatively neglected in community college planning. Although they may take no more than two or three courses and then disappear, they are replaced by newly entering students who follow a similar enrollment pattern. Thus a substantial number of people are served—a number large enough to justify explicit attention in program planning. Even though, individually, their experience in the community college is brief, collectively they are a persistent quarter of the student population.

The Coming Patterns of Community College Education

The dominant characteristics of community college students are their uncertain enrollment patterns and varied purposes. The compositions of the student population changes continually with little regard for formal program structures, except possibly for the short-term, highly structured occupational programs. The boundary between the college and its surrounding community is porous, as it should be in view of the community colleges' primary purpose.

Despite the easy flow of students into and out of the community colleges, neither the colleges nor the students are comfortable with the process. The colleges continue to emphasize preparation for transfer and structured occupational programs while considering attrition rates an indicator of failure. The students, most of whom have major commitments outside college, tend to be uncertain about how best to use their college experiences. While they report being satisfied with what they have found in college and can be shown to have advanced occupationally, the sheer variety in the patterns of courses they take makes the connections between their programs and their presumed benefits difficult to identify and describe.

Responding to their students' part-time and intermittent patterns of enrollment may be the most important task facing community colleges. Curricular patterns might be adjusted to form self-contained groups of three to six courses that could be completed over several semesters with a recognized point of completion. Various combinations of such groups might constitute higher levels of accomplishment short of a degree that could also be given formal recognition as coherent educational accomplishments. A search through any college's catalogue will reveal a large number of possibilities for such clusters of courses. An analysis of students' transcripts will show how students have formed such clusters in their course enrollments, not always in response to program requirements. Formal acknowledgment by the college of students' completion of course clusters and of integrated groups of clusters would give many students a sense of accomplishment that would encourage them to continue. It would also give the college a way to document its own accomplishments in taking students to identifiable educational goals more immediate than a degree.

Several characteristics of community college students—their age, part-time enrollment, attendance close to home, intermittent attendance, concern for occupational preparation and growth, and commitments outside college—point to a second direction for community colleges: The involvement of the colleges directly with their surrounding communities should be developed more fully. Many colleges are already moving in that direction with collaborative programs with local businesses and industry. As corporations increase their commitment to employee training, collaborative efforts involving colleges, corporations, and students/ employees grow in their appeal. Such programs will not necessarily be wholly occupational. Understanding psychological principles related to employee supervision, for example, as one aspect of managerial development draws on academic capabilities while fulfilling corporate purposes.

The need is not for community colleges to learn the training needs of businesses in the neighboring communities and then provide them; occupational requirements shift so rapidly that short-term training is best done on the job. Rather, colleges and employers in collaboration can identify the kinds of general learning, best provided in an academic setting, that will give employees the basic kinds of understanding needed to adapt to changing work roles and requirements. The arts and humanities thus may find a larger role in programs developed collaboratively with the surrounding community—with community groups, local government, and museums as well as with business and trade groups. They are likely to be less sharply differentiated from occupationally oriented courses than are present arts and humanities programs. Rather than being pursued in isolation from other parts of the curriculum, learning in history, literature, philosophy, and the social sciences may best be acquired in conjunction with learning related to the immediate social, political, and occupational needs of the neighboring communities.

The rising age of the community college population will require changes from some traditional instructional practices. Older students are more committed than younger ones and respond more fully and precisely to their instructors' directions, but they are less comfortable with broadly stated or loosely defined class requirements. They want clarity from their instructors in purpose and direction and are critical of classes they cannot fit readily into their own educational purposes. They feel that they have little time for interesting but peripheral diversions. Not only must courses be internally coherent and directed toward explicit goals, but they must also clearly fit with other courses in the students' programs. A curricular objective of some importance may be to help students develop the ability to find useful connections that are not immediately apparent between courses that differ in content and purposes.

The role of community colleges as open-door institutions and the current trend in four-year colleges toward more rigorous admission standards suggest that academic remediation, long an important function of community colleges, will require still greater attention. Community college courses intended to bring entering students to acceptable levels of proficiency in reading, writing, mathematical, and study skills may need to become more diversified in order to serve different kinds of students with different educational purposes and deficiencies. For instance, reading classes for Southeast Asian refugees will differ from those for slow-reading native-English-speaking students. Thirty-five-year-old students who have avoided any unnecessary computation since leaving high school but who now want to study marketing have different preparatory mathematics needs from twenty-year-old students who have not had high school algebra but who are interested in computer science. To accommodate students varying widely in educational purpose and current level of ability, remedial or preparatory courses varying in focus, length, and intensity are required. For some students, a two- or three-week refresher course may be enough if it is directed to specific student deficiencies. For others, extended courses with high school content but adult applications may be required. Courses shorter than a semester will require other curricular adjustments to accommodate the programs of students and college to the semester calendar. A standard remedial course for all students who fall below the cut-off score on a placement test is not adequate. The skills needed to perform acceptably in any particular group of courses, and their assessment for placement in the proper class, first need to be clearly differentiated for different parts of the curriculum and then related to pertinent test scores.

By far the most pressing need expressed by the 10,000 students in twenty widely scattered and varied colleges described earlier was for more help in defining their purposes, exploring options, finding programs that will serve their purposes, and negotiating the educational system. That need has been repeatedly confirmed in other studies. Almost 3,000 students who responded to the Community College Goals Inventory in eighteen geographically dispersed colleges stated that counseling and advising should be the college's most important goal (Cross, 1981b). It was ranked ahead of vocational and technical training, general education, and personal development. Counseling and other support services have been described as particularly critical for returning women (Scott, 1980) and part-time students (Zwerling, 1980). Actions that would improve the success of adults in college include improving the accuracy of the information provided about the college and its programs, helping adult students find student support groups, recognizing and responding to the low self-assessment of some, removing unnecessary administrative barriers, and responding to the variety of purposes adults bring (Cross, 1981b).

Community colleges and their students have collaborated in putting together an educational institution that has developed far beyond its early form. How that continually evolving institution is now functioning and how it might continue to change can best be seen through detailed observation of the paths students follow in moving through their college experiences and integrating them with their lives outside and after college. Broad pictures of enrollments, completion rates, and transfer success are not sufficient.

The declining relevance of the term *two-year college* (Cohen and Brawer, 1982; Knoell, 1976) points up the need for community colleges to go even further than they have in developing flexible and varied educational programs to match the purposes and needs of their students. Having acknowledged more fully the variety and complexity of the purposes for which students use their community college experiences, the colleges should then find more direct methods for assessing their short-term accomplishments. Accomplishments in terms of the satisfaction of community needs as well as the needs of individual students, and the integration of those two missions, are taking on greater importance in the fifth generation of community colleges.

References

Alba, R. D., and Lavin, D. E. "Community Colleges and Tracking in Higher Education." *Sociology of Education,* 1981, *54,* 223–237.

Andersen, C. J. *1981–82 Fact Book for Academic Administrators.* Washington, D.C.: American Council on Education, 1981.

Astin, A. W. *Minorities in American Higher Education: Recent Trends, Current Prospects, and Recommendations.* San Francisco: Jossey-Bass, 1982.

Astin, A. W., Hemond, M. K., and Richardson, G. T. *The American Freshman: National Norms for Fall 1982.* Los Angeles: University of California, 1982.

California Postsecondary Education Commission. *Update of Community College Transfer Student Statistics: Fall 1982.* Sacramento: California Postsecondary Education Commission, 1982.

California Postsecondary Education Commission. *California College-Going Rates: 1982 Update.* Sacramento: California Postsecondary Education Commission, 1983.

Cohen, A. M., and Brawer, F. B. *The American Community College.* San Francisco: Jossey-Bass, 1982.

Cross, K. P. *Adults as Learners: Increasing Participation and Facilitating Learning.* San Francisco: Jossey-Bass, 1981a.

Cross, K. P. "Community Colleges on the Plateau." *Journal of Higher Education,* 1981b, *52* (2), 113–123.

Dearman, N. B., and Plisko, V. W. *The Condition of Education.* Washington, D.C.: National Center for Education Statistics, 1980.

Eckland, B. K., and Henderson, L. B. *College Attainment Four Years After High School.* Washington, D.C.: National Center for Education Statistics, 1981.

Educational Testing Service. *Student Reactions to College: User's Manual.* Princeton, N.J.: Educational Testing Service, 1974.

Friedlander, J. "An ERIC Review: Why is Transfer Education Declining?" *Community College Review,* 1980, *8,* 59–66.

Grant, W. V., and Eiden, L. J. *Digest of Education Statistics 1982.* Washington, D.C.: National Center for Education Statistics, 1982.

Knoell, D. M. "Challenging the 'Model and the Myth.'" *Community and Junior College Journal,* 1976, *47* (3), 22–25.

Lenning, O. T., and Hanson, G. R. "Adult Students at Two-Year Colleges: A Longitudinal Study." *Community/Junior College Research Quarterly,* 1977, *1,* 271-287.

Morstain, B. R., and Smart, J. C. "A Motivational Typology of Adult Learners." *Journal of Higher Education,* 1977, *48,* 665-679.

National Center for Education Statistics. *Two Years After High School: A Capsule Description of 1980 Seniors.* Washington, D.C.: National Center for Education Statistics, 1984.

Pincus, F. L. "The False Promises of Community Colleges: Class Conflict and Vocational Education." *Harvard Educational Review,* 1980, *50,* 332-361.

Renkiewicz, N. K., and others. *The Reverse Transfer Student: An Emerging Population.* Sacramento, Calif.: Los Rios Community College District, 1982.

Roelfs, P. "Teaching and Counseling Older College Students." *ETS Findings,* 1975, *2* (1), 5-8.

Scott, N. A. *Returning Women Students: A Review of Research and Descriptive Studies.* Special Monograph. Washington, D.C.: National Association of Women Administrators, Deans, and Counselors, 1980.

Sheldon, M. S. *Statewide Longitudinal Study.* Part 5. Los Angeles: Los Angeles Pierce College, 1983.

Smallwood, K. B. "What Do Adult Women College Students Really Need?" *Journal of College Student Personnel,* 1980, *21,* 65-73.

Tough, A. "Interests of Adult Learners." In A. W. Chickering and Associates, *The Modern American College: Responding to the New Realities of Diverse Students and a Changing Society.* San Francisco: Jossey-Bass, 1981.

U.S. Bureau of the Census. *Characteristics of American Children and Youth: 1980.* Current Population Reports. Special Studies Series P-23, no. 114. Washington, D.C.: U.S. Bureau of the Census, 1982.

U.S. Bureau of the Census. *School Enrollment—Social and Economic Characteristics of Students: October 1981.* Current Population Reports. Population Characteristics. Series P-20, no. 373. Washington, D.C.: U.S. Bureau of the Census, 1983.

Zwerling, L. S. "The New 'New Student': The Working Adult." In G. B. Vaughan (ed.), *Questioning the Community College Role.* New Directions for Community Colleges, no. 32. San Francisco: Jossey-Bass, 1980.

4

Chester H. Case

Supporting
Faculty Leadership
for Change

What does the future hold in store for the professional lives of community college instructors? What might it be like to be a teacher in the community college of tomorrow if the many transformations and changes advocated in this book come to pass? How might trends and contemporary situations interact to influence the teacher's work, career, sense of reward and incentive, and participation in college processes of governance? Indeed, can a particular, preferred faculty future be shaped by present actions? If the fifth-generation community college is to be realized, concerns for the role, vitality and effectiveness of the faculty must be addressed, because the faculty is the key to quality, productivity and responsiveness of a college.

In the pages that follow, three scenarios are presented. Each depicts a possible but not equally probable future for community college faculty. Proposals for achieving the preferred scenario are offered after a discussion of salient trends and contemporary situations in the teacher's professional life.

Before undertaking this look to the future, a few words of qualification are needed. Discussing the professional life of today's community college instructor, much less projecting possible and probable futures, is difficult and frustrating. For, as important as faculty is for the effectiveness and responsive adaptability of an institution, there is a notable lack of research and applicable theory. There is, however, an abundance of "common knowledge"—the store of understandings, shared beliefs, anecdotes, lore, and language that teachers and those who know about teachers use when they talk. I have drawn on the common knowledge as I have learned it in some thirty years of educational experience in a variety of roles, including community college manager, staff development facilitator and consultant, and teacher. I have used this common knowledge with proper caution, as it can be biased, misleading, partisan, contradictory, and banal. At the same time, it offers extraordinary insights, perceptions, and wisdom. It can scarcely be ignored. It is a principal medium, after all, for the professional socialization of community college instructors.

Another difficulty in writing about possible futures of faculty lies in the fact that teaching takes place in the nested context of classroom, college, and community over which teachers historically have had little influence. Changes in the context send changes reverberating toward the teacher. Teachers are receivers (and resisters) of change, rarely initiators. Whether teachers can influence their future is an open question. Finally, a caution to the reader: Because of the diversities among the colleges, their contexts, and their some 250,000 teachers, full and part time, all generalizations should be read with the expectation of exceptions in mind, and the scenarios should be read as imaginative composites.

The Professional Life of Community College Faculty

Ask a group of teachers to reflect on their professional lives and tell about them. Likely, they will tell of things quite unique to themselves, but they will comment as well on commonalities regarding the work of teaching, the career of teaching, rewards and incentives, and faculty participation in governance and other college processes. I believe these four topics would be prominent in the discussion, as they are at the center of the professional life of the teacher, have pronounced trends, and are replete with issues and developments that could eventuate in quite different futures.

These four of the myriad aspects of the teacher's professional life and the culture of the community college are by no means the only ones of importance and influence. There are other important aspects that cannot be discussed here or will be discussed only indirectly. The personal and private lives of teachers have great influence on how they work, play out a career, respond to rewards and incentives, and choose whether to become involved in governance. However, there are so many variables, such wide diversities, and so much idiosyncrasy involved in the intricate connections between the personal life and the professional life that it would require a study far greater in scope than this to even begin to make sense of them.

Another important topic that will not be taken up for similar reasons is the complex matter of interpersonal interactions of teacher and student. Full explication of the subtleties and intricacies of the mutual influences of teacher, student, and school setting will perhaps require the perceptions and artful representations of novelists, such as Dorothy Bryant in *Ella Price's Journal* (Bryant, 1972), or the painstaking accounting of nuance, pattern, and context of ethnographers, such as Howard London in *The Culture of a Community College* (London, 1978). Other aspects that will be addressed only indirectly, though essential to the work and career of teaching, are pedagogy and curriculum. A wealth of literature exists on each of these topics, but they can be only alluded to here.

The Work of Teaching. In the midst of the changes that characterize the movement of the community college from the first generation to the present fifth generation, there has been a remarkable sameness in the work of teaching. As in previous generations of the community college, the essential work of the teacher is the management of the teaching and learning transaction. It is complex work. When it is done seriously, it demands a wide range of competencies, knowledge, and stamina. The work can generate intense interpersonal interactions. Integral to the work is the selection, preparation, and organization of teaching methods and materials. The teacher must learn about learners and about the consequences of learner characteristics for curriculum and instruction. Formative and summative evaluation of learner outcomes and the teaching process itself is an essential aspect of the work. Teaching can occur in a variety of settings, including the classroom, lecture hall, shop, laboratory, clinic, office, playing field, or game court.

Inherent in the work of teaching are properties that promote teacher isolation and individualism. Commonly, colleges deploy teachers in classrooms that, though side by side, rarely connect in respect to the work of teaching and learning. Over the generations of the community college, there has been little in the ethos of teaching by way of vibrant and compelling norms and values to urge teachers to initiate and maintain colleague networks or support systems conducive to the sharing of knowledge and experience. Past efforts at innovation and experiment in curriculum, instructional procedures, integrated programs, or special subunits within the college have run up against tendencies of isolation and individualization (Cohen and Brawer, 1982, cf. chap. 6).

In the work of teaching, the teacher is called upon to exercise professional judgment regarding what to teach, how to teach it, and at what levels of expectation. Behind a sound professional judgment must be a firm knowledge of the subject matter, knowledge of instructional methods and curriculum design, and a sense of how and when people learn best. A large measure of subjectivity enters into professional judgments. The difficulty of specifying and ascertaining learner outcomes makes the work of teaching taxing and often frustrating. The difficulties in measuring learner success cause difficulties in measuring teacher success.

Teachers often display resistance to change and conservatism in their work. Conservatism arises from several preconditions fundamental to effective learning. One precondition is continuity in a course of instruction over a period of time, and another is the need for sequence in cumulative, reinforcing learning experiences. A source of resistance to change is the teacher's intellectual and emotional investment in his stock in trade—that is, knowledge of a subject and the skills to teach it. It can take a long time and much effort to bring teaching to a level of maximum effectiveness.

Teachers regard exhortations to change with suspicion and resistance when these sources of conservatism are ignored.

As complex and demanding as the work of teaching is, little is done by colleges to assist teachers in the mastery of their art and science or to help them plan, initiate, or participate in change. Little remains of the few preservice preparation programs of previous generations. Credentials, where they are necessary, require little or nothing by way of professional preparation other than subject matter knowledge or occupational skills and experience. Teachers learn to teach by trial and error, an unguided and lonely experience for the most part. Comprehensive in-service staff development programs that effectively improve instruction are rare.

Constancies and continuities in the work of teaching extend from previous generations into the present and very likely will be present in the future. However, changes are at work that could have profound effects on the future work of teaching. Pressures to change arise, for instance, from changes in the larger societal context, changes in learner characteristics and curricular choices, and changing expectations of the college and redefinitions of mission and goals, as well as changes in the occupations and bodies of knowledge that undergird curriculum. Teachers are being called upon to raise the level of sophistication and increase the productivity of their work in order to enhance the standards of quality, responsiveness, and cost-effectiveness of their colleges. Ironically, teachers all too often are called upon to be creative, responsible change agents with little or no support or guidance in how to perform this complex, demanding role.

Teachers are under pressure to expand and diversify their role as new tasks and goals are assigned to the colleges. For instance, colleges undertaking learner assessment and referral systems, sometimes called matriculation models, draw the teacher out of the classroom. Teaching work traditionally has included assessment of learner skills, but the matriculation model can demand a much greater extent of expertness in, say, preparing and administering assessment instruments and interpreting and disseminating the results. To make effective learner referrals to developmental personnel or developmental facilities, the teacher will need to have something of the counselor's skills and a comprehensive grasp of the structure and operations of the college. In time, the teacher's work may routinely include ongoing interaction with the college's counseling and developmental personnel in the coordination, planning, and evaluation of assessment, referral, and developmental systems.

Teachers once had a virtual monopoly on the role of manager of the teaching and learning transaction. Today, the monopoly is being challenged as the work of teaching is diffused throughout the college. Consequently, new roles come into being to share in the work of teaching. For instance, telecommunication technology has made "distance learning" a widespread phenomenon in community colleges. Phases of telecommunication-supported teaching can be managed by persons not designated as teachers and who may never have contact with the learners they affect. These roles may feed into an instructional system as curriculum specialists, instructional designers, paraprofessionals, market analysts, publicists, or evaluators. This diffusion of the teacher's role raises critical issues of control, standards, and security of employment.

Changes in society are echoed on the college campus. Of particular importance to faculty are the deep and pervasive societal changes stimulated by rapid and far-ranging developments in technology, particularly in the areas of information processing. Our time has been proclaimed the "information age" so often that the assertion has the virtual stature of fact. Faculty are challenged to respond creatively and effectively to changes set in motion in the larger society. Curriculum requires updating and new curriculum has to be developed. Technology beckons to be incorporated into teaching and learning.

The Career of Teaching. As the community college continues into the fifth generation, among its most important concerns should be the character of the career it offers its teachers and the quality of its cadre of career professionals.

Ordinarily, career refers to both a span of time and a sequence of events. In its idealized form, a career follows a sequence of signal events as it progresses through stages from entry to exit. A person begins his or her career upon presentation of requisite qualifications and an initial employment. Then comes further socialization to the norms of the profession and its ethos. During the early years, there is mastering of the knowledge and skills of the work and a settling in. Over time, rewards increase and competence grows. Recognition, status, a claim on the job, and opportunities for advancement come to pass. At a time of readiness, a fulfilled career ends with the worker's dignified exit from the profession. However, present trends, unless checked, promise to carry the career of teaching far from the logic, orderliness, and predictability of this idealized conceptualization.

In earlier generations of the community college, the career of teaching followed more closely the idealized portrayal. Historically, however, the career has lacked a clear identity when contrasted to that, for instance, of the university professor or the high school teacher. It lacks exacting entrance requirements, imperatives for continuing growth in the profession, and rigorous standards and procedures to enforce accountability for performance. In respect to credentialing, qualifications other than academic background or occupational experience have been minimal, and aspiring faculty members have been assumed ready to teach upon employment.

The career of community college teaching has had positive and attractive aspects. Historically, community college teaching offered higher salaries, better working conditions, and more prestige and status in the community than public school teaching. The career offered opportunity for a scholar who preferred teaching over research. With tenure and an apparently inexhaustible demand for instructional services, employment appeared to be unshakably secure. In the era of expansion and increase in the number of colleges, career mobility enabled a teacher to improve his or her position or to seek more congenial settings.

Fiscal stringencies, enrollment shifts, changing societal expectations, competition from other education providers and other developments described elsewhere in this book have undermined the positive, attractive aspects. Negative aspects have intensified, contributing to declining morale, lowering productivity, alienation, and disillusionment. Reductions in force and reductions in programs have dispelled any illusions of security of employment. Termination and threat of termination are a part of the contemporary milieu of teaching. In some areas, teachers have been compelled to seek retraining in other subject areas or occupations in order to continue teaching. Due to steady state or cutback, career mobility has virtually vanished. With the loss of mobility there has been a loss of a sense of career opportunity and open-endedness.

Other problems are perennial and inherent. The organizational structure of a college leaves little room for advancement within the role of teacher. As the role conventionally has been structured, a teacher could begin a career at age thirty and still be performing essentially the same work at age sixty-five. There are few, if any, rungs in the teacher's career ladder. Differentiation of responsibilities within the role of teacher with commensurate compensation are virtually unknown. As the "common knowledge" instructs, the path toward salary improvement and advancement leads out of the classroom.

Faculty demographics in one state point to changes that have important consequences for the character of the career of teaching and the instructional cadre. A study of age distributions over a three-year period found the cadre of California's full-time faculty to be shrinking and aging (Case, 1984). In the fall of 1983, close to 40 percent of the full-time faculty were fifty years of age or older. Some 21 percent of full-time faculty were eligible for retirement, having reached the age of fifty-five or older. Another 18 percent were between the ages of forty-five and fifty. By 1994, when the fifth-generation community college should be flourishing, some 40 percent of the full-time faculty could be eligible for retirement, with another 18 percent only several years away from eligibility. From 1981 to 1984, the number of younger, entry-level faculty decreased slightly, reflecting the decrease in new hires and contributing to the increasing average age of faculty as a whole.

A survey of California community college districts (Case, 1984) found an accelerated shrinking of the full-time faculty cadre in the academic year 1983–84. For that year, the number of separations (retirement, resignation, termination, or death) approached three times the numbers of the two previous years. Retirements accounted for 80 percent of the separations. Numerous individual decisions to retire were undoubtedly catalyzed by the one-time, special retirement incentives offered by many districts, which included cash stipends or bonuses of up to $15,000 in a few unusual instances, as well as promises of continuity in medical and insurance benefits and opportunities for part-time professional work in teaching, counseling, consulting, or special assignments. The same survey found that, in aggregate, the estimates by districts of new hires of full-time faculty made up for only about 40 percent of the total number of separations.

The aging and shrinking of the cadre has serious implications for the career of teaching and the capabilities of the colleges. Of course, there will be an unavoidable and necessary adjustment of the numbers of full-time faculty as enrollments decline or curriculums are discontinued. But beyond these adjustments, demographics signal an impending surge of retirements that could cut deeply into the cadre.

Some replacement will be necessary. Even if the number of new hires is substantially less than the number of retirements, an excellent and rare opportunity is nevertheless presented for restaffing the cadre with persons who have talents, competencies, experiences, and outlooks that suit them well for the changing work and career of teaching. The overuse of part-time faculty poses another serious problem for the career of teaching and the integrity of the cadre. The past decade has seen an increase in the proportion of part-time instructors. Interestingly, in a short-run exception to this larger national trend, the number of persons teaching part time declined in California some 22 percent from 1981–82 to 1983–84.

Rewards and Incentives. Entwined and interacting with issues of the work and career of teaching are issues of rewards and incentives. Promising to have serious effects on the future of the teacher's professional life are the ineffectiveness and inequity of the present system, which is undiscriminating, clumsy, and obsolete. One informed observer notes that the present incentives often send wrong or inadequate signals to the teacher as to what kinds of performance and productivity are really important to the college (Roueche and Watkins, 1982).

Rewards and incentives are in both tangible and intangible forms. The most tangible reward, of course, is the salary and benefit package. Problems of low salaries and declining purchasing power are well known. A less tangible but important source of reward for teachers is the positive regard of knowledgeable colleagues, but this is difficult to obtain because of the isolation inherent in the work of teaching and the lack of opportunity for teachers to interact on the subject of their teaching. Positive feedback from students is another potent but ephemeral reward and one that is difficult to share with others. The opportunity to work with students within a subject area or occupation of personal significance remains a source of reward for serious teachers.

Learner success is a powerful motivator of teacher preparation and performance. Yet conflict and confusion have arisen as to what constitutes success. The ideology of the community college has promoted the "open door success story." It is the story of an individual student's success at overcoming odds and finding and activating personal potential. A teacher, working with the student, opens the doors of opportunity. The emphasis on individual success clashes with the present emphasis on success as measured by the aggregated numbers of student contact hours per full-time faculty equivalent. "Productivity" or "efficiency" tells the teacher to concentrate on large groups, a message that runs counter to the concept of teacher success embedded in the open door success story.

Present salary and reward systems accord equal pay for unequal work and provide little by way of incentives for sustained distinguished performance or sanctions for substandard work. The lines of accountability are tenuous and blurred, so that along with teachers who give more than the expected measure are those who do just enough and others who, for whatever reason, are below standard. Consider the spectrum of performance represented by three teachers who might, hypothetically, teach different sections of the same course in adjacent classrooms. One could be the "teacher of the year," obliging herself to live up to the highest standards. Herself a learner, she presses on with her own professional development, growing, adapting, and renewing in response to changes in clientele, subject matter, or college goals. Her neighbor could be competently but dully performing the basic necessary job of teaching. He would be described by the common knowledge as "retired on the job," a minimal performer who has found an equilibrium between the least that is expected and the most he is willing to produce. The third teacher barely gets by with outdated material, outmoded methods, negative attitudes, irregular attendance, simplistic tests, and low image and expectations of learners. She would be described as "deadwood." The irony is that all three, given the same years of experience and schooling, will receive equal pay.

Serious, stubborn problems reside in the matters of rewards and incentives. The problems are not entirely fiscal. Issues of reward and incentive in terms of esteem of colleagues and learners, personal and professional satisfactions, fulfilling relationships with colleagues, or the sense of identification, significance, and effectiveness in the institution require more than money for resolution. How faculty might be effectively rewarded for excellence in teaching and motivated for professional growth and institutional participation is a crucial issue with a strong bearing on the future.

Faculty Participation. At the beginning of this chapter, the question was raised as to whether faculty members can shape the future of their professional life. They can, if the centrality of faculty to the functioning of the college is fully recognized and understood and if faculty participation in governance continues to enlarge and become more effective. However, neither of these preconditions is foreordained by present trends.

The fourth generation saw an accelerated general trend of increased faculty participation. Academic senates began to appear in large numbers in the 1960s and took on larger roles. Collective bargaining units proliferated to make a profound impact on the policies and practices of colleges and how they are managed. Statewide and local professional organizations and associations with legislative advocates developed, as did discipline-based organizations. Faculty members have taken places on national and state commissions, committees, and task forces.

At the local, college, or district level, faculty tie in to processes of governance in a variety of ways. Faculty participate as members of a department or other subunit and may be called upon to cast votes in some form of a college-wide governance system. Teachers participate on committees, standing or ad hoc. Academic senates afford means for participation. Collective bargaining has brought a formalized, legalistic contractual means for linking faculty into governance and administrative processes. Informally, individual teachers exercise influence by giving advice and counsel to decision makers.

The general trend toward increased participation has not been without conflict or reversals. Established norms, organizational structures, and processes have been challenged. While the most visible conflicts have been over wages, hours, and working conditions, there have been no less important conflicts over matters that pertain to the work of teaching, such as pedagogy, curriculum, standards, educational policy, allocation of resources, and evaluation of personnel.

Some evidence points to a perceived decline in influence of faculty. A survey taken by the Institute of Higher Education at Columbia University's Teachers College found that the percentage of faculty agreeing to the following statement declined from 64 percent in 1970 to 44 percent in 1980 (Anderson, 1983, p. 82), "A concept of 'shared authority' by which faculty members and administrators arrive at decisions jointly, describes fairly well the college's system of governance."

In an interview, Richard E. Anderson, director of the survey, said evidence from the ten community colleges surveyed showed a "dramatic decline in institutional spirit, concern for innovation, and democratic governance" (Magerrell, 1982, p. 1). He noted that faculty members felt a loss of control and perceived that "presidents, system chancellors, and local politicians are more likely to be making the decisions" (p. 1).

Effective and responsible faculty participation is constrained. In principle, the locus of the teacher's role is at the center of the core of activity where the essential work of the college is performed. Yet in several critical ways, the teacher is peripheral to the processes of decision making, distanced by the isolating tendencies of the work, and excluded by the hardening of layers of administrative personnel who are themselves moving toward a professionalization of management. Organizational processes should be centripetal when they are too often centrifugal. Standing in the way of faculty participation are histories of conflict and legacies of divisiveness, and at some colleges entrenched lines of battle are drawn up and adversarial modes have become a way of life.

Views of the Future: Three Scenarios

It should be apparent that the teaching profession is characterized by continuity and constancy. Some might even say that it is characterized by heavy, change-resisting inertia. Yet changes are at work that could alter fundamentally the character of the profession. Where these changes might lead is conjectured in the following three scenarios, each set in the mid 1990s.

Business as Usual Scenario. The professional life of the teacher is similar to that of 1985. The work of teaching is similar for many teachers, except for adjustments in texts and other teaching materials, methods, and policy, such as grading and standards. Organizational units are set up to provide telecommunications and other instructional delivery systems. Some veteran teachers have gone along with the innovations, while others, relatively secure in traditional curricular areas, are apart and aloof. The college seems more than ever like a collection of separatist functions, housed at a common campus and held together by managers and quasimanagers. These administrators also supervise instructional teams of part-time teachers and short-term contract professionals and other specialists who undertake, among other functions, market analysis, curriculum design and delivery, and evaluation. The work of teaching is dispersed throughout the college.

Some faculty have moved with the trends and taken pains to find ways to develop the skills and knowledge necessary to join the instructional teams. Some teacher activists participate in governance by means of collective bargaining units and academic senates. However, there is a strong adversarial presence in management-faculty relations. Quantification of productivity has institutionalized a version of teaching success that is described, in a phrase, as "more is better."

Highly flexible, entrepreneurial teachers with a flair for systems design find rewards in their work and are motivated by a sense of accomplishment and added income for added work. Traditional teachers reconcile themselves to a less prestigious status in the faculty. They feel eclipsed by what they regard as the flashy newcomers who appear to have no loyalty or even concern for a particular college but who market their skills wherever the price is right. Incentives for early retirement are extensive and elaborate, which, though widely used, give the veteran teacher a feeling of not being wanted.

How did the business as usual scenario come to pass? During Generation 4, the colleges continued to struggle for self-definition and direction as crisis followed crisis, all with ever more constrained resources. Inertia, conservatism, self-serving pursuit of narrow, short-range interests battled inconclusively and expensively with adaptation, innovation, and attempts at leadership through-out the decade.

Neglect and Decline Scenario. The teachers are uneasy, poorly paid workers whose centrality to the teaching and learning transaction is gone. Collective bargaining units, fortified with legalistic rules and procedures, are the only remaining means for faculty participation in governance. Unions are dominated by faculty oligarchs who frequently move into management positions after a period of officership in a bargaining unit. Academic senates, committees, and other linkages have atrophied. The work of teaching is accomplished largely by paraprofessionals, technical specialists, and various professionals on short-term contracts who work under the direct supervision of managers. Strategies of marketing and the pressures of consumerism dominate the thinking and activities of a management system which regards the aging faculty as a tenured-in, unresponsive and obstructionist element.

It is not pleasant to be considered an old-fashioned, old-time teacher. The college sends learners the message that it is better to avoid these classroom-bound anachronisms with their nontechno-logical, imprecise ways of teaching. An occasional consolation to the aging teacher is an aging learner. The "Great Teacher of the Year" awards go to teacher entrepreneurs who tote up the most impressive quantifications of success.

How did this come about? One hears most often a neglect hypothesis, and the blame is placed on both faculty and managers. Faculty, it is argued, neglected to grow and develop the competencies required of them to carry on successfully the teaching and learning transaction for a changing clientele in a changing environment. Those who spoke for the institutional view and urged even greater dedication to pedagogy and curriculum development and participation in college processes outside the scope of collective bargaining generally were not heeded and eventually became still. Managers, for their part, neglected to do the hard, conflict-ridden work of developing the means and incentives for faculty participation. Managers succumbed to a marketing approach predicated on short-term survival of the institution.

This future is possible but not highly probable. The probability of its occurrence would depend on intensification of negative pressures in the environment, such as even more drastic downturns in levels of financial support, too effective competition by nonschool educative entities, or political struggles over centralization that preempt the attention and energies of administrative and faculty leaders. Negative pressures internal to the college would come from further politicization of governance processes, hardening of class lines, and intensification of adversarial relationships in collective bargaining. The main factor that would increase the probability of this scenario would be the failure of college leadership, both faculty and management, to find common grounds for collective activity and their inability to conceptualize and fund internal processes of staff and organizational processes to accomplish renewed institutional goals.

Proactive Adaptation Scenario. This is the preferred future. The comprehensive community college is in better shape than it has been for many years. Despite several years of conflict, the life of the community college teacher is, by all reports, vastly improved. Though there are still curricular islands inhabited by teachers who seem suspended in time, the overall organizational character of the college has changed and the life of the teacher with it. Teachers still teach, but in varied modes. Teachers participate in the full range of organizational processes. Participation is no longer advisory—it is substantive. Teachers are encouraged to innovate by redesigned reward and incentive systems. The concepts of "teaching success" and "the great teacher" have been redefined: Teaching success means effectiveness in facilitating learning and institutional participation. A great teacher is less the sentimental hero with rare, mystical gifts than a person who is able to orchestrate effectively a wide repertoire of organizational skills, interpersonal skills, knowledge of subject matter and pedagogy, and strategies for curricular design.

Because the work of teaching and the sources of effectiveness are better understood, specifications and expectations for the varied aspects of the teacher's role are delineated explicitly. Development of human resources has a top priority and a strong claim on college resources. Its importance is manifested in recruitment efforts precisely targeted to highly desirable talents, competencies, and traits, as well as in pre- and in-service development programs and career counseling and development program offices.

The locus of the teacher's role in the organizational scheme of things has been shifted from the periphery to the centers of decision making and policy formulation. Stronger linkages are in place, with a delegation of responsibility to the teachers that brings them into vital participation in governance. The role of the teacher is central to the college by virtue of a broadened scope of operations and the greater depth of knowledge and skills acquired.

Early retirement incentives are elaborate and effective, and they serve the interests of teachers who cannot or do not want to adjust to the fifth-generation community college. It is scarcely possible anymore to "do my thing" in the isolation of the classroom. This loss of autonomy distresses some teachers, as does the presence of numerous teacher colleages who clearly do not fit the mold of the old school. Extensive colleague interaction and teamwork are involved in the work of teaching, and this rides poorly with some teachers. For others, the opportunity to vary the work of teaching provides novel experiences and energizing incentives. For the short or long term, on an ad hoc or regularized basis, teachers can be researchers, for instance, or curriculum designers, evaluators, market analysts, mentors, staff development facilitators, or project directors.

Proposals to Achieve the Proactive Adaptation Scenario

Realizing the preferred future, the proactive adaptation scenario, will demand much of college leaders. Funds will be in short supply, competition from public and private education providers will stiffen, and enrollment fluctuations will present problems in the fifth generation. Leaders will have to be resourceful and wise as they cope with these problems, as well as with organizational rigidities and obstacles lodged in a college's history and culture. Some proposals are offered for consideration.

Meet the Challenges of New Work and New Roles. Faculty should be encouraged to expand their competencies and motivated to take up the kinds of teaching-related work brought to the college by the assignment of new tasks and expectations, such as those related to matriculation and assessment models and new instructional technologies. For the new work, job descriptions need to be developed by participatory planning. Output and performance standards need to be made explicit and tied to learner outcomes. Within systems such as learner assessment and referral models, cross-role training and exchanges would improve mutual awareness of function and improve system operation. Planning for curriculum and instruction should incorporate effective, collegial strategies for goal setting, problem solving, evaluation, interpersonal relations, and communication. Up-to-date, well-funded staff development must be provided to enable existing faculty to acquire needed competencies and knowledge. Personnel policy and practices must be geared to bring in those human resources necessary for the new kinds of work. Faculty, trustees, and managers need to work together to evolve shared understandings on policy and practices for the recruitment, preparation, and continuing development of new faculty. The "more of the same" approach must give way to policies that support the securing of new talent for new work.

Diffusion of the teacher's monopoly on the delivery of instruction can be turned into an enhancement of the role of teacher by establishing instructional teams with leadership roles for teachers. Teams should be flexible and ad hoc. To facilitate team functioning, process consultants should be made available. To preserve the benefits to the college and learners of necessary stability and continuity, conventional roles should be maintained and honored for the work they do best.

To move positively and constructively into the future, faculty will need to respond to large-scale social changes, such as the rapid development and applications of technology and the advent of the information age. Faculty resistance to technology, however, should be recognized as a response that has a rational basis: Technology brings change, and change threatens. The value of technological innovation to instruction has been oversold in the past. However, threat diminishes with familiarity. Future shock is abated when a teacher gains perspective on where change might lead and what it could mean to the individual and to the institution. To promote familiarity, the college can develop its own curriculum on societal change, its consequences, and possible futures. This kind of learning can become an essential element in a college's strategic planning. Faculty can be encouraged to be instructors as well as learners in a study of social analysts and commentators who assert the advent of the information society and trace its potential implications through society onto the college campus and into the classroom.

The community college needs to fully appreciate its potential importance in the information society. The college traffics in knowledge and skills essential to the emergent society and can offer in its general education the skills of learning, adaptation, and social and personal awareness necessary for the survival and welfare of the individual.

Resistance to technology as a tool of instruction can be abated through familiarization with and illustration of its uses. For instance, faculty can participate in staff development workshops on computer literacy conducted by other faculty and learn from demonstrations by other faculty of how the computer or other technologies have been incorporated into instruction.

Enhance and Upgrade the Career of Teaching. The present character of the teaching career needs modification. Practices of private-sector research and development companies and other high-tech industries should be gleaned for ways to facilitate career entry and exit, maintain and enhance skills, and attract promising candidates. Rungs should be added to the teacher's career ladder. Career stages should be recognized, for instance, by institutionaliz-ing mentor roles. Qualifications for entry should be examined and, with equity and reasonableness, upgraded. Qualifications, de facto and de jure, informal and formal, must be realigned to lead to a preferred future. Faculty replacements simply must not be clones of the old school models. Qualifications for the fifth-generation faculty will include talents, competencies, and outlooks that are presently scarce or nonexistent.

The impending shortage of teachers must be anticipated. Each retirement offers an opportunity to build a stronger fifth-generation faculty; restaffing and maintaining the cadre must result in much more than merely the replication of the present faculty. Since universities cannot be relied on to provide preservice training other than in academic specialties, the colleges must develop their own professionals. Colleges need to establish intake and preparation programs to recruit, screen, prepare, and evaluate new faculty in an ongoing, in-service internship induction type of model. Part-time instructor pay and amenities should be upgraded and proportionately more should be expected of them. At a minimum, staff development should be mandatory to orient parttimers to the community college, impart basics of planning curriculum and instruction, and provide support and evaluation, preferably by faculty mentors.

Reward and Motivate Quality Performance. The many problems of rewards and incentives will not be solved by simply providing more money, though securing adequate basic salaries, especially at entry levels, and equitable pay for part-time instructors is a necessary first step. Nor is it likely that any combination of rewards and incentives will guarantee, person by person, job satisfaction. Brawer argues that job satisfaction reflects the quality of life a person experiences outside the working situation more than it does the interaction between the workplace and that person (Brawer, 1979). Yet rewards and incentives must be overhauled to motivate, to the extent possible, performance and professional growth.

As the work of teaching diversifies, differentials in pay can be attached to differentials in the kinds of work performed. In effecting differential pay schemes, simplistic merit pay incentives based on dubious evaluation plans, popularity contests, or favoritism must be avoided. Diversification and expansion of the role of teacher can provide opportunity for rewards of an intangible nature by affording faculty opportunity to undertake short-term, out-of-the-classroom assignments. Quasimanagerial positions, such as project director, evaluator, researcher, coordinator, grant writer, team leader, planner, or futurist, for example, will energize faculty members with the challenge of learning and using new skills, acquiring new knowledge and perspectives of the college and its functioning, engaging in new relations, and self-discovery. Faculty members enjoy the respect of their colleagues and the opportunity to interact as fellow learners. Faculty lecture series, seminars, and symposia can bring together faculty to teach one another in a community of learners.

Burnout, to the extent possible, should be prevented and abated. While burnout is a widely used term validated by the teacher's common knowledge, it is difficult to define and analyze. Cohen links it to job satisfaction and notes its sources and incidence (Cohen and Brawer, 1982). Burnout can arise from very personal, individual sources unreachable by any efforts of the college. It also arises from college-related circumstances that can be reached, such as an environment of protracted stress and conflict, bureaucratic indifference to individual needs and differences, meager rewards and unclear expectations, isolation and alienation. While the college cannot become a therapeutic community, it can identify and denote resources for faculty who need help and offer, through humane, reality-based counseling, ways to renew interest in teaching, to develop new skills, or, in some cases, to leave the profession. Delineating and implementing evaluation procedures capable of identifying incompetence and procedures capable of dismissing incompetent personnel are challenges to management and faculty leaders.

Disincentives and negative rewards should be sought out and counteracted. Bureaucratic unfairness and "one size fits all" policies that bear down on the innocent together with the guilty dampen individual will to perform and breed cynicism. Inequitable distribution of resources, favoritism, and star systems discourage productivity. Barriers and discouragements of institutionalized sexism, racism, and agism need to be removed.

Participate Effectively and Constructively. As recent years will attest, issues of faculty participation in institutional affairs can generate very serious consequences for both the forms of participation and the substantive matters of participation. Proposals for effective and greater faculty participation are made on the premise that it will enhance college vitality and shape the future of faculty in a preferred direction. In the preferred future, the faculty is a proactive faculty, participating constructively and effectively. There should be no illusion that change in this area will be cheap or that it will be achieved without great effort.

Senates and bargaining units need to clearly delineate between their respective scope and functions. Innovations in the forms of participation can be stimulated by new approaches to management and awareness of participatory modes in industry and business. To do what they do well, committees should continue to be a vehicle for participation, but their limitations of politicization, lethargy, and least-common-denominator compromises need to be transcended by other modes, such as task forces, single-purpose one-time groups, or ad hoc teams that self-liquidate upon completion of an assigned task.

Participatory modes can be shaped around the new kinds of work the fifth-generation colleges are striving toward, such as open, consultative, consensus-building processes for budget development and review, college goal setting, or strategic planning, as well as more commonplace work now made all the more imperative—such as program review, curriculum development, and establishing systems for personnel evaluation and staff and organizational development. As faculty participate, it is important that they be more than advisers. Authority commensurate with responsibility needs to be assigned. Leadership development for faculty leaders is as important as management development. To ensure the functioning of modes of participation, new or old, programs in staff and organizational development are necessary.

Cultivate Human Resources: Key to Preferred Future. A recurrent note in these proposals has been the need for staff and organizational development. Staff and organizational development can be the keys to unlock many of the issues and problems discussed here. By staff and organizational development, I do not mean either the top-down indoctrinations inspired by management that were so familiar to previous generations or the easy-answer panaceas all too often offered up as the means for improving instruction and college functioning. I refer to structured, well-funded and staffed programs supported by management commitment and faculty participation—

programs that build on the considerable body of existing theory, practice, and experience. Staff development should focus on human resources while organizational development focuses on organizational processes and interpersonal relations.

The fifth-generation community colleges require fifth-generation staff and organizational development. There should be an intensification of self-study by colleges to help them better understand their own cultures and the impact of culture on organizational success. There should be newly designed and energized university-based programs for advanced study and research. Colleges should be as interested in their cultures as corporations are in theirs. Colleges should seek collaboration with those elements in the private sector in which continuing education, innovations, improved organization and conditions of work, management of information, and development of human resources have become integral to their functioning.

From among the colleges, models of the most successful efforts and most interesting failures in staff and organizational development, rewards and incentives, participation, and the work and career of teaching should be gathered and disseminated. Lastly, faculty and managers should realize that they do, in fact, help shape the future of their colleges. Essential to the achievement of a desirable future is present planning and action. In this, teachers and teaching are of vital importance.

References

Anderson, R. E. *Higher Education in the 1970s: Preliminary Technical Report for Participating Institutions.* New York: Institute for Higher Education, Columbia University, 1983.

Brawer, F. B. "Personality Attributes of Two-Year College Instructors." *Community College Frontiers,* 1979, 7 (3), 22–26.

Bryant, D. *Ella Price's Journal.* New York: New American Library, 1972.

Case, C. H. "Impending Faculty Staffing Problems: What the Figures Tell Us." *FACCC Bulletin,* 1984, pp. 4–5.

Cohen, A. M., and Brawer, F. B. *The American Community College.* San Francisco: Jossey-Bass, 1982.

London, H. B. *The Culture of a Community College.* New York: Praeger, 1978.

Magerrell, J. "Decline in Faculty Morale Laid to Governance Role, Not Salary." *Chronicle of Higher Education,* Nov. 10, 1982, p. 1.

Roueche, J. E., and Watkins, K. "A Commitment to Great Teaching." *Community and Junior College Journal,* 1982, *53* (1), 22-25.

5

Richard A. Donovan

Creating Effective Programs
for Developmental Education

One of the most important phenomena in postsecondary education during the past decade has been the sudden growth of developmental education. When unprecedented numbers of underprepared students arrived on college campuses in the early 1970s, they posed a dramatic challenge to faculty who themselves were often underprepared for such a task. Yet developmental educators responded with energy and creativity, producing, in slightly over ten years, a wide range of innovative classroom strategies, instructional materials, and learning environments that offered students a legitimate chance to succeed. It was the profession at its best.

  Like John Naisbitt (1982), I believe the most valuable way to anticipate the future is to understand the present. In this chapter, I will briefly trace the history of developmental education, survey the most notable advances that emerged during the 1970s, and then discuss the directions I believe colleges are and should be heading in the fifth generation.

103

History of Developmental Education

Although K. Patricia Cross (1976) traces the roots of developmental education back to a precollege mathematics course offered at Wellesley College in 1894, it wasn't until the 1970s, in the fourth generation of community colleges, that developmental education assumed an identifiable form. Fortified by the moral fervor of the civil rights movement, pushed by the activists of the 1960s, and convinced that "success" in high school had been too narrowly and rigidly defined, frustrated students and faculty forced colleges to open their doors wider, thereby expanding access for minority students and for all students who had been ill-served by the secondary system. This effort was so successful that by the mid 1970s, fully 95 percent of two-year colleges and 41 percent of four-year colleges identified themselves as open-access institutions (Roueche and Snow, 1977).

The national rush into developmental education was perhaps symbolized by the open admissions experiences of the City University of New York (CUNY), a mix of eight two-year and nine four-year colleges. Because of the dimension of CUNY's effort and the speed with which the university implemented its decision, the open admissions programs of the seventeen CUNY colleges attracted national attention. In 1970, with less than six months' advance warning, CUNY's freshman class rose to 35,000 students, a 75 percent increase from the previous year. The majority of these new students would not have been admitted on the basis of traditional university criteria. As a consequence, in the fall of 1970, 39 percent of the freshmen at CUNY's senior colleges and 66 percent of the freshmen at the community colleges were open admissions students (Lavin, Alba, and Silberstein, 1981). As CUNY struggled with great numbers of underprepared students, other colleges in different areas of the country were responding to similar pressures and began to revise their curricula, revamp or initiate supportive services, and, sometimes, rethink their educational missions.

Many of the students entering through expanded access programs lacked the academic skills and study habits that colleges had traditionally, though perhaps incorrectly, assumed students brought with them as freshmen. Basic skills courses and support systems had to be developed if severely underprepared students were to stand an academic chance, particularly during the inevitable dislocation and adjustment of the freshman year. The courses, services, and learning environments created for these underprepared students have become known as developmental education. While my discussion will largely focus on developmental education at the community colleges, such an emphasis is somewhat arbitrary. All but a handful of four-year colleges and universities have been affected by expanded access programs, and the "lessons" of developmental education apply directly, if not equally, to all types of institutions.

For the most part, developmental educators in the 1970s were sailing uncharted waters. Without many role models and without much of a literature to draw on, faculty improvised and learned while they taught. The proliferation of developmental education conferences since 1975 testifies, among other things, to the faculty's eagerness and need to seek confirmation that they were "on course," and to adjust that course as new information and new strategies emerged. Clearly, this was a different direction for higher education. Some faculty might claim that the course was an unwise one, but no one could deny that a major new journey had begun.

It was not without navigational problems. The transition from selective to nonselective admissions policies was as difficult for faculty as for students. In fact, Martha Maxwell (1979) refers to the "trauma" that both faculty and the more prepared students experienced at the outset. As the decade progressed and as the proportion and number of underprepared students increased, many colleges experienced the further difficulties of budget hardships and many faculty, particularly at the community colleges, began to teach more and larger developmental courses. Few community college faculty entered college teaching expecting to teach predominantly developmental courses, and as the implications of expanded access became clearer, the "acceptance" of developmental education by many faculty became grudging and sometimes bittersweet.

However, legitimate and exaggerated faculty worries should not obscure the real progress that was made. Although it may be unwise to date the legitimatization of developmental education, surely the publication of Mina Shaughnessy's *Errors and Expectations* in 1977 announced to the world that developmental education was attracting first-rate teacher-scholars like Shaughnessy, that a generation of faculty were lavishing on the composing process or mathematics anxiety the same rigor and attention that other faculty devoted to the subplot in *King Lear* or to the implications of Yalta for twentieth-century diplomacy.

Developmental programs became more sophisticated, too. Colleges became adept at analyzing the needs of entering students, rethinking instructional procedures—at least as they applied to developmental courses—and determining when students had completed a developmental or precollege sequence. The popularity of mastery learning (Cross, 1976) indicates a growing commitment to document the progress and success of developmental students.

Many colleges now realize that since they are not likely to be relieved of the responsibility for developmental education in the forseeable future, this newly won expertise will be a valuable commodity. Three reasons dominate colleges' thinking. First, there is little evidence indicating that the tightening of high school standards will greatly affect the number of recent high school graduates underprepared for college-level work (Ribaudo, Roellig, and Lederman, 1982). The state of New Jersey, for example, recently announced that freshmen entering public colleges have not improved meaningfully in mathematics skills over the past five years. State officials estimate that fully 61 percent of New Jersey's freshman class in 1982 lacked proficiency in algebra. While it is true that current high school students are doing better at simple arithmetic than they have in the past, they show little or no gain at applying these skills to mathematical problem solving (Maeroff, 1983b).

Second, as the number of recent high school graduates declines, it is increasingly unlikely that many colleges facing enrollment shortfalls will deny admission to underprepared applicants. College officials are usually committed to institutional survival. With fewer prepared applicants, it is inevitable that the balance will be filled by less prepared ones.

Third, one of the salutary benefits of open admissions has been the increased attention that colleges now pay to assessing the needs of entering students. As colleges began to test all freshman, they discovered that many students whose high school averages indicated that they were prepared for college lacked essential skills. This conclusion has been reinforced by the steady decline in and now the leveling off of Scholastic Aptitude Test scores (Cohen and Brawer, 1982). Roueche (Roueche and Snow, 1977) notes the emergence of reading laboratories and developmental writing courses at such bastions of preparedness as Stanford and Berkeley as indicators of this trend. Students are equally underprepared in mathematics. A national survey of universities and four-year colleges found that enrollment in remedial mathematics increased 40 percent from 1970 to 1975 and 72 percent from 1975 to 1980 (*Remedial Education in College*, 1983).

Finally, with the dramatic increase in the number of minority students in the 1970s, there will be substantial pressure not to retreat from postsecondary education's new and belated diversity. If the "fairness" principle continues, the most cursory look at demographic projections indicates that Hispanic Americans will join blacks as a dominant minority group as the fifth generation evolves. Differences in language and culture make it clear that precollege and supplemental help must be offered if substantial numbers of Hispanics are to be offered a fair opportunity to succeed.

Emerging Trends in the Fifth Generation

The gains made by developmental educators in the 1970s become all the more noteworthy when the relative youth of the basic skills movement is considered. Despite those who claim that it is too early to make value judgments, promising approaches have been identified (Schaier, 1977; Donovan, 1976; Cross, 1976; Trillin and Associates, 1980; Cohen and Brawer, 1982), and the screening process used by foundations and selective federal agencies such as the Fund for the Improvement of Postsecondary Education indicates that the initiatives of some well-regarded programs warrant a close look. My survey of the literature, foundation and federal awards, and direct observation suggest that distinct progress has been achieved in five major areas: instruction and counseling, program administration, in-service programs, educational collaboration, and assessment. In this section, I will review recent trends in each of these areas.

Instruction and Counseling. Virtually every observer of developmental education in the 1970s commented on the energy and time that colleges committed in their attempts to match instructional strategies to the needs of underprepared students (Maxwell, 1979; Roueche and Snow, 1977; Lavin, Alba, and Silberstein, 1981; Trillin and Associates, 1980). Cross (1976) goes so far as to characterize this national effort as "the instructional revolution." Seldom, it seems, had the art of teaching mattered so much to so many.

One of the most significant features of classroom instruction was the decentralization of authority. While the responsibility of faculty was in no way lessened, efforts to determine how faculty could function most effectively led frequently to a rejection of the lecturer-listener model that many of the faculty themselves had experienced as students. Perhaps representative of this approach was the teacherless writing class described by Peter Elbow (1973). While Elbow in no way trivialized the role of the classroom instructor, he did emphasize the value of the teacher as participant in class activities and stress the need for students to further their own learning by accepting more responsibility for it. The "collaborative learning" approach of the 1970s, still popular in the 1980s, is one practical variant of Elbow's theory.

The expanded use of peer tutors and peer counselors is consistent with collaborative learning and with the decentralized classroom. Here again, the role of the instructor (or the counselor) is more fluid, with peers assuming some of the elementary and diagnostic work with students. Faculty who use peer counseling programs comment on the collegiality of the classrooms and emphasize that the intervention by peers is invariably perceived as less threatening by students (Maxwell, 1979; Arkin and Shollar, 1982). Institutions that have attached tutoring or laboratory components to reading, writing, and mathematics classes underscore the importance of peer tutors, peer counselors, and learning center staff.

Perhaps the chief reason for the emphasis on collaborative or interactive learning, and the insistence on the value of tutoring and learning center assignments, was the desire of colleges to create a positive learning environment. Faculty in practically all disciplines learned to respect and address the academic anxieties of students. While *mathematics anxiety* became a popular term early in the decade, soon others were mentioning writing and reading "blocks" that interfered with student learning. It was the near unanimous conviction that if these different anxieties were not addressed, classroom achievement would be seriously hampered.

Beyond combating specific or generic anxieties, however, the desire to create and sustain an environment in which students were encouraged to succeed prevailed. Arthur Chickering (Hall, 1982) and others stressed the importance of students attaining self-confidence and a sense of competence if they were to do well in college. Cross (1981) claimed that high self-evaluations of underprepared adult learners were critical to their progress. In an attempt to create a supportive environment, colleges tried to bring instructors and counselors into working harmony. Often the first collaboration occurred in precollege and first-semester orientation programs for high-risk students or academic "bridge" summers for such students prior to their freshman year. The purpose of these different programs was the same: Colleges reasoned that if students were more familiar with their institutions and with each other, and if they could have successful precollege academic experiences, they were more likely to begin their freshman year with confidence and to persist.

Program Administration. In their desire to offer high-risk students the maximum opportunities for success, many colleges reassessed and altered existing administrative practices. For example, colleges had to decide whether developmental courses should be offered by existing departments or divisions or whether new ones should be created. While Richardson, Fisk, and Okun (1983, p. 165) argue that creating special developmental studies departments virtually "insures discontinuities between remedial and advanced courses in the same field," Lavin, Alba, and Silberstein (1981) and Roueche and Snow (1977) note that there has been no clear resolution to this debate.

In the critical area of the allocation of institutional resources, Donovan (1976) notes that colleges have found imaginative ways to fund developmental programs. For example, Oscar Rose Jr. College in Oklahoma assigned the bulk of its federally funded counseling hours to first-semester freshmen. Other colleges made similar allocations. They reasoned that since the first semester was critical for most underprepared students, concentrating institutional resources and services on this key semester made sense.

Colleges began to realize, too, that the problems of developmental students were highly complicated and interlocking. For example, since developmental students were likely to be required to take courses that carried partial or no credit toward their graduation, everything from financial aid to what constituted satisfactory academic progress had to be reexamined in light of the necessarily slow progress many students would make (Lavin, Alba, and Silberstein, 1981). It became clear that developmental students began the freshman year at such a disadvantage that colleges would have to augment the typical instructional program by offering the students more time and additional help if they were to be successful.

To maximize the chances for success, colleges allocated funds for expanded tutoring programs and learning centers. Trained tutors proved to be a flexible, economic resource, and by the end of the decade many colleges had established the peer counseling programs described in the last section as well. Learning centers, while costly, provided a versatile resource both for faculty seeking to personalize and diversify instruction and for students attempting to learn new material at their own speed (Maxwell, 1979).

In-Service Programs for Faculty and Administrators. While pedagogical and organizational innovations abounded in the 1970s, institutions initiated concurrent efforts to increase their staffs' skills. Two areas that attracted considerable interest were the efforts to broaden the faculty's academic responsibilities and to enhance their teaching abilities.

Before the 1970s, a wide gulf had separated the developmental faculty laboring with basic skills courses and the faculty teaching intermediate and upper-level courses, who were largely sheltered and absolved from the responsibilities of dealing with such problems. To many, though, it became clear that if the skills learned during prefreshman courses were not reinforced in subsequent courses, these newly won competencies would atrophy and students would be back where they started. Few efforts of the 1970s were as noteworthy or as promising as the inservice efforts to promote basic skills instruction in college-level courses.

The first breakthrough occurred in the area of writing. Pioneering institutions, such as Beaver College in Pennsylvania and the University of Michigan, developed writing-across-the-curriculum projects—projects that encouraged and trained faculty in disciplines other than English to respect and attend to the writing needs of students in their courses. Efforts to redistribute the responsibility for promoting good writing addressed the lament by many faculty that graduates of developmental writing courses did not write well enough in subsequent biology or history courses.

Efforts to involve other academic departments in writing assessment deserve note as well. Johnson State College in Vermont, for example, was one of several colleges to develop a program whereby faculty from all departments were trained to assess students' writing proficiency and place students in the appropriate first-year writing courses based on these assessments. The decision by the University of Minnesota and other institutions to postpone the second half of the traditional Freshman English course until the junior or senior year was promising, too. Junior or senior writing courses attempted to tailor writing assignments to the student's academic major and encouraged faculty from different departments to discuss what constitutes effective writing and sometimes to help shape the curriculum.

Such attention to the continuing writing needs of students led to attention to the other competencies as well. Perhaps the most ambitious program was initiated at LaGuardia Community College in New York. There the Integrated Skills Reinforcement program provides a comprehensive program that systematically builds in basic instruction to intermediate and upper-level courses, thereby reinforcing earlier gains and distributing basic skills responsibility to all members of the faculty.

The different programs to reinforce newly acquired basic skills dramatized the attention paid to making classrooms as flexible and responsive as possible. Sheila Tobias (1978) and others insisted that student anxieties with particular subjects interfered with their progress. They argued that faculty had to attend to the affective as well as the cognitive needs of students and suggested that faculty inexperienced in such matters might need assistance in providing this help. While programs differed from college to college, the counselors typically became more identified with and involved in the instructional process. At some colleges, faculty and counselors would collaborate in the same classroom—to combat math anxiety, for example—whereas at other institutions counselors might become part of an interdisciplinary, instructional "team" that would meet regularly to design complementary assignments and to review students' progress. Counselors provided such teams with information that might explain student failures or poor attendance.

During the 1970s, institutionally sponsored workshops enabled faculty to practice new teaching techniques, blend student tutors into classroom work, integrate learning center assignments into the syllabi, and in general diversify faculty talents. Between 1972 and 1975, for example, the Vocational Education Act enabled Bronx Community College to offer over twelve different workshops to faculty, staff, administrators, and students in such areas as alternate teaching strategies, administrative decisionmaking, communication skills, and even the allocation of support services money.

Educational Collaboration. The rapid growth of developmental education and its relative youth encouraged institutions to collaborate with and learn from one another. Early in the decade, these collaborations were largely confined to postsecondary institutions. While two- and four-year colleges tried to work together to formulate articulation policies that would ease the transfer of students from one system to another, they also shared equipment and materials, addressed regional and local problems collaboratively, and participated in joint research projects. As the dimensions of the remedial problems of students were acknowledged, the collaboration extended to the secondary schools as well.

Proliferating developmental education conferences brought educators together to discuss local problems, share classroom strategies, and discuss future plans. Annual meetings held by the

National Association of Remedial and Developmental Special Programs, Networks, the Community College Program of the University of Texas, Appalachian State University, and the regional, federally funded TRIO associations (consisting of Upward Bound, Talent Search, and special services) represented only a few of the more popular conferences. Information and exemplary approaches were also shared in regular publications, such as Appalachian State's *The Journal of Remedial and Developmental Education* and the City University of New York's *Resource.* As the data base began to expand, such publications devoted special issues to more focused topics, such as innovations in English as a second language instruction (Gonzales, 1981) and reports on curricular and assessment projects which grew out of summer training institutes (Adelman, 1983).

Colleges also collaborated on research projects. A widely publicized effort was the Fund for the Improvement of Postsecondary Education's (FIPSE) National Project II: Alternative to the Revolving Door (NP II). For NP II, FIPSE selected five two-year and four four-year expanded-access institutions from 250 applicants and awarded them research monies to try to identify the variables critical to the success of their award-winning programs (Schaier, 1977). Projects like NP II helped legitimize the research efforts of developmental educators at the same time that it furthered collaboration.

Partnerships were established to address local problems as well. For example, Wellesley College and Wesleyan University joined forces in an attempt to reduce the mathematics anxiety of women students, a project that influenced several others and indicated that math anxiety was neither a problem confined to women nor one that could be addressed simply. The University of California at Berkeley collaborated with high schools in the area of writing. The Bay Area Writing Project (BAWP) trained high school English teachers to become better writing teachers by becoming better writers themselves. The influence of BAWP was extraordinary: By 1984, over ninety such collaborative writing projects had been established throughout the country.

Assessment. Researchers such as Cross (1976), Roueche and Snow (1977), and Lavin, Alba, and Silberstein (1981) have noted the increased attention that colleges devoted to determining entering student needs during the 1970s. Colleges were less likely to be satisfied with gross measures of previous success (high school rank, for example) but sought to discriminate among different student needs. While ACT and SAT test scores are still used at some colleges for admission and placement, many colleges employed disciplinary tests to validate the results of the standardized tests in writing, reading, and mathematics. Occasionally, such tests were administered in the natural and social sciences as well. More and more colleges, dissatisfied with standardized tests, developed tests of their own. In fact, Roueche and Snow (1977) discovered that 95 percent of community colleges used locally developed placement tests in at least one area. Ribaudo, Roellig, and Lederman (1982) note that 75 percent of their respondents relied heavily on local tests as the major determinants for remedial placement.

Institutions began to devote much time to determining students' affective as well as cognitive needs. In 1976, Cross noted the trend toward developmental programs that included affective and social as well as educational components. Community colleges in particular recognized that students with a previous record of failure were unlikely to enter college glowing with academic confidence. Astin (1975) indicated the high correlation between student attitudes about themselves and subsequent success in college. He also noted that only 22 percent drop out for poor academic performance. Murtha, Kaufman, and Warman (1981) reveals that financial difficulties are often the critical element as to whether students decide to remain in college. As a result, colleges began to develop sophisticated orientation programs to allay some of the students' anxieties. Many colleges established financial aid offices with well-trained personnel to provide quick and flexible assistance and encouraged faculty to integrate both affective and cognitive strategies into instructional programs.

Perhaps nothing helped legitimize developmental education more than the efforts of colleges to assess their programs' success. Although some writers were able to link success in remedial programs with achievement in subsequent courses (Hoban, 1983, and McCadden, 1983, show that their developmental students did better than students at their colleges who required no remediation), most researchers tend to relate success in remedial programs to retention. Lavin, Alba, and Silberstein (1981) note that in the giant, multicampus CUNY effort, success in remediation could only be linked with subsequent persistence in college. Cohen's (Cohen and Brawer, 1982) review of hundreds of studies confirms that the only conclusive effect of remedial programs nationally is the tendency to lower the student dropout rate. However, high attrition rates do not necessarily spell failure. Attrition rates mask at least three important groups of students: those who transfer anonymously to other institutions; those who drop or stop out of college before returning; and those who leave before graduation but have benefited significantly from their exposure to college. Chickering (Hall, 1982) contends that dropouts may be satisfied and therefore should not be counted as failures.

Such interpretations of attrition do not mean that dramatic improvement in retention is not possible. Brannan (1982) feels that the persistent efforts of Miami-Dade Community College to determine indicators of student progress that are both tough and reasonable are critical if students are to be guided through the open door rather than caught in a revolving one. Because of the vast implications for financial aid, the impetus for carefully defined rate-of-progress guidelines is increasingly likely to emanate from state legislatures. What is especially promising, though, is the dramatic progress that has been achieved in slightly more than ten years in understanding the parameters of academic "success" for students who have entered college with severe and heretofore fatal disadvantages.

Directions in the Fifth Generation

During the remainder of the fifth generation, I believe that the innovations in instruction, counseling, and program administration and the growing sophistication in assessment that began in the fourth generation will continue. Because fourth-generation gains in these areas were so substantial, their future growth is likely to be incremental. However, I predict that major advances will be made in three areas: Instructional technology will burgeon, educational collaborations will increase dramatically, and faculty development programs, expanded to emphasize career assessment and health, will come to play a dominant role in higher education.

Instructional Technology. In the early 1970s, some community college mathematics departments debated whether students should be allowed to use pocket calculators to solve arithmetic problems. In 1983, a spokesman for the National Assessment for Educational Progress urged high school teachers to require the use of calculators for basic arithmetic tasks to free students to concentrate on the inferential reasoning skills essential to understand more sophisticated material (Maeroff, 1983b). The debate over pocket calculators appears to have been resolved.

Today higher education is awhirr with flashing computers and humming word processors, equipment that has scarcely begun to reveal its instructional potential. Government sources indicate that the number of microcomputers in high schools has tripled since 1980, and American colleges and universities now spend an estimated $300 million a year on computers (Reed, 1983). By the mid 1980s, Carnegie-Mellon University plans to create a total computer environment on campus by requiring all students, faculty, and administrators to have their own personal computers (Gavert, 1983). Signs from Congress reveal strong bipartisan support for increased funding for the National Science Foundation, and Reed (1983) counted twenty-four different bills before the 98th Congress that pertained to mathematics and science instruction for the use of technology in instruction.

Certainly computers and other forms of technology have a vivid future in developmental education. One inner-city community college in California reports that student reading skills can jump five academic years in one semester through the use of a computer system (California Postsecondary Education Commission, 1983). Even departments traditionally as remote from computers as English have begun to utilize computers for practice exercises, and some writing programs use word processors as essential parts of the composing process. Similarly, technology seems to have a distinct future in the general area of language acquisition. The widespread conviction that the language skills of English as a Second Language

(ESL) students need to be continually reinforced opens numerous possibilities for the use of technology and new software in college resource centers. The growing emphasis on reasoning skills as a prerequisite for success in college-level work indicates that some problem-solving exercises may be suitable for technology, too.

Despite the promise of technology, however, growth in its use with underprepared students probably will be gradual. Recent studies have shown that the average college student spends fewer than ten hours a year on a computer, and other studies reinforce the common sense observation that low-income students are less likely than their more affluent peers to have access to computers (Reed, 1983). Since students in developmental programs are not likely to be affluent, they are not likely to be experienced with computers, either. It seems clear, too, that colleges will purchase equipment principally for courses related to high-technology curricula. It is also clear that colleges lack adequate software in most curricular areas, a fact likely to be gradually remedied as publishing houses mount concerted efforts to develop quality software (McDowell, 1983). In any case, while technology will play a strong role in the future of postsecondary education, faculty in developmental programs will be competing for growing but limited resources with many others.

It would be paradoxical if colleges prepared students for a technological society and allowed their faculty and staff to remain largely innocent of it. While computers have played an ongoing role in the management of community colleges, particularly with registration and financial aid, faculty and staff not connected with these tasks have had little incentive to become more adept with current technology. At some community colleges in the New York area, recent courses in computer literacy for faculty and staff have proved popular, and one college has even begun a "curriculum" to enable faculty to acquire additional skills. Bronx Community College, for instance, offers three sequential minicourses to its faculty and staff: an introduction to microcomputers for instructional support, a follow-up, hands-on microcomputer workshop, and a workshop in micro-CAI software design. It is likely that such courses in technology will proliferate.

While it may be desirable for faculty to learn about technology to increase their instructional options, viewing instructional technology as the sole answer for students is wrongheaded. In the early 1970s, colleges learned that interdisciplinary teams and cluster programming helped combat a tendency to identify students as exclusively math anxious or as suffering only from writing blocks. With such experience behind them, community colleges will be reluctant to embrace new technological options as a quick, let alone exclusive, educational "fix" for students. If the core curricula at community colleges are revised to include courses in computer literacy, the curriculum should not expand at the expense of literature or philosophy or courses that encourage students to develop reasoning skills, pursue new fields of inquiry, or question or reassert their personal values.

New Collaborations. The many collaborative programs begun during the fourth generation are likely to continue to increase in quality and quantity as the fifth generation continues. The collaboration among faculty within two-year colleges will grow, as will efforts to develop programs with four-year colleges, with high schools and, eventually, with elementary schools as well. Many of these projects will be curricular, and by the end of the 1980s Kindergarten–14 and even Kindergarten–16 sequences in writing, reading, and mathematics should be established. More and more educators at all levels are determined to make the "fit" between precollege, college, and postcollege work more exact. To fashion this fit, community colleges and higher education in general will increasingly seek to collaborate not only with school systems but with corporations as well.

Whereas interdepartmental collaborations to reinforce basic skills were launched in the 1970s—such as Beaver College's writing-across-the-curriculum project—the reach of such programs in the 1980s will probably be even greater. One key to these efforts is the attention being paid to English as a Second Language students. Growing ESL populations, combined with the burgeoning understanding of language acquisition and concerns about retention, may spur institution-wide efforts to help ESL students persist once they exit from ESL courses. At Hostos Community College in Bronx, New York, for example, ESL faculty regularly interact with other faculty to plan language-related support for ESL students in courses that traditionally have not been designed to meet the needs of any ethnic group. The Hostos experience may herald others.

Although collaboration with secondary education has grown recently, it will increase enormously in the future. One reason is that access is still a fundamental issue in higher education, and it dovetails with a very pragmatic concern. As the United States becomes more and more conscious of the need to augment its supply of mathematics and science educators, it will increasingly reach out to the high schools to identify and attract such students. Happily, the consciousness of higher education and of society has been raised sufficiently to encourage access in fields of need to groups traditionally underrepresented there. In 1980, for example, the University of Connecticut began a program with the Hartford public school system to identify, support, and attract minority high school students to the university's health sciences cluster. In 1981, the University of California at Berkeley began to work with the National Hispanic University to attract Hispanic students to math-related curricula at Berkeley.

Community colleges will be active, too, particularly with the least prepared students. In North Carolina, the National Model Dropout Information and Service Project, a network established by nine community colleges, contacts dropouts from twenty school districts. Dropouts are encouraged to enroll in one or more of several community college programs that prepare students for high school equivalency examinations and different types of vocational education (Maeroff, 1983a). Students attend classes at six community college campuses to prepare for the equivalency examination and to have access to various college services.

Such emphasis on access will not mean that the curricular gains will be lost or slowed. By now, secondary-postsecondary curricula patterns have been established and programs such as the Queens College writing project, planned and initiated jointly by the college and major feeder public schools, has become one of the many models that other colleges can borrow from. The Queens project showed that it is possible for students to receive sequential instruction in writing from high school through Freshman English in college.

It is inevitable that teacher training, particularly at the elementary school level, will borrow heavily from the existing secondary-postsecondary training programs. For example, one of the most influential partnerships in the fourth generation was the Bay Area Writing Project in California, discussed previously. The goal of the project, to increase the effectiveness of high school writing teachers, applies logically to elementary teachers as well. It seems inevitable that the most successful secondary-postsecondary models will be adapted and extended as a consensus emerges that quality basic skill instruction is most essential at the beginning rather than at the end of a student's educational journey.

Collaboration will not be limited to the formal education system. As federal and state contributions to public education decrease or remain fixed, community colleges will be attracted to academic partners beyond the formal education system. Industry-university cooperation in research and development has long been a way of life at the graduate level, and recently some corporations began programs to attract women and minorities. In 1982, for example, the Westinghouse Educational Foundation awarded over $400,000 to minority education programs (Gavert, 1983). Now that partnership is likely to be extended to undergraduate and developmental education as well. Community colleges in particular will reach out to corporations for equipment, facilities, and personnel, especially since colleges now belatedly concede that many corporations have substantial educational experience of their own.

Staff Development. During the remainder of the fifth generation, community colleges will move in creative ways to retrain and renew their faculties. This need seems particularly acute in developmental classrooms—where stress may resemble combat neurosis, with severely underprepared students often demanding much time and attention, yet frequently disappointing faculty. Community colleges will be more sympathetic to sponsoring internships that enable faculty to gather more expertise about instructional technology or that enable some faculty to leave education for noneducational jobs, or both. The new, broadened roles of community college faculty, coupled with the benefits of career assessment programs, will encourage two-year colleges even more to diversify the teaching and administrative responsibilities of their developmental staffs.

With heavily tenured faculties likely to be teaching an increasingly high percentage of developmental courses (Lavin, Alba, and Silberstein, 1981), it seems inevitable that efforts to retrain faculty from underutilized disciplines to teach developmental courses in reading, writing, and mathematics will burgeon. It is likely, too, that community colleges will intensify their efforts to distribute developmental responsibilities throughout the college. For example, the college-wide writing assessment at Johnson State College described earlier suggests one model for drawing other faculty into the developmental program. Successful efforts to integrate basic skills instruction into subject area classes also will spread. LaGuardia Community College's faculty engaged in the Integrated Skills Reinforcement (ISR) project recently began to train other area two-year and four-year faculty in the ISR methods. Those faculty in turn became instructors and mentors for their own colleagues.

Since faculty workloads at community colleges will probably remain heavy and teaching assignments will be largely constant, institutions will have to address the problem of an overworked, aging faculty. Loyola University of Chicago and Gordon College of Massachusetts have both implemented career assessment programs that provide teaching faculty with time and assistance to assess their own careers in light of their career goals. Through seminars and workshops, Loyola and Gordon provide information about opportunities for administrative or nonacademic careers and support faculty as they pursue and practice second or new careers. Such programs are less directed at reducing the work force significantly than they are designed to revitalize faculty who will return refreshed, with new skills, to their classrooms.

But the expanded or new professional roles, however important in themselves, do not comprehensively address the problem of stress so frequently associated with developmental classrooms. The diagnosis and control of excessive stress will become a priority for community colleges in the decade ahead.

Corporate America discovered some time ago that health programs for workers were cost-effective (Manuso, 1982). As higher education is concerned with quality teaching, it seems inevitable that colleges will call upon experts in nutrition, exercise, and stress management already on their faculties or consult with outside experts. Community colleges will begin to offer a variety of health services for their staffs, as they do for their students. While the personal lives of faculty have long been sheltered by the traditions of privacy and autonomy cherished by higher education, the national emphasis on health, the growing concern of faculty unions as well as administrations, and the realization that good health benefits everyone make it likely that acceptance of health programs is possible. The long-standing success of comprehensive, confidential health programs, such as the University of Missouri's Employee Assistance Program, illustrates that campus-based programs are much needed, can be effective, and, if given a chance, will flower.

Any prophecies about the future directions of developmental education, however, must be tempered by reminders of the very real problems affecting postsecondary education today. First of all, in the early and mid 1970s, most institutions accepted the fact that small, remedial classes and extended support services would be costlier than most other college programs. With operating costs escalating and state and local support dwindling, developmental programs must compete with other campus programs if they are to be designated an institutional priority. Institutions are less likely to be as generous now as in the past. For example, the University of Utah announced that after the mid 1980s, it would no longer offer remedial courses as part of the regular university program. President David Gardner explained that developmental programs drained too many resources from the university and threaten "the quality and rigor of our teaching programs and the national respect which we presently enjoy" (Maeroff, 1983a, p. 14).

Second, key policymakers outside higher education may be overly optimistic in anticipating the benefits from the minimum competency laws now operating in at least thirty-eight states. State legislatures may balk at providing sufficient resources to colleges under the mistaken impression that students will be graduating from high school prepared for college-level work. In Florida, the

Postsecondary Education Planning Commission called for the phasing out of remedial education at the college level by 1988 (Maeroff, 1983a).

Third, staff development programs may be threatening, too. Unless faculty unions are sympathetic to expanded and sometimes revised roles for teaching and nonteaching faculty—and they have actively supported some initiatives already—community colleges that are overloaded in areas of declining student interest may be discouraged from initiating retraining programs to enable faculty to be redeployed more realistically.

Finally, in light of the tightened job market, community colleges must recognize that voluntary faculty attrition will be slight and that staff development programs must be started if the faculties are to remain vital and productive.

I believe, however, that these problems will be addressed. Never have developmental faculty been more skilled at their professions, and never have so many models for growth and change been so accessible.

Recommendations

In the areas of instructional technology, new collaborations, and staff development, eight recommendations seem to me particularly germane to community colleges in the fifth generation.

1. Community colleges should use technology to expedite and simplify students' nonclassroom lives. Rather than troubling overworked counselors with questions that could be efficiently answered by technology, students should use computers. Miami-Dade Community College is well known for its Advisement and Graduation Information System (AGIS), a sophisticated, computer-based advisement system that provides students with information about their standing in each class as well as information about their progress toward graduation with a view toward upper-division study at Florida's four-year colleges. AGIS may command more resources than most community colleges can afford, but few institutions can afford not to delegate certain discrete tasks to the computer.

2. Community colleges should use technology to reinforce basic skills instruction and should offer introductory computer courses to both students and faculty. There is widespread agreement already that various language and computational tasks can be performed effectively on computers. As faculty comfort with technology grows, computers will play an increasingly sophisticated role in basic skills classrooms and support laboratories. Institutions should encourage faculty and student acceptance of computers by routinely offering introductory courses to both groups.

3. The emphasis on basic skills instruction should be complemented by the creation of interdisciplinary courses that promote critical thinking, synthesis, and independent learning. The interdisciplinary, team-taught honors and transfer programs at the Community College of Philadelphia offer models for institutions wishing to follow basic skills courses with a curriculum that demands intellectual rigor. At their best, such collaborative programs enable faculty to challenge the students intellectually at the same time they reinforce the basic skills acquired during developmental courses.

4. Community colleges should interact regularly with feeder high schools and embark on curricular innovations with them. While conversations about goals and student needs represent a logical first initiative, curricular partnerships seem to be the critical next step. In Ohio, Cuyahoga Community College has initiated a high school-to-baccalaureate project. Curricular "ladders" are being developed in business, engineering, and health careers so that students will proceed with a coherent curriculum from high school through the community college to a four-year institution. Such collaborations make it more likely that students will receive sequential basic skills instruction too.

5. Since many two-year students eventually transfer to four-year colleges, collaborations between these institutions are critical. The best partnerships will likely address student skills, as the faculties at Compton Community College and the nearby University of California at Los Angeles have done by conducting joint workshops in mathematics and writing. Alternatively, partners might attempt to demystify the postsecondary bureacracy,

as South Mountain Community College and its neighbor Arizona State University have done by jointly creating an orientation course for prospective transfer students, which is offered on the South Mountain campus.

6. Community college links with industry should be strengthened. Since many two-year colleges regularly communicate with companies employing their graduates, programmatic collaboration is realistic. The Lockheed-Compton Community College Math/Engineering Program represents one promising model to increase the number of minorities in high-tech fields. Lockheed provides scholarships and training for Compton students who demonstrate academic progress in course work and who satisfy the requirements for upper-division standing in engineering at the California State University.

7. Community college faculty must develop additional teaching and administrative specialties. At colleges at which there is a mismatch between student needs and faculty competence, faculty must acquire additional expertise. Retraining programs should be established to enable faculty in underutilized areas to become proficient in areas of student need—usually basic skills courses. This expansion of faculty talents offers institutions a second benefit—a more diversified professional life for faculty who may be suffering from the repetitiveness of teaching assignments.

8. Community colleges should promote health programs for their faculty. With workloads increasing and a tightened job market rendering faculty and staff less mobile, colleges must anticipate the needs of a stable, aging professoriate. Institutions might follow the lead of Dundalk Community College in Maryland, which has established a Voluntary Stress Management Program for its faculty. Such programs will respond to the predictable needs of faculty by helping them develop career plans, explore nonteaching and nonacademic assignments, and receive basic health information. Community colleges will discover that their personnel are no less susceptible to the stages and frustrations of adult development than are professionals in any other field.

The expertise already exists to sustain the momentum of the past decade and to build on its notable achievements. Already community colleges are mastering the new technology for their instructional programs; they are cementing old links and forging new ones with public school systems and with industry; and they are becoming aware that it is costly not to offer faculties additional skills and the opportunity to rejuvenate themselves. If I am correct, instructional technology, educational collaboration, and staff development will be pivotal areas during the remainder of the fifth generation, and American higher education will grow stronger as community colleges refine and expand on the pioneering programs already in place.

References

Adelman, J. "Practicum Summaries." *Journal of Developmental and Remedial Education*, 1983, *6* (special issue), 24.

Arkin, M., and Shollar, B. *The Tutor Book*. New York: Longman, 1982.

Astin, A. *Preventing Students from Dropping Out*. San Francisco: Jossey-Bass, 1975.

Brannan, D. "An Interview with Robert W. McCabe of Miami-Dade Community College." *Journal of Developmental and Remedial Education*, 1982, *5* (3), 18.

California Postsecondary Education Commission. "Promises to Keep: Remedial Education in California's Public Colleges and Universities." Sacramento: California Postsecondary Education Commission, 1983.

Cohen, A. M., and Brawer, F. B. *The American Community College*. San Francisco: Jossey-Bass, 1982.

Cross, K. P. *Accent on Learning: Improving Instruction and Reshaping the Curriculum*. San Francisco: Jossey-Bass, 1976.

Cross, K. P. *Adults as Learners: Increasing Participation and Facilitating Learning*. San Francisco: Jossey-Bass, 1981.

Donovan, R. A. "The Southwest Institutions of National Project II." *Alternatives to the Revolving Door* (newsletter no. 2), 1976, *2*, 1-6.

Elbow, P. *Writing Without Teachers*. New York: Oxford University Press, 1973.

Gavert, R. V. "Business and Academe—An Emerging Partnership." *Change*, 1983, *15* (3), 23.

Gonzales, B. "Teaching ESL at CUNY." *Newsletter of the Instructional Resource Center, The City University of New York,* 1981.

Hall, R. "An Interview with Dr. Arthur Chickering." *Journal of Developmental and Remedial Education,* 1982, *5* (2), 16.

Hoban, M. "Developmental Studies: A Model Program." *Journal of Developmental and Remedial Education,* 1983, *6* (3), 6.

Lavin, D., Alba, R., and Silberstein, R. *Right Versus Privilege: The Open-Admissions Experiment at the City University of New York.* New York: Free Press, 1981.

McCadden, J. F. "Team-Teaching: Quality Circles for Teacher." *Innovation Abstracts,* 1983, *5,* 1.

McDowell, E. "Publishing: The Computer Software Race is On." *New York Times,* Apr. 22, 1983, p. 27.

Maeroff, G. I. *School and College: Partnerships in Education.* Princeton, N.J.: Princeton University Press, 1983a.

Maeroff, G. I. "High Schools and Public Colleges Stiffening Requirements for Pupils." *New York Times,* Feb. 7, 1983b, p. A1.

Manuso, J. S. "Stress Management and Behavioral Medicine: A Corporate Model." Paper presented at the conference "Faculty Burnout: Faculty Renewal" held at City University of New York, March 1982.

Maxwell, M. *Improving Student Learning Skills: A Comprehensive Guide to Successful Practices and Programs for Increasing the Performance of Underprepared Students.* San Francisco: Jossey-Bass, 1979.

"Most College Freshmen in Jersey Fail Math Test." *New York Times,* Dec. 19, 1982, p. 47.

Murtha, J., Kaufman, B., and Warman, J. *Outcomes of Educational Opportunity: A Study of Graduates from the City University.* New York: Office of the Deputy Chancellor, City University of New York, 1981.

Naisbitt, J. *Megatrends: Ten New Directions Transforming our Lives.* New York: Warner Books, 1982.

Reed, S. "Technology Still a Novice in Classrooms." *New York Times,* Mar. 27, 1983, Sec. 12, p. 47.

Remedial Education in College: The Problem of Underprepared Students. Issues in Higher Education, no. 20. Atlanta, Ga.: Southern Regional Education Board, 1983.

Ribaudo, M., Roellig, L., and Lederman, M. J. "Basic Skills Assessment and Instruction at the City University of New York." Paper presented to U.S. Department of Education, Washington, D.C., Apr. 1982.

Richardson, R. C., Jr., Fisk, E. C., and Okun, M. A. *Literacy in the Open-Access Colleges.* San Francisco: Jossey-Bass, 1983.

Roueche, J. E., and Snow, J. J. *Overcoming Learning Problems: A Guide to Developmental Education in College.* San Francisco: Jossey-Bass, 1977.

Schaier, B. *The Final Report of National Project II.* New York: Bronx Community College, 1977.

Shaughnessy, M. *Errors and Expectations.* New York: Oxford University Press, 1977.

Tobias, S. *Overcoming Math Anxiety.* New York: Norton, 1978.

Trillin, A. S., and Associates. *Teaching Basic Skills in College: A Guide to Objectives, Skills Assessment, Course Content, Teaching Methods, Support Services, and Administration.* San Francisco: Jossey-Bass, 1980.

Part Three

Assessing Programs
and Services

Community colleges have undergone significant changes and developments in their service programs through the previous four generations. Student services and community services especially have reached a point at which major policy and program decisions are confronting community college leaders. In addition, the rapid growth of linkages between community colleges and other organizations has emerged as a fundamental and controversial issue.

Jane E. Matson and William L. Deegan review in Chapter Six the evolution of student services programs in community colleges and the basic assumptions and theoretical foundations that have guided these services through four generations. They then discuss the changes in students and their needs that affected student services programs so profoundly in the fourth generation. The final section of the chapter presents a number of alternative strategies for community college administrators to consider as they analyze the need for and delivery of student services for fifth-generation community college students.

In Chapter Seven, Joseph N. Hankin and Philip A. Fey
review the emergence of the community services function and the
philosophy and forces that have led to its becoming a predominant
and growing emphasis in community colleges across the country.
Hankin and Fey discuss major policy and program issues, such as
demographic trends, life transition programs, course proliferation,
organization, and finance, and conclude the chapter with an
analysis of the potentials and problems of community services
programs in the fifth generation. While citing the tremendous
opportunities ahead, they caution that community college leaders
need to carefully examine the degree of commitment their
institutions ought to make to community service programming.
This examination, they warn, needs to be made not in the context
of generalities about public service and civic responsibility but in
light of the hard realities of institutional mission and resource
allocation.

Marvin Feldman follows the community services chapter
with an analysis of a specific and growing phenomena—the
increasing number of linkages between community colleges and
other educational providers. In Chapter Eight, Feldman reviews the
increasing needs of society for these kinds of arrangements and the
leadership position community colleges hold as primary "hubs" in
these networks. He then analyzes the major types of other learning
environments and the forms of linkages before he concludes the
chapter with his views of both the values and the problems that
increased linkages will present in the decade ahead. He sees both
promise and peril in increased linkages with other learning
environments and cautions that the question of whether these
linkages will lead to more effective education or to a loss of values
may become "the" issue to be resolved by community college leaders
in the fifth generation.

6

Jane E. Matson
William L. Deegan

Revitalizing
Student Services

Student support services, or student personnel services as they have
been traditionally known, have been part of two-year colleges since
their inception in the early part of this century. Throughout the
history of community colleges, student services have always faced
something of an identity crisis about their role and contributions.
For most of this century, student services were based on the concept
of "in loco parentis," with staff serving as counselors and authority
figures. The student protest movement of the 1960s and the
increased diversity in students' age ranges and attendance patterns
challenged many of the roles student service administrators had
traditionally played. The 1970s saw the profession search for a new
conceptual basis. We began to hear more about "student
development"—a concept that remains vague, undefined in
practice, and largely unimplemented in community colleges.

Coupled with the problems of defining role and identity were
the fiscal crises that struck so many colleges in the 1970s and early
1980s and that are predicted to continue in the decade ahead. The
combination of these problems has frequently led to a downgrading
or even elimination of many student service functions. Many new

social forces are now emerging and presenting student service administrators with difficult choices—choices that will have profound influences on the future direction of the profession. The choices must be made at a time when pressures for both expansion and contraction are increasing (Deegan, 1982). In view of these challenges, the objectives of this chapter are to examine the basic assumptions and theoretical foundations that have guided the development of student service programs in community colleges, to review changes that have affected the need for traditional student service programs, and to offer a review of alternative strategies in programs and management that student service professionals might consider as they enter the fifth generation.

Foundations of Student Services

To gain insight into the nature of student services, it is essential to review the basic assumptions that provide the rationale for these activities and to look at the major sources that contributed to the design or evolution of student services in two-year colleges. The statements of the basic, underlying assumptions come primarily from the literature of the four-year college. This is understandable, considering the longer history of these institutions and the forces that contributed to their development. In 1937, when two-year colleges made up a relatively small portion of postsecondary education, the American Council on Education sponsored the development of a statement titled, "The Student Personnel Point of View." In this statement, emphasis was placed on a humanistic approach to education: "This philosophy imposes upon educational institutions the obligation to consider the student as a whole, including intellectual capacity and achievement, emotional make-up, physical condition, social relationships, vocational aptitudes and skills, moral and religious values, economic resources and esthetic appreciations" (Delworth and Hanson, 1980, p. 26). The statement was revised in 1949 to take into account the emerging social changes and the new roles for postsecondary education at that time. This statement has since served as a primary philosophical basis for the offering of services to students over and beyond traditional classroom instruction.

Student services as a professional field has developed with no well-defined theoretical framework that could provide guidelines for practice. In the late 1960s and early 1970s, concern was evidenced for a systematic approach that could be used to apply the ideas that evolved in the practice of student support services. The term *student development* came into popular usage, largely as an effort to denote more accurately the emphasis on the facilitation of a climate most conducive to learning.

Since the late 1960s, a number of models and theories of student development have emerged in the literature. Several writers have presented seminal ideas which have had a significant impact on thinking regarding the place of student development in the educational environment. Erik Erikson (1968) has been instrumental in focusing attention on psychosocial development and has described the sequence of developmental stages that define the life cycle. Other theorists, such as Kenneth Keniston (1971) and Arthur Chickering (1969), have made significant contributions to the theoretical structure, basing their work largely on the constructs of Erikson. Douglas Heath (1968) has centered his work on the development of models of the maturation process. K. Patricia Cross (1971) has done pioneer work in analysis of student behaviors. Her work has been of special value to the community college in calling attention to and defining the "new students" who are not commonly seen in postsecondary institutions and who have come to the community college in recent years in large numbers.

Many of these theoreticians have developed models designed to assist the practitioner in solving everyday problems. Most of the models focus on the typical college student in terms of age and socioeconomic background, and for the most part they were devised by persons relatively unfamiliar with the nature and mission of the community college. However, even in the four-year college, most of these models have not been implemented in such a way as to significantly affect the practice of providing student personnel services. As has been pointed out by Delworth and Hanson (1980, p. 111): "The use of theory to implement practice and intervene in the development of college students has been described as a dilemma, a paradox and a problem. The dilemma of using theory is that theory building requires the abstraction of a few elements from the whole of the human experience while intervention and practice require concrete and specific behavior in complex situations. To create a researchable model of how a person develops, we must choose and select those parts we wish to study and ignore the rest of the person, but the practitioner must work with the whole person in real-life situations. . . . Thus the dilemma is that our practice is too complex for theorizing and our theories are too simple to be useful in practice."

No universally agreed upon model of student services has been accepted in the world of education—nor is one likely to be in view of the rapidly changing environment in which the world of postsecondary education exists. No sector of postsecondary education has gone or is undergoing such rapid change as the community college, with its mission that is continually being redefined. There is, however, a general consensus about which of the various activities of a college are identified with the term *student services,* as it is commonly used. In 1965, the findings and recommendations of a national study of student personnel services funded by the Carnegie Corporation and sponsored by the American Association of Junior Colleges were reported. The study was the first—and to date the only—effort to examine and evaluate a major function of a total sector of postsecondary education. A taxonomy for student services was devised which attempted to minimize the multiple interpretation of commonly used terminology (Collins, 1967). While the data collected in this study cast doubt on the effectiveness of student services as provided at that time, the functions have persisted in more or less traditional form, and most are still found in the majority of two-year colleges.

Student Services and Changing Needs

A number of changes took place during the fourth generation of community colleges (1970 to 1980) which have had a significant impact on the need for student services. These changes brought into question both the kinds of programs student services offer and the way student services are managed. Many of the changes have been discussed in other chapters in this book (see Chapters One and Three), but any discussion of student services must take into account these changes as well: (1) the significant increase in the number of students underprepared for college work, many from ethnic groups underrepresented in higher education, (2) changes in patterns of attendance and the increase in part-time attendance, (3) the development of new delivery systems that may limit students' presence on campus, (4) the increase in the number of older women returning to college, (5) the growing number of displaced workers, many of whom never expected to return to college, (6) the increase in the average age of students, (7) the developments in technology, which offer both new opportunities and new problems, and (8) the increased involvement with the private sector—both through contract training programs and in competition as more companies develop educational programs.

Accompanying all of these changes, which have put enormous stresses and strains on the community college, has been a decrease in financial support. While the proportion of revenue received by the colleges from the state government has varied markedly from state to state, that proportion has been steadily increasing as local tax rates have failed to produce adequate revenue to maintain the colleges' previous level of services. At the same time, federal funds, which have supplemented local and state funding, are becoming increasingly limited, and community colleges are undergoing the painful process of adjusting to reduced budgets while attempting to develop new thrusts to enable them to more adequately meet new educational needs. The student services area has been severely affected by this critical situation, and it has often been one of the first targets of budget reductions.

As the environment of the community college has changed, the student services programs have undergone changes in response, presumably, to the forces acting on them. Ideally, these changes should have come about as the result of predictable shifts in the focus of the college. In most cases, however, they came after the fact and constituted reaction to the new situations rather than conscious efforts to redesign policies and services to more adequately meet the needs of the new student constituencies. These changes included shifts in organizational patterns, such as moving the counseling component to the jurisdiction of the chief instructional officer, presumably in an effort to more closely integrate the instructional process with student services. In other cases, financial aid was moved to the purview of the chief business officer. Other significant changes included involving the counseling staff in the teaching of courses in the "affective curriculum" designed to enhance personal development and the use of substantial numbers of paraprofessionals to supplement the work of the professional staff.

But these changes were not enough to stave off the "raiding" of student services as a major source of budget cuts. Because student services were not and never have been an important source of revenue in most colleges, it was logical to seek ways to reduce costs in these areas. Some student support services, of course, are essential to the operation of the college. Every college must have some system of admitting students and maintaining essential records. The availability of financial aid and its efficient administration are needed to maintain opportunity for education for sizable numbers of students. The placement of students in classes in which they are most likely to achieve success and attain their educational objectives is important to the maintenance of the instructional program. But many of the traditional services are perceived as being ancillary to the central thrust of the college and are considered largely expendable in many colleges.

Alternatives for Student Services in the Fifth Generation

In view of the problems and changes confronting student services administrators, a number of major alternative strategies have been developed for revitalizing both the programs and the management of student services in community colleges. While no single alternative will meet the needs of all community colleges, the alternatives can serve as a useful focus for analysis as student services administrators consider future directions. It should also be noted that none of these alternatives is mutually exclusive and that the revitalization of student support services may be found in the integration of several or all of the suggested strategies.

Divestiture of Certain Functions. It may be argued that the rapid growth of student services, which occurred concurrently with the growth of community colleges, has resulted in an "empire" that has grown beyond bounds that are reasonable, given the present financial and programmatic circumstances in community colleges. As financial support has been steadily reduced, all possible means of better distribution of limited resources have been sought. One strategy that may alleviate the situation to some degree is to divest some student support service functions that are considered nonessential to the achievement of the college's mission. Some functions, such as admissions and records, are obviously essential for the continuing operation of the institution, but there may be others that, while desirable and beneficial, may be determined to be less than essential. The services to be divested will vary from college to college, depending on such factors as demography of the community, the availability of alternate sources of service, and the political climate within the community in terms of attitudes and values attached to the student services program.

Elsner and Ames (1983) suggest three categories of student services in colleges: (1) institutionally based services—those services that are essential to the functioning of the college, such as admissions; (2) situationally based services—those that may be required because of special circumstances, such as childcare; and (3) special interest or developmental services—which provide assistance to special groups, such as support services for reentering women. The argument could be made that many student service programs, especially those in the situationally based or special interest categories, could be handled in one of two ways: they could be discontinued or they could be divested (Chait, 1983). The decision to discontinue certain functions would be made after a review of campus-wide needs, priorities, and fiscal resources. Other functions, such as clubs, special services, or some cocurricular activities, might be divested to student groups. These functions could be run by student interest groups as needed. In other cases regarding such services as health care, some financial aid, or some personal counseling, students could be referred to resources in the community, where liaison relationships could be developed. As an example, many of the student services in England are either run by the students themselves or provided through community agencies. If the need for budget redirection continues, this alternative has the advantage of allowing colleges to concentrate limited resources on the essential institutionally based functions and leave the situationally based and special interest-based services in the hands of other providers as demand dictates.

Contracting for Services. A second strategy for coping with the changing needs in community colleges would be to contract with private entrepreneurs or public agencies or to create consortia to provide certain services for community college students. While the availability of these services would vary from community to community, the concept seems to be applicable on a broad basis. In some cases, existing public agencies may be utilized with or without a fee arrangement. For example, services such as health, placement, some personal counseling, or testing might be particularly adaptable to such an arrangement. Even financial aid might be provided through a contract agency or through consortia. Contract agencies or consortia staff could, in time, offer certain services and management at least similar in quality and perhaps more expert and cost-effective than is often found now in community colleges. Obviously, any decision to create consortia or contract for services must be made in the context of a larger strategic plan that considers alternative costs and benefits and the use of resources that might become available if a contract program were established. It is hoped that more community colleges will experiment with this alternative to provide a basis for identifying those areas that can most effectively and efficiently be administered on a contract or consortia basis.

Extension of Services to the College and the Community. The practice of opening some college programs and services to the entire community served by the college has been common for the past twenty years. The most obvious example is that of intercollegiate athletics, which has been a significant source of revenue for many colleges. Another example is cultural programs, such as lecture series and dramatic and musical productions. These have been used to further the image of the college as a community institution serving a variety of needs in the population served by the college.

Precedence for the extension of such services as counseling and assessment to the general community was established at a number of colleges in the 1960s. While this practice did not become as widespread as might have been expected, its feasibility has been well established. Fees were charged for these services, which were provided for the most part by full-time student service staff of the college, frequently for extra compensation and, in other cases, as a part of a regular assignment. In many communities, such services are not readily available. Providing counseling, including personal, vocational, and educational planning, under a modest fee structure would not only serve the community but would also enable the student services to improve their financial contribution to the college.

In addition to extending services to the community on a fee basis, some student service staff could take leadership responsibility for one of the most pressing needs facing community colleges—staff development (Deegan, 1984). An increasing body of literature produced throughout the past decade has called attention to the need for more effective organizational and staff development. The problems of "tenured-in" faculty, rapid changes in technology, and the increasingly diverse student population all demand institutional adaptations that can be greatly facilitated by an effective staff development program. Unfortunately, many staff development programs have been piecemeal, cosmetic, and often unrelated to institutional or individual needs. One of the problems of translating staff development theories into practice is the absence of any unit in which responsibility for campus-wide needs assessment and program development is fixed. While many departments and units make efforts, staff development tends to remain a peripheral and ad hoc activity. This strategy for student service programs would see the development of a second thrust for student services—the responsibility for managing a campus-wide staff development program. Again, this alternative would require a firm setting of priorities, some reallocation of resources, and strong support from the president of the college.

Much of the training in human development and program management that student service professionals receive could readily apply to the development of this second thrust. While critics will point to a potential loss of emphasis on student programs, the setting of clear and limited priorities and responsibilities and the allocation of resources for this dual thrust could lead to benefits for both students and staff. Putting limited resources into priority needs in two important areas may be more useful to the college than scattering resources over a wide range of questionable priorities in only one area—especially if some resources can be freed through the use of contracts for services, divestiture, or reorganization and use of paraprofessionals. Community colleges will need to make more progress in organizational and staff development in the next decade than perhaps at any other time in their history. Programs that lead to institutional, professional, and personal development and that grow from the needs of the institution will be among the most important efforts of community college personnel. Assigning responsibility for this function to student service professionals and critically examining functions that could be replaced to make room for this responsibility could pay significant long-term dividends for the institution and could give student services a new importance through this dual thrust.

Management Alternatives

In addition to considering alternatives for program development, we need to consider alternatives for management development in student services. While management development decisions should grow out of assessment of institutional needs and program priorities, there is a growing awareness of the need for reassessment of program priorities and for better integration of student services into mainstream campus activities. Several concepts from the American corporate world and from Japanese management theory may have special applicability for student service administration as the fifth generation continues (see Pascale and Athos, 1981; Deegan, 1982; Peters and Waterman, 1982; Deegan, 1984; Ouchi, 1981). Let us review three such concepts that may be particularly relevant for community college student service administrators as they consider directions for the future.

Integrated Strategic Planning. Richardson and Rhodes present a comprehensive discussion of the need for and character- istics of strategic planning in Chapter Twelve of this book, and readers are referred to that chapter for a discussion of the rationale and benefits of the concept. A critical first step for student service administrators is to make sure that they are effectively engaged in the strategic planning efforts of the *total* institution. Too often, in the past, student service programs have been relatively over- looked in many of the key decisions that affect the entire college. Student service leaders in the fifth-generation community colleges must be involved in the serious study of institutional priorities and the role of student services within those priorities. It will not be enough just to pursue the old priorities with increased effort; the relevancy and role of student services must be critically reviewed in terms of community, institutional, and student needs.

A concept that may help achieve that goal, and one that is receiving a good deal of attention in both the corporate and nonprofit organization literature, is the use of a comprehensive governance audit as a basis for integrated strategic planning (see Ouchi, 1981; Deal and Kennedy, 1982; Deegan, 1985). The governance audit is a technique that can be used to analyze the needs, norms, and values of an organization, to generate issues of substance and process, and to place strategic planning decisions in a broader and more integrated framework. Much of the impetus for the concept came from the work of Pascale and Athos (1981), who concluded that one of the keys to success in effective organizations is an emphasis on analyzing and managing a wider range of variables. Thus, rather than placing the emphasis on managing one or two variables, such as strategy or structure, Pascale and Athos present what they term the "7-S" framework as a conceptual scheme for analysis. The seven "S's" are: superordinate goals (the large values guiding the organization), strategy (planning activities), structure (organization), systems (communication systems and routine processes), staff (personnel and their abilities), style (the cultural values of the organization), and skills (distinctive capabilities of the organization).

Deegan (1985) has used the Pascale and Athos work as a basis to develop a framework for governance and decision-making analysis. Table 1 shows the Deegan framework. The framework can be used in two ways. First, it can be used to conduct a comprehensive analysis of decision making and planning issues. This could be done about every three years to generate an analysis of both substantive issues facing the college (and/or the student service division) and processes needed to effect change. The framework can also be used to analyze issues in any single area, such as the need for a change in mission or a new program proposal. The analysis could be done by outside consultants or by teams of campus personnel, who would ensure participation of all interest groups on campus and who would operate under the direction of a strategic planning committee. The framework would generate an analysis of the present condition of the college and the unit, an assessment of changes needed, recommendations on how to most effectively implement those changes, and an analysis of the costs and benefits of the proposed changes. The advantage of the framework is that it forces analysis and recommendations to be made in a more comprehensive and integrated manner. Thus, proposed changes in goals or structure would have to take into account the impact on the other major areas in the framework and the processes needed to ensure implementation. This comprehensive and integrated analysis should help student service leaders make more effective and *implementable* strategic planning decisions. Too often, decisions concerning student services have been made without consideration of broader institutional needs and consequences. A more comprehensive analysis of organizational needs that leads to a more effective strategic plan could produce the kind of decisions and programs that will restore student services to a leadership position in community colleges in the fifth generation.

Matrix Organization. A concept that may complement integrated strategic planning efforts is matrix organization. As discussed, a frequent criticism of student services is their limited coordination and integration with academic divisions and departments. This problem often exists because of a lack of interest and effort on the part of faculty and the absence of effective structural vehicles to enhance integration and cooperation. A

Table 1. A Framework for Decision-Making Analysis.

	Where We Are	Change Needed	Process (How)	Costs Benefits
Superordinate goals				
Strategy				
Structure				
Staff				
Style				
Skills				
Systems				

Source: Adapted from Deegan, 1985.

number of authors have written about the need for organizational flexibility in order to provide more effective responses to rapidly changing client and program needs. A problem that hinders effective organizational responses is the development of rigid organizational fiefdoms within which staff are unable or unwilling to respond to changing needs and tasks.

One organizational vehicle proposed to provide more effective responses and flexibility in student service programs is matrix organization. Matrix organization is controversial because it violates traditional organization principles, and therefore it often encounters resistance. Matrix organization can provide organizational flexibility, specialized knowledge, responsiveness to changing needs, and a better balance between time, cost, and performance. These advantages must be weighed against the potential problems of conflict, stress, complexity, and politics that can occur in a poorly managed matrix organization. Yet reductions in resources, changing student needs, and the need to maximize the use of scarce resources suggest that the time may be ripe for more experimentation with matrix organization in student affairs divisions. The increasing emphasis on attracting students and, more importantly, on retaining them calls for greater collaboration and team efforts than the "separate jurisdictions" model of student affairs organizations can provide.

Traditionally, student services have been organized in a line-staff structure. But as Appleton, Moore, and Vinton (1978, p. 373) have concluded, "student affairs activities require an organizational structure that places responsibility for meeting student needs on *both* the academic unit and the division of student affairs, that links central services to the academic units, that accommodates differences among academic units, and that coordinates academic units so that general policy and programming can be established and central resources optimally utilized." In theory, matrix organizational patterns hold the potential to fulfill these conditions and needs. What is needed is more experimentation with matrix organization in student services work so that we may more effectively assess the potentials and limits of this concept.

One major matrix organizational model that has been proposed for student services is team organization. Figure 1 shows such a model. In this model, each academic division would designate a person responsible for coordination of a particular project—for example, counseling, orientation, placement, or student activities. That person would work with both the project (team) leader from student affairs and staff in his or her own division to help coordinate the particular function. Depending on the campus climate, the functions could either be decentralized and offered in the academic division with the help of student affairs staff or remain centralized but with better information and coordination provided by the divisional representatives on the teams. Obviously, this decision must realistically take into account prevailing reward systems for faculty and administrators and the potential problems and benefits of the concept for the particular college. Given the need for more effective coordination and communication that enhances student retention and better integrates student services programs and academic programs, the matrix structure is a concept that student services staffs should seriously consider as they face the challenges of the decade ahead.

Job Rotation. A third management concept that may help improve morale and productivity in student services administration is job rotation. Job rotation is an important component of Japanese

Figure 1. Team Organization.

Vice-President   Vice-President
for Academic Affairs   for Student Affairs

Divisions

(D1)   (D2)   (D3)   (D4)   *Teams*

1	1	1	1	→	(T1)	←	*Counseling*
2	2	2	2	→	(T2)	←	*Placement*
3	3	3	3	→	(T3)	←	*Orientation*
4	4	4	4	→	(T4)	←	*Activities*

Source: Deegan, 1984.

management theory (Ouchi, 1981), and it is gaining increasing attention in many American organizations. While the concept of job rotation is not new, the economic conditions and job market projected for higher education administrators in the decade ahead may now make it an attractive management development concept.

Research on human motivation has indicated that people need new challenges and incentives to enable them to continue to be effective and productive members of the work force (Hershey and Blanchard, 1982). In the past, higher education, through its various employment practices, has encouraged career mobility through staff changing institutions periodically. This employment pattern will always exist in American higher education, but because of economic conditions restricting mobility, organizations have seen the need to develop the leadership potential of their own staff members through planned professional development experiences within the organization. Job rotation in a student service unit might take one of three forms: rotation between units in the student service division, rotation of staff to work in the office of the vice-president for student services as project directors, or rotation/exchanges of student service staff with other units of the college, such as academic affairs or computing operations. Implementation of this concept would require clear policies regarding duties, goals, and financial arrangements (see Deegan, Steele and Thielen, 1985), but it may provide staff with a more comprehensive perspective on needs and resources of the college and it may enhance teamwork, productivity, and a better integration of student services programs in mainstream campus activities.

Job rotation will not be productive for either the individual or the organization if the experience does not enlarge or expand the individual's perspectives. Hershey and Blanchard (1982) stress that giving an employee a little of this and a little of that does not necessarily result in motivation. Job enrichment needs to be made a part of the rotation *plan* by deliberately developing experiences that will have meaning and challenge to the employee. A critical leadership issue that will need to be faced in the latter 1980s is the task of motivating and stimulating the highly skilled and productive staff member. In the past, that was not as much of a problem. Effective staff could renew their personal and professional motivation by moving up in the organization or on to another institution. Because of the short-term, and maybe long-term, economic conditions, the future will be perceived as a nonmobile time, even by the best people on the staff. When aspiring people feel blocked and stagnant, management will have difficult morale problems to solve. As we face the prospect of a limited job market for student service administrators during the next decade, serious consideration should be given to job rotation as part of a staff development plan. This emphasis may enhance staff morale and productivity and provide many long-term benefits to the institution in return for a minimum financial investment.

Conclusion

K. Patricia Cross, in Chapter Two of this book, suggested five themes that presently dominate discussion regarding the two-year college's mission: the comprehensive focus, the vertical focus, the horizontal focus, the integrative focus, and the remedial focus.

While Cross does not take a definitive stand regarding which of these five themes may dominate the 1980s and 1990s, she points out the problems inherent in pursuing each of them. The specific role, program, and management strategies of student support services in the fifth generation can be defined only after a college has determined its mission and the priorities within that mission. Once that has been done, long-range strategic planning can begin and the role of student support services can be made a major part of that strategic plan. The role, however it is defined, can be effectively implemented only through greater effort toward the integration of teaching and student services in such a way that the most productive learning environment is created for the broad spectrum of students who will use the community college as one means of achieving their life goals.

The first four generations of student support services in community colleges were often dominated by lofty theoretical statements and principles that have rarely been translated into practice for any significant numbers of students. The future of student support programs in community colleges must be tied more directly to the future of colleges generally. What is needed is a reassessment and agreement on mission and priorities, a strategic plan to achieve those priorities, and an analysis of the costs and benefits of alternative program and management strategies that more effectively integrate student services as mainstream activities. We hope to see this kind of strategic planning more broadly implemented in community colleges and the emergence of a new conceptual basis and effectiveness for student support programs in the fifth generation.

References

Appleton, J., Moore, P., and Vinton, J. "A Model for the Effective Delivery of Student Services in Academic Schools and Departments." *Journal of Higher Education*, 1978, *49*, 371–381.

Chait, R. "Student Affairs Strategies in an Age of Education, not Regulation." *Chronicle of Higher Education*, Mar. 23, 1983, p. 88.

Chickering, A. *Education and Identity.* San Francisco: Jossey-Bass, 1969.

Collins, C. C. *Junior College Student Personnel Programs: What They Are and What They Should Be.* Washington, D.C.: American Association of Junior Colleges, 1967.

Cross, K. P. *Beyond the Open Door: New Students to Higher Education.* San Francisco: Jossey-Bass, 1971.

Deal, T., and Kennedy, A. *Corporate Cultures.* Reading, Mass.: Addison-Wesley, 1982.

Deegan, W. L. *The Management of Student Affairs Programs in Community Colleges: Revamping Processes and Structures.* Washington, D.C.: American Association of Community and Junior Colleges/ERIC Clearinghouse for Junior Colleges, 1982.

Deegan, W. L. "Revitalizing Student Services Programs." *Community and Junior College Journal,* 1984, *54* (8), 14–17.

Deegan, W. L. "Toward a New Paradigm: Governance in a Broader Framework." In W. L. Deegan and J. F. Gollatscheck (eds.), *Ensuring Effective Governance.* New Directions for Community Colleges, no. 49. San Francisco: Jossey-Bass, 1985.

Deegan, W. L., Steele, B., and Thielen, T. *Translating Theory into Practice: Implications of Japanese Management Theory for Student Personnel Administration.* Monograph series, no. 3. Columbus, Ohio: National Association of Student Personnel Administrators, 1985.

Delworth, U., and Hanson, G. R. *Student Services: A Handbook for the Profession.* San Francisco: Jossey-Bass, 1980.

Elsner, P., and Ames, W. C. "Redirecting Student Services." In G. B. Vaughan and Associates (eds.), *Issues for Community College Leaders in a New Era.* San Francisco: Jossey-Bass, 1983.

Erikson, E. *Identity: Youth and Crisis.* New York: Norton, 1968.

Heath, D. *Growing Up in College: Liberal Education and Maturity.* San Francisco: Jossey-Bass, 1968.

Hershey, P., and Blanchard, K. *Management of Organizational Behavior: Utilizing Human Resources.* Englewood Cliffs, N.J.: Prentice-Hall, 1982.

Keniston, K. *Youth and Dissent.* San Diego: Harcourt Brace Jovanovich, 1971.

Ouchi, W. G. *Theory Z: How American Businesses Can Meet the Japanese Challenge.* Reading, Mass.: Addison-Wesley, 1981.

Pascale, R. T., and Athos, A. G. *The Art of Japanese Management: Applications for American Executives.* New York: Simon & Schuster, 1981.

Peters, T. J., and Waterman, R. H. *In Search of Excellence: Lessons from America's Best-Run Companies.* New York: Harper & Row, 1982.

Joseph N. Hankin
Philip A. Fey

7

Reassessing the Commitment to Community Services

As community college leaders contemplate the fifth generation, an increasingly dominant issue is the role their institutions will play in providing community services. The quality of thinking about this issue and the new visions of melding education and service that emerge from it could significantly alter the mission and configuration of today's community colleges. Until the 1960s, community colleges had been concerned primarily with transfer and career education. However, underlying these primary foci of attention had been a persistent and growing demand for community services. Currently, the demand is intensified by a new set of societal forces that affect broadly and intensely today's adult population. The fifth generation should be a time in which a convergence of the community college's philosophical commitment to community services, along with a new set of societal forces, shifts institutional gravity toward a greater, and perhaps even predominant, concern with providing community services.

Rapid Change and the Need for Increased Community Services

One of the more significant characteristics of contemporary society is the dominance of change. Change is widespread in our society and increasing at a dramatic rate. This increasing rate of change has both horizontal and vertical dimensions. Horizontally, change crosses more and more areas of our lives. Vertically, its influence is being felt more deeply in everyday activities. While change and its increasing rate of acceleration are affecting all aspects of our society, three areas have particular significance for community colleges and community service programs in the fifth generation: science and technology, demographic trends, and life transitions.

Science and Technology. The progress that has been achieved in science and technology is noteworthy not only for its accomplishments but also for its rate of accomplishment. Achievements in science and technology have propelled us into an "information age," the chief characteristic of which is the generation and use of knowledge. This new knowledge and the ways in which it is being used are changing the definition of work and the requirements for getting and holding a job. Increasingly, more and more of us must absorb new knowledge, use it, reject it when it becomes outdated, and replace it with newer information if we are to be effective in our jobs and careers. This cycle of updating knowledge and skills is no longer limited to the professions; it applies equally to blue-collar jobs. By current estimates, there are twelve million professionals in the United States who require continuing education to avoid knowledge obsolescence. What is even more striking are the findings of the U.S. Department of Labor, which tell us that the average adult worker must acquire completely new job skills every ten years. By projecting this trend, futurists have determined that many adults entering the work force today can expect to be fully retrained up to seven times within his or her work life. This new environment for education, with its increasing emphasis on continuous education as necessary and complementary to preparatory education, opens up unprecedented opportunities for community college community service programming in the fifth generation.

Demographic Trends. A second area of societal change that has far-reaching implications for community service programming in the fifth generation focuses on demographic changes. Not only is the general configuration of our society changing, but specific entities within it are gaining new prominence. One particularly important development is that America is getting older—and all the indications suggest that this trend will continue. In the fourth generation, one out of eight Americans exceeded 64 years of age, and one-half of the children born in that decade will reach and live beyond 73 years of age. The median age, currently 30.3, will continue increasing to 34 by 1990 and reach over 37 by the end of the fifth generation. Advances in the prevention and treatment of disease, better health care delivery systems, and increased understanding of the role of exercise and nutrition in maintaining physical and mental well-being have extended the life expectancy from 40 or 50 years to 74.6, all in a few short decades in this century.

On the other side of the population equation, an equally powerful set of economic and social changes, ranging from the cost of raising a child to the phenomenon of living alone as a legitimate life-style, has kept birth rates down. This increase in the aged population without replacement by youth suggests an interesting new set of implications ranging from the bankruptcy of the Social Security system to a diminished capacity for national defense. Not the least of these implications is the impact of the new demographics on community college community service programming in the fifth generation. An aging population will make large-scale demands on community service programs for help in areas ranging from adjusting to retirement and understanding the aging process to leisure education and volunteer opportunities.

The general demographic shift toward an older population is accompanied by specific changes in two subpopulations in our society: minority groups and women. Ethnic minority populations, in particular blacks and Hispanics, are increasing in our society and will continue to do so. Blacks, now totaling 26 million, or 11.8 percent of the United States population, will increase to 30 million, or 12.2 percent by 1990. Hispanics currently are the nation's fastest-growing minority group, now totaling more than 12 million, or 6 percent of the population.

Perhaps the most dramatic and far-reaching change in any subpopulation in our society can be found in the new role of women. Again, starting in the fourth generation, 19 million women joined the labor force, accounting for 60 percent of its growth.

During that same time, the nation added 3 million new jobs, and 66 percent of these went to women. Also, of the women in the twenty-five to thirty-four-year-old range who entered the work force, 70 percent had dependent children. In the fourth generation, women comprised almost half of the work force, and half of the women of working age either had or were seeking full- or part-time employment. The evidence seems clear that this trend will continue as the fifth generation reaches maturity.

Community colleges, with their democratic, open-door orientation and their outreach, needs-oriented community service programs, have played a major role in helping minorities and women move into the mainstream of American life. The programmatic response has been eclectic, including English language training, job-coping skills, adult basic education, women's reentry programs, specific job and career training, and counseling and placement services. As these subpopulations increase in numbers and in influence, we can anticipate even greater demands on community service programs in the remainder of the fifth generation for an increasingly diverse offering of courses and services.

Life Transitions. A third area of societal change that will significantly influence community service programming in the fifth generation is the number of Americans in life transition. In a 1978 study published by the College Board (Arbeiter, Aslanian, Schmerbeck, and Brickell, 1978), it was determined that forty million adults in the United States were in the process of making a job or career transition. Sixty percent of them, some 24 million, felt that they would need additional learning to successfully complete the transition. In a later study (Aslanian and Brickell, 1980), College Board researchers expanded the definition of life transition to include all changes from one stage of adulthood to another. This more comprehensive definition of life transition led to the conclusion that 126 million adults twenty-five years of age or older are in transition, moving from one stage of adulthood to another. Again, learning was found to be important in facilitating a smooth transition.

The expansion of our understanding of human growth in adulthood has significant implications for community service programming. Initial concepts of adulthood as a plateau in which the very achievement of adulthood by the early to mid twenties constitutes the end point of human growth and development have given way to a more fluid definition of what it means to be an adult. A more precise examination of adulthood reveals that it is a period of dynamic growth and human development and that adults are continuously in transition from one life stage to another at different age points. In addition, adults are coping with various life situations, many of which are stressful, such as the loss of a loved one, the breakup of a marriage, entering the world of work, or changing a job or career. Learning is an important ingredient in successfully negotiating transitions from one life stage to another and in coping with unfamiliar life situations.

In the fifth generation, developing state-of-the-art education and service programs centered around life stages and life transitions present community service program developers with an entirely new set of challenges and opportunities. Concepts of life stages and life transitions can constitute a highly useful framework for lifelong learning; it is the community service program developer who will be called upon first to prove this hypothesis.

The Evolution of Community Services in the Community Colleges

Trying to capsulize the history of community services is futile. In one sense, the community service idea dates from ancient Greece, for Socrates took his wisdom into the street and the marketplace. Among the first forms of adult education in America, we find the proposals of Thomas Jefferson for the University of Virginia, the land-grant colleges and agricultural extension movement fostered by the Morrill Act of 1862, the Chautauqua lecture series, public forums, the Wisconsin Idea and university extension public service, and correspondence schools—*not* formal classes.

In the days of immigration and World War I, during the first generation, there were "Americanization" classes. Adult education seemed to have caught on in the public schools but not in the community junior colleges. In fact, the prominent studies of two-year colleges in the 1920s and early 1930s make no mention of the concept. As early as 1931, as the second generation emerged, Walter Crosby Eells identified service to the community as an important function of the blossoming two-year colleges (Eells, 1931), but it was not until 1934 that the *Junior College Journal* editorialized and encouraged it. In 1935, at the American Association of Junior Colleges (AAJC) annual meeting, Eells, as executive secretary, encouraged the growth of continuing education (Brick, 1963).

As community junior colleges increasingly oriented their work toward their communities rather than toward senior colleges and universities, it became clear that the education of adults was beginning to fall within their sphere. Also, the Depression of the 1930s made it essential to provide training for high school graduates who could not afford to enroll in day classes. World War II brought demand for special training and more people with advanced education. As Atwell points out, The Truman Commission report admonished the colleges and the universities to "cease to be campus-based. It must take the . . . college to the people . . ." (Atwell, Vaughan, and Sullins, 1982, p. 9).

Atwell and his coauthors cite Jesse Bogue, as executive secretary of the AAJC, advancing the cause of adult education in the 1950s as "an emerging concept for the community college . . ." (Bogue, 1950, p. 215; Atwell, Vaughan, and Sullins, 1982, p. 10). During the beginning of the third generation, in the 1950s, there was a developing interest in the field; Medsker, in his classic textbook of 1960, showed that 90 percent of the 243 community colleges in the study *were* performing functions we would classify today as part of adult or continuing education, if not community services.

Still, as late as 1963, Michael Brick of Columbia University's Community College Center, in his history of the AAJC and the junior college movement, could write: "While it is not the peculiar responsibility of junior colleges, those two-year institutions that are truly oriented to community services should perform a major share of the nation's total program for adults. With the increased emphasis on the value of education throughout life, with more leisure time, and with the increased need for retraining, continuing education is a new frontier in American education" (p. 141).

By the end of the 1960s, as the fourth generation was dawning, this frontier was indeed being explored by hundreds of two-year institutions. One of the pioneers in the field, Ervin L. Harlacher, wrote a book, *The Community Dimension of the Community College* (1969), which quickly became the "bible" of the movement. That same year, the National Council on Community Services for Community and Junior Colleges was founded, and by 1971 it began to publish its own journal, *The Community Services Catalyst.* (Note: the council has since changed its name to the National Council on Community Services and Continuing Education.)

During the 1970s and into the 1980s, community service programs grew and developed, but not without problems. Critics began to question the validity and quality of some community service offerings, while some supporters began to call for community services to become the central mission of community colleges (Cohen and Brawer, 1982; Vaughan and Associates, 1983).

Current Problems and Issues in Community Services

Obviously, such continued growth will bring not only positive prospects but problems and issues as well. For example: Will the colleges' personnel continue to respond to an increase in enrollment in a positive manner? Will the new groups of students served place special burdens on the institution? Who will decide how an institution's resources will be allocated among different groups of students? Will proprietary institutions, as well as other private and public institutions at all levels, compete to such a degree as to diminish the trend in increasing enrollments? Will unions and other faculty representative groups reduce the capability of the colleges to respond flexibly? Will sufficient attention be given to the differing learning styles of these new students? Will facilities be adequate? Will use of community learning centers continue as is? Will the state and other funding agencies continue to support what *they* perceive not to be a major mission of the colleges?

In many respects, the problems of the fifth generation were with the colleges in the fourth generation, too. In order to assess that perception, we took what we had considered to be a list of problems and issues facing community services ten years earlier and sent them in late 1981 to all fifty state directors of community and junior colleges, asking them for their comments and for prominent examples in their states in which institutions had responded with community service programs that were worth calling to the attention of community college practitioners in the field. In the process, we received responses from half of the states in the nation.

The first problem reported was the *lack of a clear definition* in many minds over what is included in the rubric *community services.* (For a more extended discussion of this problem, see Atwell, Vaughan, and Sullins, 1982, pp. 13–15, 69–70). There is no better definition of what should be included in community services than that of Harlacher (1969). For simplicity's sake this is restated as including: community use of college facilities and services, community educational services, community development, and cultural and recreational activities. Part of the definition problem is that we have had a muddying of the waters in this enrollment-conscious age and there has seemed to be no structure to many of our community service programs. However, when we use the term in this chapter, the preceding definition is intended. It should also be noted here that Harlacher himself changed the definition over time from his earlier writings.

A second problem is an extension of the first: A lack of a clear definition in many people's minds has led to a *proliferation of progams and competitors,* of which more will be written later in this chapter. Another issue that emerged was that *many community college educators do not themselves accept the community service concept,* and they sometimes see it as a "watering down" of the more formal academic offerings. Many faculty seem to be concerned that noncredit courses and services may not be of college caliber and thus may detract from the image of a community college.

Sometimes the services offered become college rather than community oriented, and on some campuses regular faculty see themselves as being "drafted" to serve. Where solely part-time faculty are used, the issue of *possible overuse of part-time faculty* has been raised. Some faculty see resources being drained off instead of being used in the "regular" program. A fifth problem has to do with the *planning of programs,* the *identification of community needs and interests,* and the *evaluation of the function* at the colleges. Some feel that the decision to provide a specific course or service is based on little more than the hunch of some staff member, that any expressed need or interest often triggers the launching of a program whether or not it has long-range value, and that such programs or courses are planned hit-or-miss or are based on ability to enroll numbers of students and generate state aid rather than around some organizing principle. Seemingly, few programs have built-in programs of evaluation.

Still another set of criticisms revolves around *organization, administration, and supervision.* Should there be a separate organization, or "one college," or both? Is there consistency of policy and procedure between community service programs on the one hand and the other offerings of the college on the other? How can the colleges best integrate learning outreach centers with campus life? Are the programs really offering adequate student personnel and other services, including counseling, library facilities, and other services to the same degree? Should they? What kind of communication exists among the parts of the campus and college? Is there internal flexibility or credentialism?

Seventh, and far and away the greatest problem area (a decade ago it was just beginning to become a problem; see Evans, 1973) articulated was that of *finance.* Dale Parnell (1982), president of the American Association of Community and Junior Colleges, put this problem in focus by asking the question "Will Belly Dancing Be Our Nemesis?": There isn't anything innately wrong with teaching belly dancing. . . . But if those programs are skewing the college's image, distorting the pictures in people's minds, then I suggest we examine some alternatives. . . . Is it written in tablets of stone somewhere that community colleges *must themselves* give people everything anyone wants, be all things to everyone? . . . We can't afford any kind of nemesis which undermines ·he 'bread and butter' programs of our colleges" (pp. 4-5).

The Brookings Institution study conducted by Breneman and Nelson (1981), which has come under fire from so many sources in recent months, had this to say about community services: "Offerings in the community services category are valuable primarily for their consumption, rather than their investment, benefits. Making students more productive members of the labor force and enhancing their earnings potential are generally not the main purposes of these activities, although some students may learn skills that they then use in the workplace. Community services primarily enhance the nonmonetary quality of life." (p. 52).

No wonder there has been resistance by the public and by the funding agencies. Funding, which during the third generation had been no problem, became one during the era of tightening resources in the fourth generation. The issue has seemed to polarize into two camps: those states in which support is given, except for where courses are seen to be avocational, recreational, or of a social group nature (for example, North Carolina and New York) and those states in which little or no state support is forthcoming (such as California and Massachusetts) and in which such programs are being made to be self-supporting. There are a number of people around the country in states and colleges which, they fear, during the fifth generation will be made to conform to the latter; they are presently looking for good examples of colleges that have been able to run their programs on a self-sustaining basis. (See James Wattenbarger's Chapter Eleven in this volume for a fuller exploration of funding in the community colleges.) Because the community service offerings are seen as a frill by many, including those at the colleges themselves, they are often the first to be cut. Moreover, they are not always afforded the best space, and many staff have come to feel like "second-class citizens."

For the Fifth Generation—A Community Service Agenda

What we hope to do in this section is to present a scenario of how we see the future unfolding for community services. Anyone who attempts to project the future has biases or preferences, so forecasts are based on a mixture of fact, belief, and value judgment. To a great extent, we have actually taken current examples of what is possible and projected that more institutions will be doing them in the future. We do project, however, that community services enrollments will grow.

Robert Scott (1982), director of academic affairs for the Indiana Commission for Higher Education, in an article entitled "The Significance of Noncredit Educational Programming," tells us that in a survey of 3,165 higher education institutions, the National Center for Education Statistics (NCES) found that almost three-quarters of them (or 2,285) provided some form of adult and continuing education and that in 1979 there were 12.3 million noncredit registrants in higher education—almost twice the 6.9 million full-time students that year.

The American Association of Community and Junior Colleges only began reporting community education enrollments in its *Directory* commencing with the 1975-76 academic year. These figures have been summarized for the period from 1974 to 1984 in Table 1.

Reports from the states confirm the growth shown in Table 1. In recent correspondence to the authors, Larry Blake, former president of the North Carolina State Board of Community Colleges, wrote that while his system had 180,758 curriculum

Table 1. Community Education Enrollments in American Community and Junior Colleges, 1974 to 1983.

Year	Enrollments
1974-75	3,259,972
1975-76	2,852,673
1976-77	3,078,079
1977-78	4,299,149
1978-79	3,422,058
1979-80	3,977,050
1980-81	4,088,513
1981-82	4,359,941
1982-83	3,520,126
1983-84	3,724,529

Source: American Association of Community and Junior Colleges, 1985.

students, to use his terminology, the system served 426,893 extension students. The state of Maryland reported that during 1981 more than 120,000 residents enrolled in 5,741 different state-supported community college continuing education courses (Maryland State Board for Community Colleges, 1980b).

We have applied regression analyses to the national noncredit enrollment data and have projected enrollments to 2000–2001. These data are summarized in Table 2. Given this projected growth, it is obvious that we face tremendous changes ahead of us, just as we have weathered tremendous changes behind us. We will be facing trends in society, such as population shifts away from the current center cities to small towns, suburbs, and small cities. Aiding and contributing to this particular trend has been the decentralization of manufacturing, the rebirth of the family farm, the development of rural recreational and retirement areas, and, most importantly, revolutionary developments in communication technologies. We now have optical fibers, two-way interactive cable television, and home computers. To a certain extent, we are now capable of taking care of, in the home, entertainment, shopping, employment (the office in the home), some types of medical care, and, important for this reading audience, *education.*

Major issues that community service professionals and community colleges themselves must confront in the fifth generation will include the following.

Values. A central issue facing community college community services professionals in the fifth generation is the development and articulation of a systemic set of values that guides and informs their conceptualization of community services. As community service programs become more central in a learning society and interact more closely with other providers of lifelong learning, the need for a fundamental set of values that provides a rationale for thinking and action will become increasingly important to a coherent, cost-effective community services effort.

Community service professionals need to rethink the mission and role of community services in an information age. An essential part of this reflective process is for community service professionals to articulate their responsibility to their institutions for program

Table 2. Community Education Enrollments in American Community
and Junior Colleges Projected to 2000–2001.

Year	Projected Enrollments
1983–84	4,255,939
1984–85	4,376,959
1985–86	4,497,979
1986–87	4,618,999
1987–88	4,740,018
1988–89	4,861,038
1989–90	4,982,058
1990–91	5,103,078
1991–92	5,224,098
1992–93	5,345,118
1993–94	5,466,137
1994–95	5,587,157
1995–96	5,708,177
1996–97	5,829,197
1997–98	5,950,217
1998–99	6,071,236
1999–2000	6,192,256
2000–2001	6,313,276

Source: Joseph N. Hankin, Philip Fey, and Mark Gesoff.

direction and success with their responsibility to adult learners for
holistic growth and development. The results of this reflection must
be translated into a clearly stated set of values that constitute the
guiding force behind the philosophy of and program development
for community services. This set of values must be articulated and
interpreted to constituencies both within and outside the college. In
so doing, community service practitioners lay down the basis on
which they function and relate to others. In addition, they exercise
their professional responsibility as administrators and adult
educators for proactively shaping the future of community services
rather than simply reactively responding and allowing the future to
be designed by others.

As the community service dimension of the community
college gains more attention in the larger society and internal and
external pressures build in intensity and diversity, a carefully
thought out, clearly articulated set of systemic values becomes

essential to program integrity. Values that influence long-range strategy and inform day-to-day development and implementation are crucial if the college is to mount a manageable, financially feasible, coherent program of community services and if community service professionals are to play a significant role in shaping the future.

Coordination of Offerings. State government agencies are not necessarily the bogeymen they have been made out to be. They need more data during the fifth generation, for after all they are being asked to coordinate programs to avoid funding duplication, and they will be asked to make decisions on what is fundable. The state of Maryland has developed a manual (Maryland State Board for Community Colleges, 1980a) and a record keeping system on continuing education students so that intelligent decisions can be made, and we believe that this will become more commonplace during the remainder of the fifth generation.

In California, where Proposition 13 did its damage, Jackie Ireland of West Los Angeles College and treasurer of the National Council of Community Services and Continuing Education, reports (personal communication, Feb. 18, 1982; Ireland, 1980, 1982) that despite the loss in revenue, the community services programs have not suffered that greatly. We agree that this seems directly attributable to the strength of the programs themselves and to the degree of public loyalty that has been gained by the community colleges through such offerings. The danger, of course, is twofold: (1) there has been a move away from cultural events and recreational classes and conversion to classes, and (2) the states may now be dictating the offerings for what grew up as community-based institutions.

The fifth-generation community college is finding that it is not the only agency offering community service programs. Not only are there school systems and four-year colleges, but as we have been regularly reminded over the last three decades, business and industry, the church, and civic groups all provide some form of adult and continuing education. It is said that 60 million Americans now find themselves in some form of instructional setting, with 46 million of them outside our formal school and college systems. Business and industry alone spend billions annually on training and upgrading. Even the College Board has an office of adult learning services, which offers workshops entitled "Marketing to Adult Learners" and "Making Business and Industry Your Clientele."

So the first message is that we are not in the community service business alone. Indeed, one trend we have noticed through our correspondence, which we believe will intensify as we become more interested in saving resources and money and inducing efficiencies, is the establishment of consortia: We will have more consortia like the State University of New York's Public Service Network, which coordinates the availability of resources; the Capital Region High-Tech Conference, which shares the cost of providing programming; the Illinois Interagency Network; the Dixie Area Lifelong Learning Project; and the New Hampshire Continuing Education Network of twenty-one institutions, which groups small numbers of available students from industry into critical masses large enough to teach and which has already serviced more than seventy-five program needs by asking the institutions themselves to submit competitive bids when an area of need has been determined. The theory behind these efforts is that of *synergism*—the idea that the whole can be greater than the sum of the parts. This synergism will also be evidenced in agreements between community colleges and arts councils, libraries, historical societies, and other agencies, including public school districts, which have common interests in serving the public. Because of this synergism, the fifth-generation colleges may be forced, if they do not agree voluntarily, to coordinate their local planning through joint community surveys.

Use of Community Resources. Greater use of community resources—facilities and people—will become obvious in the remainder of the fifth generation. The fifth-generation colleges, for example, will be using community volunteers both for teaching and for providing necessary services, in order to reduce costs. Volunteerism will be reflected in their programs, as well, as is seen at Vincennes University (a two-year college), where members of the Young Adult Conservation Corps help the state of Indiana in its conservation work. Community service professionals will take the lead in canvassing the community for such opportunities and suggesting creative ways to utilize available resources in order to maximize the benefits to the taxpayer.

Instructional Evaluation. The fifth-generation college must also look hard at its instruction and make evaluation of it a priority, or it will lose its customers. We will no longer be able to continue doing things the way we did them yesterday. This does not mean that we must change things for change's sake, but there are things happening all around us of which we must be cognizant: population changes, electronic media innovations, changes in taste, economic forces. To ignore these is perilous at the least. More effective use of evaluative personnel will be introduced; faculty members who do not perform adequately will not be reemployed if they are part time and without tenure; and consumerism will become more apparent throughout the fifth-generation community colleges.

Use of New Media and Delivery Systems. We know that the rental costs for specialized facilities will continue to rise, but we also know that by 1990 about one-fifth of all retail sales will be accomplished by a combination of the telephone and the computer and that by that year some thirty million homes will be so equipped. We know that many colleges are participating in the courses-by-newspaper program and that the newspaper is now capable of being delivered into the home via television. In the future, more and more homes will have videophones and facsimile production of letters, drawings, newspapers, and books. There are already examples in Alaska of two-way interactive schoolrooms in community college education.

Videocassette recorders, audiotape recorders, videodisc players, home computers, and other devices may give people in their homes access to lectures on virtually any topic, courses in any subject, and degrees if they want them. If we couple the availability of the technology with such developments as four-day work weeks, the cause of additional learning in the home may be further developed. Bergen Community College in New Jersey and many other community colleges have television studios on their campuses, some of them maintained by the cable companies themselves. We believe that cable television connections will soon allow for computer-assisted instruction between the campus and the home computer. Already in Oregon during the fall of 1981, some thirty-seven credits were offered and made available to 90 percent of the state's citizens.

Moreover, we may have overlooked the possibility of radio productions—far less expensive than television. Many campus FM stations are now broadcasting educational programs. With the prevalence of SONY Walkman-type receivers and car radios, as well as home radio receiving sets, why not reinvestigate the potentials of educational radio? There also may be increased use of the audiocassette. For the past seven or eight years, one of the authors has been listening to tapes in his automobile. He has already exhausted his own college's collection of about 800 tapes twice and has rented books from several companies on both coasts. Although he lives only twelve minutes from his office, in one week that amounts to two hours of listening. Just between home and office he logs in 100 hours a year—or the equivalent of two three-credit courses, not counting the longer trips to the state capital. It would be possible for colleges to tape faculty messages, even course teasers if not whole segments of courses, on cassettes for students to absorb. Some years ago, the other author of this chapter made mention of a "cassette college," although the dream has yet to become a reality.

Colleges may also explore the medium of "telephone tapes," which currently give information to callers on subjects of law, medicine, and consumer issues. Why not make telephone tapes on college subjects? Some colleges already have the capability of linking the telephone and the computer in order to register older students so that they need not come to the campus. Why not use the same media to give instruction at a nursing home for local shut-ins, such as is being done with traditional media in English literature by George Wallace State Community College in Alabama?

The computerized home, ballyhooed in the media today, will be a reality tomorrow. Through the use of videotext, we can already have news, weather, sports, retrieval of special resources (such as all the articles on one topic), and interlibrary loan information. A new, experimental videodisc encyclopedia combines written text, four-color illustrations, film clips, and sound recordings to create an interactive "talking" reference work. Students may read about the music of a particular period and listen to it at the same time. How far are we from using the same technology as a more extensive teaching tool, first for shut-ins and then for members of the general learning public? Radio took two decades before it became a household product, but the introduction of television was much quicker. How soon will the home computer become prevalent? It will happen sooner than any of us thinks. How many of us are planning for it?

We boast now about our weekend courses, our 7 A.M. courses for workers on the way to their place of employment, and courses given in-plant for factory workers on a night shift. But think how much more we can do with the new technologies. The community college of tomorrow will engage in continuing education for its own graduates, much of it utilizing some combination of "distance learning"—that is, instruction elsewhere with printed materials, computer programs, and telecommunications materials produced at the colleges, bolstered by occasional brief periods of formal study at the college itself.

Economic Development and Use of College Resources. The fifth-generation college is still focusing many of its resources on the economic development of its service area. It may be using more of its resources in helping to solve community problems. For example, its placement office may serve community residents, not just students. Its library resources may be open to the public, and several colleges may actually have public library branches on the college premises—more of the cooperation to which we alluded earlier. Some say that the college library eventually will not even be needed at all. For example, John Strange has forecast that "much of what we now consider to be available only in libraries will be available inexpensively in homes: within five years you will be able to purchase for less than $500 the equivalent of 10,000 books on videodisc or microcomputer storage" (Strange, 1981, p. 17). If this proves true, how can the fifth-generation college fit in?

In true community service spirit, the college will make its computer resources available for hire by small businesses in the community which could not afford their own. The data-processing faculty and the faculty in other disciplines will be used as consultants through the speaker's bureau and through department use. Small businesses that cannot afford an advertising agency may well "employ" the college's marketing survey and other business classes to assist them. For example, Lane Community College in Oregon has a productivity center available not only for on-campus use to facilitate the establishment of quality circles but presumably also to help disseminate productivity principles to the community as well.

More and more, we shall see the community junior college acting as a catalyst in its community. Harford Community College in Maryland, for example, sponsored a program to help the community focus on food stamps versus the Donatable Food program; Westchester Community College in New York held a cable television seminar to help local governmental and industrial groups learn how to use that new medium; Pitt Community College in North Carolina has helped people build stills in its farm alcohol fuel seminars, and Dundalk Community College in Maryland has taken 2,000 steelworkers through rescue training. Every college will produce examples of its own throughout the fifth generation.

Life Stages and Transitions. More and more programming will focus on critical life stages, skills, and needs as colleges focus more on courses that meet adult requirements and as faculty focus more on how to incorporate adult resources and requirements into the courses they teach. Carol Aslanian, in a book with Henry Brickell entitled *Americans in Transition: Life Changes as Reasons for Adult Learning* (1980), focuses on twelve critical life stages around which we believe we see more course programming already, with even more such programming expected in the future. These twelve stages are: (1) getting married, (2) becoming pregnant, (3) children moving through school, (4) getting divorced, (5) moving to a new location, (6) acquiring a new house or apartment, (7) increase in family income, (8) direction from friends or family, (9) rising cost of living, (10) injury or illness of a family member, (11) retirement of a spouse, and (12) death of a family member (Aslanian and Brickell, 1980, p. 72).

Examples of these kinds of programs are already in place. For instance, Johnson County Community College in Kansas offers "The Secret of Staying in Love," "The Joys and Isolation of Having Young Children," and "Living with Children and Maintaining One's Sanity." Other colleges offer courses for the growing single population, for preparing for retirement, on the "Myths and Realities of Senility," and, "Getting Fired May Be Beneficial to Your Wealth." Whether they be courses on motorcycle safety for the midlife crisis man or on changes in the income tax law for the woman contemplating going to work, the incidence of such courses in the fifth-generation college will increase just to stay abreast of the needs of the community and to meet many of them.

Competition. If the fifth-generation community college does not respond positively to the learning needs of individuals or to the needs of society, other colleges or learning centers will do so. A growing number of "learning networks" have begun to offer courses of practical use to the population. For example, New York's Network for Learning attracted 52,000 students during 1980, grossing $1.9 million, and its chief competitor in New York, the Learning Annex, claimed 60,000 participants and a revenue of $1.1 million in the same period. Lambert (1982, p. 27) quoted the annex's director as saying that "What we're looking at is the McDonald's of adult education." There is even an association of such learning centers, and its national coordinator estimated that during 1981 about 500,000 Americans registered for minicourses offered by 200 "learning networks." The courses, which do not offer credit, generally last one to four sessions and cost $20 to $50 each. Lambert's article (1982, p. 27) went on to indicate that although the networks often pay teachers between $100 and $300 per hour of instruction, they usually require teachers to arrange their own classroom space. Some of these entrepreneurial institutions are beginning to offer franchises for $40,000 to $60,000 each, and one of them recently introduced a line of audiocassette courses being sold in a nationwide bookstore chain. Another has signed a contract with a cable television company to jointly produce four courses and accompanying cassette discs for cable television. Some of these networks are nonprofit organizations sponsored by community groups and even colleges. A quick look at some of their offerings reveals courses entitled: Investing Deals and Steals, Pregnancy After Thirty, Saturday Opera Seminar, Hot Air Ballooning, How to Manage Stress, How to Set Priorities, Selecting and Motivating People, How to Make Money in Real Estate, Career Change, Being a Successful Two-Paycheck Couple, Computers for Kids, Owning and

Operating a Successful Restaurant, Mail Order and Direct Mail, Understanding the Financial Page, and Correcting Your Speech or Accent.

It is obvious that many of these offerings are similar to courses found in community colleges, and it is equally obvious that many more traditional colleges that have not offered courses with this content or format in the past have been influenced to follow this successful model. (See "Adult Education Courses Tap a New Market," 1982). The lines among colleges and even other organizations offering higher education are becoming blurred more than ever, and a combination of home study courses, four-year and two-year colleges, and learning centers are seeking the same market and may even attempt to do so together. What cannot be denied is the allure this market has had for business and educational entrepreneurs. Among the new courses in one of the learning center catalogues was "How to Start Your Own Adult Education Program," which enrolled 119 people the first time it was offered (Lambert, 1982)! If fifth-generation community services professionals do not begin to offer these kinds of short courses and learning experiences, they can expect to lose enrollments to those institutions that do.

New Populations and Social Trends. The fifth-generation college will increasingly be seeking to serve new populations— English as a Second Language students, senior citizens, women preparing for work, civil servants who wish to take review tests for job advancement, boards and community groups, educated citizens (for example, at Montgomery College in Maryland, 51 percent of its adult students already have a bachelor's degree), the clientele served by Johnson County Community College's College Learning Experiences for Adults with Retardation program in Kansas, the homebound students serviced by Queensborough Community College in New York, or the deaf students served by a captioned films for the deaf series (LaGuardia Community College in New York is a leader in this field of education of the deaf). Of this latter population, in Westchester County, New York, alone there are 56,000 hearing-impaired individuals, many of whom are unserved by higher education. Possibly in the future we will devise ways of delivering instruction into the homes of the deaf by way of teletype or other media. As we increasingly meet new groups, additional attention will have to be given to the adult development and varying characteristics of these adult learners.

College planners in the fifth generation need to look at census and population statistics and social indicators more closely. Among the population trends that have import for program planners in community services are the continuing decline of death rates coupled with increases in longevity and life expectancy, low fertility rates, increases in the population aged thirty to forty-four and decreases in the fifteen- to twenty-nine-year-old age group, increases in the numbers of divorces and in the number of unmarried couples living together, increases in the percentage of women who are working, especially those with younger children, the sharp rise in illegal and refugee immigration, the reverse migration from urban to rural areas, the growth in size of minority groups—especially in urban locations, the lack of sufficient growth in real income for many workers, the continued trek to the Sun Belt, and the shrinking size of households. Fifth-generation community service professionals will be most successful when they assess community needs by paying attention to appropriate social indicators.

Central Themes for Community Services in the Fifth Generation

As we reflect on past accomplishments and consider possible scenarios, several central themes emerge that will influence community services in fifth-generation community colleges. Community college leaders need to carefully think through the degree of commitment their institutions ought to make, and are prepared to make, to community service programming. This thinking needs to be done not in the context of generalities about public service and civic responsibility but in light of the hard realities of institutional mission and resource allocation. Each institution needs to define community service with particular reference to pressing needs in its service area and to articulate a clear set of community service objectives. Tough-minded consideration needs to be given to the allocation of human and material resources. Issues such as the scope of the college's community service effort, the percentage of the total college budget allocated to community service proramming, new roles for full-time faculty in community service programs, and the organizational structure of the community service effort need to be confronted and addressed. It is in the resolution of such issues that a college's true commitment to community service is forged.

Fifth-generation community colleges engaging in community services need to focus on achieving excellence. The center of attention has to be riveted on developing and delivering high-quality, consumer-satisfying, cost-effective programming that will enhance the image of the college and justify the allocation of resources in financially tight times. Such issues as integrating full- and part-time faculty members in ways that maximize their respective strengths and capitalize on their potential contribution and exploring creative uses of new technology to enhance and expand delivery options need to be fully thought through. Community colleges must exhibit a willingness to coordinate and collaborate with other educational and helping agencies to eliminate duplication, enrich program offerings, and develop funding strategies. Evaluation systems that measure and ensure both program quality and cost-effectiveness need to be constructed. The viability and expansion of community service in fifth-generation community colleges is integrally tied to demonstrated excellence.

Finally, fifth-generation community colleges engaged in community service need to address the issue of providing leadership for the learning society. As continuous learning becomes more central in our society, deciding who will provide the leadership for organizing an articulated and coordinated effort becomes more urgent. As local institutions concerned with educational needs in a specific geographic area and oriented toward screening people in rather than out, community colleges are in an ideal position philosophically and pragmatically to provide that leadership. Community colleges have the potential to play a central role in helping each community orchestrate its educational and service efforts to provide maximum opportunity for the entire community. Commitment, excellence, and leadership are the central challenges facing community services in the fifth generation. If these challenges are successfully met, they may lead to a redefinition of the community college in American society.

References

"Adult Education Courses Tap a New Market." *New York Times,* Oct. 17, 1982, p. 50.

American Association of Community and Junior Colleges. *1985 Community, Technical, and Junior College Directory.* Washington, D.C.: American Association of Community and Junior Colleges, 1985.

Arbeiter, S., Aslanian, C. B., Schmerbeck, F. A., and Brickell, H. M. *Forty Million Americans in Career Transition: The Need for Information.* New York: College Entrance Examination Board, 1978.

Aslanian, C. B., and Brickell, H. M. *Americans in Transition: Life Changes as Reasons for Adult Learning.* New York: College Entrance Examination Board, 1980.

Atwell, C. A., Vaughan, G. B., and Sullins, W. R. *Reexamining Community Services in the Community College: Toward Consensus and Commitment.* Los Angeles: ERIC Clearinghouse for Junior Colleges and National Council on Community Services and Continuing Education, 1982.

Bogue, J. P. *The Community College.* New York: McGraw-Hill, 1950.

Breneman, D. W., and Nelson, S. C. *Financing Community Colleges: An Economic Perspective.* Washington, D.C.: Brookings Institution, 1981.

Brick, M. *Forum and Focus for the Junior College Movement: The American Association of Junior Colleges.* New York: Teachers College Press, 1963.

Cohen, A. M. and Brawer, F. B. *The American Community College.* San Francisco: Jossey-Bass, 1982.

Eells, W. C. *The Junior College.* Boston: Houghton-Mifflin, 1931.

Evans, A. M. "The Funding of Community Services." *Community Services Catalyst,* 1973, *3* (2), 17–22.

Harlacher, E. L. *The Community Dimension of the Community College.* Englewood Cliffs, N.J.: Prentice-Hall, 1969.

Ireland, J. "The California Community Services Challenge." *Community Services Catalyst,* 1980, *10* (2-3), 11-14.

Ireland, J. "The Role of Community Services in a Time of Fiscal Constraint: A California Perspective." *Community Services Catalyst,* 1982, *12* (3), 11-15.

Lambert, P. "Popularity of Minicourses Is Growing." *Wall Street Journal,* June 3, 1982, p. 27.

Maryland State Board for Community Colleges. *Maryland Community Colleges: Continuing Education Manual.* Annapolis: Maryland State Board for Community Colleges, 1980a.

Maryland State Board for Community Colleges. *Maryland Community Colleges: Continuing Education Study.* Annapolis: Maryland State Board for Community Colleges, 1980b.

Medsker, L. L. *The Junior College: Progress and Prospect.* New York: McGraw-Hill, 1960.

Parnell, D. "Will Belly Dancing Be Our Nemesis?" *Community Services Catalyst,* 1982, *12* (3), 4-5.

Scott, R. A. "The Significance of Noncredit Educational Programming." *Continuance,* 1982, *2,* 1.

Strange, J. H. "Adapting to the Computer Revolution." In American Association for Higher Education, *Current Issues in Higher Education.* Washington, D.C.: American Association for Higher Education, 1981.

Vaughan, G. B., and Associates. *Issues for Community College Leaders in a New Era.* San Francisco: Jossey-Bass, 1983.

8

Marvin J. Feldman

Establishing Linkages with Other Educational Providers

Nothing will more clearly distinguish the fifth generation of the community college than its consciousness of the community's other learning resources and its awareness of the need to work out new collaborative relationships with them. In its first four generations, the community college was concerned, primarily, with its vertical linkages—those with high schools and universities. Now, in the fifth generation, the emphasis is shifting to include its horizontal linkages—those with the community's other learning resources.

In its first generation, when the community college was perceived as an extension of the high school, its overwhelming concern was with high school articulation. It existed as an alternative to the university. In the second generation, as the community college began to develop an identity of its own, it became conscious of its linkages with the universities and its close linkages to the schools began to show signs of strain. By the third generation, the separation from the schools was complete and community colleges were accepted as essential parts of methodically planned "systems" of education. The fourth generation was a generation of transition, as patterns of collaboration between the

175

community college and the university gave way to a sometimes destructive competition. Now, in the fifth generation, additional concerns with vertical institutional linkages necessarily continue, but the new consciousness of the community's other learning resources is defining a new and unfamiliar agenda of linkage opportunities.

The character of linkages is also changing. It is no longer a question of forging interinstitutional links and settling jurisdictional disputes about where one institution's responsibility leaves off and another's begins; it is becoming a question of orchestrating a remarkable variety of learning resources. In this fifth generation, the community college is emerging in a new role: as a coordinator or facilitator of a newly discovered and almost unmanageable diversity. The fifth generation will be a generation of a new awareness of other learning environments and new linkages to them, a new coordinating role for the community college, and a new agenda of unfamiliar problems.

In the years to come, education will become more comprehensive. The economic system is beginning to invite and reinforce abilities of an unfamiliar order. A fashion industry executive said recently that while for years the industry wanted people who would do what they were told, now they need people who will do what, in a sense, they cannot be told. The emerging economic order needs people with imagination, courage, confidence, and independence. As the systems begins to reinforce and reward these qualities, working people are reaching for a larger educational experience. And the way they reach, both in terms of the choices they make for additional education and the form it takes, will have profound consequences for community colleges in the fifth generation. Many community colleges already interact, compete or cooperate with the other learning environments discussed in this chapter. There is no one dominant pattern of relationship. What does appear as a dominant issue is the need for community college leaders to develop policies and plans to enhance, change, or limit relationships with these other learning environments in the future. There is a danger of an ad hoc and piecemeal drift into relationships, especially those with business and industry, which may not be in the long-term best interests of the college. Linkages should be considered in a more comprehensive way than they have often been in the past in order to preserve the integrity of the institution. Policies need to be developed concerning not only what community colleges will do in their linkages, but, perhaps as important, what they will *not* do. The following discussion of other learning environments is intended to provide a focus for analysis for administrators as they consider the kinds and forms of linkages for the future.

The Other Learning Environments

Technology is altering the educational task in two elemental ways: There is much, much more to learn than ever before, but we are also discovering that there are many new ways to learn. Some of these ways are older than community colleges; a few uncommonly important ones are newer. We learn a lot by ourselves—unassisted—and electronics is widening the scope of that process. Scholars are causing us to remember the central, indispensable and perhaps irreplaceable role of the family as educator. Families teach the oral language, so naturally they are unaware of it and thus take on the most elemental educational task and surely one of the most difficult. Thomas Jefferson once said that the best way to learn a new language was to live for a while with a family with young children—that they were the best language teachers of all. We learn from friends; we learn from an increasingly complex thicket of educational institutions—some public, some private, some proprietary.

There has been a progressive delegation of responsibility to educational institutions. As the industrial revolution progressed and as the society became more complex, ever more responsibility was, almost thoughtlessly, assigned to the nation's educators. Jefferson's concept was that schools should teach literacy and nothing more. Then the rapid democratization of America suggested that the same liberal education traditionally available to a tiny handful of aristocrats should be available to all. At the same time, the nation's educational institutions were expected to provide skilled manpower for a more complex and sophisticated industrial establishment. And along the way, educators were asked to teach manners, sex, and driving, and, for good measure, to mold character. Every special interest group in America, however exotic or bizarre, began to pound on the schoolhouse door demanding that a course in the subject of its concern be added to the school curriculum. As a result, institutional educators took responsibility for more than they could deliver. That led first to overload, then to a deeply alarming crisis of confidence in schooling. Now a wholesome reformation is underway, and at the center of it is a recognition that any of the community's educational institutions is only one of its educational resources—that a community's educational effort is best when it succeeds in going beyond its institutions and drawing on *all* its educational resources. Let us review now the nature of these resources and opportunities for linkage that will play an increasing role in the fifth generation.

Business and Industry. The most dramatic growth area has been in the educational effort of business and industry. The total educational effort of corporate America is astonishing in size. Marsha Levine and Denis Doyle (1982) of the American Enterprise Institute for Public Policy Research point out that industry spends almost as much for education as do *all* public postsecondary institutions. The American Society for Training and Development puts the figure at $30 billion a year, not including the wages and salaries of those being trained. If wages and salaries were included, the figure could reach $100 billion. Before the recent breakup, American Telephone and Telegraph Company (AT&T) was spending more than $700 million a year for education. The company employed thousands of instructors in hundreds of training centers (Luxenberg, 1978–1979). The General Motors Institute (GMI), with an enrollment of 2,300, is the only fully accredited college in the United States operated by a corporation. Three General Motors presidents have been graduates, as are four of its top fifteen executives. GMI offers a five-year program, alternating work and study in twelve-week modules. The college has seven applicants for every slot in the freshman class; they are paid $8,500 a year, less $1,200 tuition. About a third of its entering classes are women; about a fifth are minority group members. General Motors is not obligated to offer graduates jobs, nor are the graduates obligated to take them if they are offered. But most do, and 60 percent of them have spent their whole working lives with the company.

Four corporations now confer bachelor's degrees: IBM, Xerox, General Electric, and AT&T. The Arthur D. Little company can confer a master's degree in business administration, and more corporations are moving toward the GMI model and forming colleges. When Wang Laboratories could find only two master's programs in software engineering in the whole country, it launched a program of its own, now approved by the Massachusetts Board of Education. The Arthur D. Little company also grants degrees that are approved by that same agency (Levine and Doyle, 1982).

Community colleges are increasingly being drawn into linkages with business and industry. The importance of the fiscal and educational issues involved in these relationships only magnifies the need for planning and policies to guide relationships as they develop in the fifth generation.

The "Open-University" Networks. People are increasingly taking education into their own hands. One highly symbolic form of this phenomenon is the so-called "open-university" network, with programs emerging all across the land. These networks offer dozens of ungraded, unaccredited classes to all comers. One estimate reported 300,000 participants in 251 groups in 1981 (Free University Network, 1981). The catalogues of these tiny learning exchanges, usually in tabloid form, are distributed free of charge in supermarkets, newsstands, and bus stations. They list dozens of courses—some frivolous, some frankly exploitative, some deadly serious. These organizations not only are colleges without walls, they are colleges with few formal facilities at all. People with something to teach list it in the catalogue. Those who want to learn what is taught come to these self-designated teachers—in their houses or workplaces.

Voluntary Community Agencies. There is also a new recognition of the educational capacities of the voluntary agencies—that great, half-invisible sector of American society that has added so much to its character and texture. Benjamin Franklin was one of its pioneers. Long before the Revolution, he and his fellow tradesmen met in Philadelphia to form the "Junto"— meaning simply a self-appointed committee—for mutual education. Soon they began to buy books to pass around among themselves, and thus began, long before the nation was formed, a tradition of voluntary educational activities. This sector exists now in a great auxiliary network consisting of thousands of libraries, study groups, and organizations to extend literacy, vocational training, and instruction in every subject from lifesaving to bookbinding to local history to survival training. Chautauqua is still functioning in upstate New York, a reminder of the great traveling tent shows of an earlier time which sought to bring culture and instruction to a generation of ordinary Americans hungry, then as now, for self-improvement.

Precise estimates of the extent of educational activities of voluntary community agencies are almost impossible to make because of the size of this sector and the rapid changes that take place within it, but a 1974 report of a national survey of organized adult education activities in private, nonprofit community organizations found the following (National Center for Education Statistics, 1974, p. 3):

1. Twenty-nine percent of America's churches and synagogues offered organized adult education activities (more than a fourth in nonreligious subjects) to 3,604,000 adults.
2. Other religious organizations (national church groups, the Salvation Army, and so on) served another 474,000 persons.
3. YMCA and Red Cross chapters provided adult education for 3,050,000 persons at some 3,360 sites.
4. Civic organizations, such as senior citizen groups, political groups, and neighborhood centers served a total of 1,175,000 adults in organized educational programs.
5. Social organizations, such as social and literary societies, theater and music groups, and other "miscellaneous" organizations provided adult education to 370,000 participants.

Voluntary community agencies are clearly a major force in providing education, a force that is likely to grow in importance in the fifth generation.

Unions. Labor unions represent another important and growing educational sector. Organized labor has 21.5 million members spread among 200 unions, and as many as 500,000 members may participate in apprenticeship programs alone (Peterson, 1979). The University and College Labor Education Association identifies four general types of "worker education." Some unions, both local and international, offer programs in cooperation with colleges and universities. International unions offer their own programs for their own members. State and county union central bodies offer their own programs with the help of educational institutions. Unions also offer programs at union-operated institutions, such as the George Meany Institute of the AFL-CIO and the May and Walter Reuther Family Education Center of the United Auto Workers. The programs offered are of different types. Some simply prepare unionists for the practical business of the union. These are expanding as contract negotiations become increasingly complex. But many union education programs are designed to help workers become "mature, wise, and responsible citizens" and to offer cultural opportunities that were for generations inaccessible to working people.

Trade Associations. Most of the 3,000 trade associations are involved in education, some of them in a substantial way. For example, the American Institute of Banking, the educational division of the American Bankers Association, calls itself an uncommon school without a campus. With a part-time faculty of almost 20,000, most of them volunteers, the institute serves 150,000 students a year, all employees of members of the American Bankers Association. Other major industries, such as insurance and utilities, have similar programs (Lusterman, 1977).

Proprietary Educators. Proprietary education may be education's fastest-growing sector. As the 1980s began, enrollment in the nation's 10,000 proprietary vocational schools was nearly one million. Its revenues, about $3 billion in 1981, are expected to reach $8 billion by 1990. Enrollment in correspondence schools exceeded 250,000 in 1980 and was growing. By far the largest entity in this field characterized by small entities is the National Education Corporation, which now operates about a hundred schools across the country—training secretaries, auto mechanics, dental assistants, and aeronautical, electronic, and computer technicians. Its revenues exceed $100 million a year and are growing rapidly.

More than 600 other proprietary firms offer educational products and services to corporations. Some are educational divisions of large corporations, some are large independents, and many are small, specialized firms. They offer audio- and videotapes and cassettes, slides, films and film strips, programmed instruction, correspondence courses, tests, and production and consulting services. Hardware suppliers offer a mushrooming variety of audio- and videocassette recorders and playbacks, cameras, optical multiflexors, and increasingly sophisticated computer terminals. Since most proprietary education institutions compete with community colleges, this is clearly a force to be seriously considered as community college administrators plan programs.

Self-Study and the Electronic Revolution. As discussed in Chapter Seven, electronics is vastly increasing the opportunities for self-study, whether it is entirely self-directed or overseen by a teacher, and tomorrow's textbooks will greatly enhance that process. A single videodisc carries thousands of "frames." These, displayed on a television screen, can contain text a page at a time, still pictures, static charts, animated charts, moving pictures—and all of these in any combination. Publishers are at work producing video textbooks that will bring subjects to life as no print-bound medium ever could.

The computer came into the home as a carrier of videogames. Now the interest in games is somewhat spent, but the computer will certainly stay for more serious purposes. The more enduring applications of the computer will be, in large part, educational. There was a premature flurry of interest in the educational possibilities of the computer in the late 1960s. Educational corporations were formed, and their great expectations caused some multimillion dollar mergers but too little enduring effect. Now the continuing reduction in the cost of computers and the greatly improved software capability mean that the new, more fully informed search for educational applications of the computer is certain to succeed.

The computer's interactive capability makes it a teaching tool with wonderful possibilities, and these will be greatly enhanced as the new generation of talking computers is perfected. The computer has what the most dedicated human teacher does not have—literally infinite patience. The computer will never replace teachers, but it will, in the next couple of decades, become a major complement to teaching.

Television will also bring vast new educational resources into the home. More and more programs and data bases are being made ready for distribution. It will not be long before a student will be able to bring resources equivalent to those of the world's greatest libraries to a screen on his desk just by punching a few buttons.

External Degrees. A final learning environment is the external degree program found in various forms across the country. In New York state, the board of regents accredits courses offered outside the system through its external degree program. The American Council on Education has a program on noncollegiate-sponsored instruction. It has found 2,000 courses offered by 138 corporations that deserve accreditation (Levine and Doyle, 1982), and a growing number of states are exploring this educational option.

Obviously, there is much more learning taking place outside of formal education institutions than inside. As educational developments such as external degrees, distance learning, learning contracts, and electronic linkages increase in importance, community colleges will find their roles expanded, reduced, or otherwise altered depending on how the colleges relate to these developments. The next section of this chapter examines the forms the linkages are taking and some possible implications of those forms.

Forms of Linkage

"Linkage" is a comparatively new concept joining, if not displacing, the concept of "articulation" that dominated the community college during its first four generations. Articulation is an interinstitutional concept, a vertical concept. Linkage expresses a need for collaborative relationships with a number of dissimilar, sometimes noninstitutional, learning environments. It is a horizontal concept. Linkage can take a number of forms, but three are emerging in the fifth generation as most important: contractual linkages, electronic linkages, and linkage through certification of educational results achieved by others.

Contractual Linkages. Corporate-college linkages are growing rapidly in the fifth generation, and they take a number of forms. Contract training programs with business and industry are perhaps the fastest-growing and most prominent form of linkage. The increasing needs of organizations to train and retrain staff has combined with a recognition that colleges, especially community colleges, may be able to provide effective training at a far lower cost. Small and even medium-sized business firms may have great difficulty funding a training department, and even some wealthy firms often do not want to or cannot afford to increase their training programs. This situation is even more pronounced in nonprofit organizations, which have similar needs for training but which often have little "in-house" provision for staff development.

Community colleges have been at the forefront in providing contract training programs, and four-year institutions are showing an increasing level of interest and activity in contractual arrangements. A study by Deegan and Drisko (1985) found that 69 percent of a representative national sample of American community colleges had established a contract training program as of the spring of 1983. Clients for contract training programs were: business and industry (69 percent), health care organizations (13.7 percent), government agencies (13.2 percent), and others, such as labor unions or service agencies (4.2 percent). Table 1 shows the extent of involvement, program site and credit status of contracts. Clear trends that emerged from the study included a marked increase in the number of institutions involved in contract training and an emphasis on training that is specially tailored and delivered at job sites. A large majority of respondents expressed the opinion that contract training will be of increasing importance in the future of community colleges.

In addition to contract courses, a surprising number of corporations are offering degree programs at their plants that are contractually provided by a nearby educational institution.

**Table 1. Extent of Involvement, Program Site, and Credit Status
of Contracts (in percent).**

	1980–81	*1981–82*
A. Annual Number of Contracts	N = 203	N = 231
1–5	47.3	37.7
6–10	18.2	20.3
11–20	17.2	14.3
21–30	4.9	11.7
31–40	3.0	3.5
41–50	3.9	2.2
> 50	5.4	10.4
B. Courses Offered at Job Site (Average Percent)	61.4	64.7
C. Noncredit Contract Programming (Average Percent)	59.1	60.1

Source: Deegan and Drisko, 1985.

Burroughs Corporation has a program provided by the Detroit College of Business, Aetna Life and Casualty by the University of Hartford, and First Pennsylvania Bank by Temple University, and there are dozens of others. In Connecticut, Manchester Community College has worked with United Technologies' Pratt and Whitney Aircraft Group for a number of years. The program began with a three-year, thirty-unit apprenticeship program conducted by the college at the plant. But when employees sought to complete their degrees at other colleges, they encountered a discouraging thicket of problems. The company contracted with the college to provide thirty more liberal arts credits and is extending the whole program to three other plant sites, working with three other local community colleges ("Earning an Undergraduate Degree at the Plant," 1980).

AT&T has also made contractual arrangements with a number of institutions in the New York/New Jersey area, including Middlesex Community College. W. E. Luithle, supervisor of corporate education at AT&T, says that these on-site lunch hour and after work programs have advantages far beyond mere convenience. "Faculty members have found . . . exposure to a completely new environment and a new culture of students very stimulating and rewarding. Many use the experiences shared by the students of the business world with their campus students" (Lusterman, 1977, p. 33). For more than twenty years, Union College has accredited General Electric's courses for advanced degrees in power system engineering. Nor is the movement limited to corporations. Unions, trade groups, and government agencies are also offering contract courses with college credit.

Correspondence courses are considered a last resort by most companies. One General Electric department says, "Courses taken by correspondence will be offered only if there is no comparable course made available at other educational facilities." But there are some striking exceptions, such as Cornell University's eighteen-week course home study program for the supermarket industry (Lusterman, 1977, p. 35). While not a major form of linkage, study by correspondence and in conjunction with other forms, such as the use of media, may see a resurgence as new delivery systems emerge in the decade ahead.

Research partnerships between colleges and one or more corporations are becoming commonplace. Exxon Corporation and Massachusetts Institute of Technology have a program in combustion research. Harvard Medical School works with Monsanto Corporation in cancer research and the DuPont Corporation in genetic engineering. Control Data, Burroughs, and 3M are involved with the University of Pennsylvania in research on integrated circuits (Levine and Doyle, 1982).

There are also special collaborative opportunities with smaller businesses. These smaller businesses have needs as great or greater than large businesses, but their ability to deliver educational services is limited. The fashion industry is a perfect example. It is the nation's third largest industry, but it is composed of a very large number of very small units. There are, of course, a few large companies, but they are exceptions. The ability to provide educational services internally is limited in the smaller units, so the industry is turning to educational institutions to a greater degree. The Fashion Institute of Technology (F.I.T.), a specialized community college, was founded by the industry in part for that reason. Now, as the fashion industry confronts an era in which retraining will become more or less continuous, it is turning to F.I.T. and other institutions more and more. There is a continuing expansion of the services F.I.T. provides its industry—in research and development, training and retraining, and perhaps eventually in outplacement. The line that separates this institution from its industry, already fuzzy, is continuing to blur.

Tuition aid programs have become nearly universal among corporations of any size. Of those the Conference Board surveyed in 1977 (Lusterman, 1977) virtually all companies with more than a thousand employees have some kind of tuition aid program, and 82 percent of the companies with 500 to 1,000 employees also have a program. One personnel officer said that, while these programs are only occasionally spelled out in labor contracts, tuition aid plans have become "so fixed a feature of company policy that any abrogation or major reduction of employee rights under them is, for all practical purposes, no longer a management prerogative" (Lusterman, 1977, p. 32).

A long-established method of collaboration is cooperative education. Pioneered in the 1960s by the National Commission for Cooperative Education, it has grown until now 1,000 institutions and 8,500 corporations participate in cooperative programs. This time-tested form is almost certain to continue to grow at a quickening pace.

One of the oldest and best examples of collaboration between a corporation and a community college involves Textronix, Incorporated, in Beaverton, Oregon. Textronix is the largest employer in Oregon and the most important producer of oscilloscopes in the world. In 1957, ten years after it was founded, the company established what became one of the nation's most extensive corporate education programs. Unofficially called Tex Tech, it has served 85 percent of the company's 18,000 employees at one time or another. Tex Tech was founded simply because the company could not find the skilled people it needed and there were then no community colleges in the area to train them. When Portland Community College was opened in 1968, and after careful consultations, about half the Tex Tech enrollment was shifted to the college. Now the company program operates as a separate campus, working in close collaboration with the college and other nearby degree-granting institutions.

Electronic Linkages. Many institutions are extending their reach simply by telecasting courses. But television is also a form of linkage through which community colleges can more readily collaborate with other institutions and environments. Most notable are the elaborate collaborative linkages with public television stations, such as the "To Educate the People" consortium, which offers college courses to working people through linkages within labor unions, government agencies, colleges and universities, and public television stations.

Another important linkage facilitated by television is that with other community colleges and universities. Dallas County Community College District, for example, leads a consortium of other institutions of higher education, which together have enrolled more than 40,000 students. The Association for Higher Education in North Texas joins seventeen postsecondary institutions and twelve corporations to broadcast four courses an hour, fourteen hours a day, to corporate classrooms with one-way video and two-way audio interaction.

Video teleconferencing is the latest form of technological link to find practical application. The National University Teleconference Network joins sixty-seven colleges and universities and the Smithsonian Institution. There were 650 participants in its first video teleconference on "Productivity in America." The American Law Institute joined the American Bar Association in a six-hour seminar which brought together 400 lawyers in fifty locations. In 1982, New York City's Hospital for Special Surgery brought a videoconference to 2,000 doctors in thirty-five locations (Gruebel, 1983).

As discussed earlier, computers communicating over telephone lines offer still another form of electronic linkage, and formal and informal networks in a variety of fields are developing rapidly (Lusterman, 1977).

Certification. A less widespread but promising method of linkage is the certification of competencies achieved in other learning environments, however informal. An increasing number of educational institutions award credit for noninstitutional experiences. Education is moving toward a pattern that awards and certifies competencies—no matter how they are achieved. Community colleges in the fifth generation will probably move increasingly toward the testing and certification of skills and competencies acquired elsewhere. One of the darkest moments in a student's life is the realization that hard-earned credits are not transferable. But a demonstrated competence should, logically, be universally transferable, and community college educators of the fifth generation will devise ways to make it easier to convert competencies into credits.

Problems of Linkage

Linkages with other institutions—particularly commercial institutions—raise some ethical issues. None of them is new, but they have a new importance, and the fifth-generation community colleges will need to resolve them. First, some of the traditional roles of institutions may be severely challenged. A growing segment of the corporate effort is remedial. Beverly McQuigg (1980), a Bell System training supervisor, puts the matter plainly: "Traditionally, Americans have relied heavily on formal schools to prepare young people to enter the labor force. This reliance is fading fast. There is a growing public perception that the school system is not keeping abreast, that there is a wide chasm between the courses schools offer and the training people need for work" (p. 324).

In 1977, the Conference Board reported that more than a third of the companies they surveyed offered remedial education of some kind, some of it for employees with college and advanced degrees (Lusterman, 1977). AT&T, for example, spends $6 million a year for remedial education. Polaroid has run an extensive in-house remedial program for ten years (Levine and Doyle, 1982).

Levine and Doyle believe that the surging growth of education by industry indicates, above all, inadequacies and inaccuracies in the product of the educational establishment. "The increase in private sector investment in education," they write, "is related to qualitative deficiencies in public sector education. Too many workers are poorly prepared, and too many public schools are not offering the kind and quality of education employers need. The private sector turned to its own education and training in the 1960s and 1970s not because too few people were being educated but because those who were, were not being educated well enough. The manpower skills employers needed were not for sale in the marketplace . . . business and industry are questioning the ability of public schools to produce a competent work force that is adequately and appropriately educated" (Levine and Doyle, 1982, p. 293).

There is clearly a danger, particularly in remedial education, that the corporation is becoming a critical competitor with public institutions. Probably the corporate energy reluctantly spent in remediation might better be spent improving the performance of the public institutions. There are immense benefits in greater and more intelligent collaboration. But this must not lead to a headlong substitution of corporate for community college education.

Another problem is the potential that in that process of collaboration community colleges may lose their sense of identity and become amorphous and indistinct, unable to make a clear, compelling claim on the interest and support of the community. It will become all the more important for community colleges to know exactly whom they are educating and why. Moreover, community colleges must never compromise independence by relying too heavily on any single relationship or set of relationships. Most community colleges will continue to develop more contractual relationships with other institutions—particularly with business organizations. There is an abiding danger of excessive dependence on such contracts—a risk that the institution will become simply a supplier of educational services defined by others, indistinguishable from commercial institutions. Thus, the community college must bring to these contractual arrangements a sense of the noncommercial values that must nourish any true educational effort. Community colleges, clearly, should be more than uncritical vendors of educational services. They should not devise or offer programs that are unworthy, that do not first of all serve the student, or that are in any way unbalanced. The community college must insist that proper attention be paid to the liberal arts and the fine arts. It is not the business of educators to program and reprogram automatons, but to help people become more complete, freer of disabling limitations of every kind.

Two IBM officials, Lewis M. Branscomb and Paul C. Gilmore, raised the question in an article in *Daedalus* (1975). In one way it is enormously helpful when industry helps society meet the huge costs of its learning requirements. But, they caution, the expansion of industry's educational involvement may make it more difficult than ever for "the committed, disciplined, and managed environment of highly structured [corporate] training to be affected by the skeptical attitude of the scholar and the innovative imagination of the researcher" (p. 229).

That quality—that commitment to a larger educational agenda—is becoming more urgent than ever. Vocational educators have welcomed the shift of public recognition that has made vocationally relevant education respectable. In the first of three generations of community colleges and into the fourth, vocational education was a kind of Siberia to which young people deemed unsuited for college were sentenced as a kind of punishment for their inadequacies. Now, in the fifth generation, vocational education has come into prominence. While other enrollments are declining, enrollments in vocational programs are solidly increasing. There is a danger that that swing may go too far. It is possible to see a disturbing kind of Gresham's law at work in education—in which vocationally relevant education drives out liberal education. There is a danger that we will build a society in which everybody knows how to make a good living and nobody knows how to live a good life. Ironically, it has often become the task of vocational educators to become spokespersons for the absolute importance of the liberal component in educational programs.

The Value of Linkages

Linkages at their best work both ways. There is an easy assumption that corporations know the techniques and colleges know how to teach, but the matter is far more complicated than that. Colleges can learn from corporations about teaching, and corporations can learn from colleges about technology and even about management. For example, the corporate world is far ahead of most colleges in the use of sophisticated systems of self-instruction. Multimedia educational modules built on programmed instruction have been brought to a very high level of effectiveness. A bank official describes a typing program which brings a trainee promptly "from zero knowledge to thirty words per minute through self-instruction programs. . . . The instructors show students how to use the equipment, and students come in at their convenience" (Lusterman, 1977, p. 76).

According to the Conference Board, "Most business executives are critical of the performance of the nation's schools and colleges in preparing people for work, and deplore particularly the lack they find in communications and mathematical skills among younger employees. Most believe, further, that these institutions would do well to emulate industry in its growing emphasis on student participation—the blending of classroom study with both programmed self-study and planned problem-solving experience, the tailoring of curricula to clearly defined goals and individual needs, and the employment of advanced instructional technologies" (Lusterman, 1977, p. 66).

Learning methods that stress peer support and teamwork and that involve participation, self-instruction, and self-evaluation are often missing in the schools but are essential in a business environment. Obviously, there is much to be gained by both corporations and colleges from increased exchanges. How that potential is actualized to the benefit of all will be one of the great challenges of the decade ahead.

Toward a New Era

During his presidency, Dwight Eisenhower spoke from time to time about what he called "the Lincoln dogma"—that society should assign responsibilities at the most primary level possible. The family should do for the individual only what the individual could not do—"or do so well"—for himself. The neighborhood should not do for the family what the family could do; the town should not usurp functions the neighborhood could handle—and so on.

The Catholic doctrine of "subsidiarity" expresses the same idea in an only slightly different way. More recently, radicals like Ivan Illich (1971) have become much more harsh and categorical. Illich has written about the disabling professions that make people dependent and less competent by doing for them what they might better do for themselves. He attracted a wide audience with his suggestion that we "de-school" society. But Illich is probably the sharp leading edge of a gathering new consciousness that a society is stronger as it learns to use *all* its institutional resources—that some should not grow at the expense of others. Schools should not seek to monopolize education but to extend it.

In his landmark speech to the convention of the American Association of Community and Junior Colleges in 1974, Alan Pifer introduced the concept of the hub, suggesting that community colleges should not think of themselves as a static "sector" of the educational establishment but rather as the hub of a network of institutions and community agencies—high schools, industry, the church, voluntary agencies, youth groups, even the prison system and the courts. Pifer proposed that community colleges begin to use what these other groups have to offer on the one hand and to serve and strengthen them on the other.

The "hub" metaphor is helpful, but it conveys a more static kind of role than the fifth generation may require. The educational system of the future may be less systematic—something of a nonsystem. The centers of initiative in education will continue to multiply—electronically equipped households, churches, museums, youth groups, factories and offices, proprietary schools, apprenticeships, schools and colleges, and many more. And running in and around and through these entities like glue will be the presence of the community college—sometimes supplementing these other resources, sometimes strengthening them, sometimes moving boldly into a gap, sometimes withdrawing from a field in which alternatives are adequate, sometimes certifying the educational results achieved by other institutions or learning environments.

How and with whom community colleges form linkages will be major policy issues as community college administrators weigh alternative future programs and priorities. The temptation is to link with everyone. The danger is in allowing linkages to develop on an ad hoc or piecemeal basis without consideration of long-term consequences to the integrity of the institution. Deegan and Drisco (1985) have proposed a number of policy questions that community colleges should review as they consider linkages, especially those with business. These questions can serve as a useful focus of analysis, and they can help place decisions about linkages in a broader institutional perspective. The questions are:

- What will be the place and priority of linkages in the mission of the college?
- What impact will the linkages have on institutional values? On reward systems?
- Should linking relationships be organized as a separate unit or integrated within an existing unit? If organized as a separate unit, how can program quality and integrity be monitored?
- What role will full-time faculty play in guiding or participating in linking efforts?
- Will the college provide sufficient "risk capital" to allow staff to do the kinds of needs assessments and planning to fully implement new linking opportunities?
- Where linkages lead to new financial resources, what will be the college policy on distribution of profits? Should profits be retained in the linking unit or centralized and redistributed college-wide, or should some percentage-sharing arrangement prevail?
- How will staff and program evaluation be conducted? What role will linking agencies play in these evaluations?
- How can the college ensure that staff hired in linking arrangements will be effective representatives in the college?

There is both great promise and great peril in the opportunities for linkages between community colleges and other organizations. That linkages will be a key theme of the fifth generation seems sure. At the rate linkages are developing, the question of whether those linkages will lead to more effective education or to a loss of values may perhaps become *the* issue to be resolved by community colleges in the fifth generation.

References

Branscomb, L. M., and Gilmore, P. C. "Education in Private Industry." *Daedalus,* 1975, *104* (1), 220–234.

Deegan, W. L., and Drisko, R. "Contract Training in Community Colleges." *Community and Junior College Journal,* 1985, *55* (6), 14–17.

"Earning an Undergraduate Degree at the Plant." *Business Week,* Aug. 4, 1980, pp. 30–31.

Free University Network. *1981 Directory of Free Universities and Learning Networks.* Manhattan, Kans.: Free University Network, 1981.

Gruebel, J. "Adult Learning by Television." *The College Board Review,* 1983, *128,* 18–22.

Illich, I. *Deschooling Society.* New York: Harper & Row, 1971.

Levine, M., and Doyle, D. "Private Meets Public: An Examination of Contemporary Education." In J. A. Meyer (ed.), *Meeting Human Needs: Toward a New Public Philosophy.* Washington, D.C.: American Enterprise Institute for Public Policy Research, 1982.

Lusterman, S. *Education in Industry.* New York: The Conference Board, 1977.

Luxenberg, S. "Education at AT&T." *Change,* 1978–1979, *11* (1), 27–35.

McQuigg, B. "The Role of Education in Industry." *Phi Delta Kappan,* 1980, *52* (1), 320–324.

National Center for Education Statistics. *Adult Education in Community Organizations 1972.* Washington, D.C.: U.S. Government Printing Office, 1974.

Peterson, R. E., and Associates. *Lifelong Learning in America: An Overview of Current Practices, Available Resources, and Future Prospects.* San Francisco: Jossey-Bass, 1979.

Part Four

Strengthening Governance, Finance, and Planning

The issues of governance, relations with government at all levels, finance, and planning became increasingly complex for community college leaders throughout the fourth generation. Choices made in response to these issues could lead to fundamental changes in the ability of community colleges to fulfill some functions that evolved in the first four generations.

In Chapter Nine, Richard L. Alfred and David F. Smydra discuss the serious challenges facing community colleges as self-governing organizations capable of making independent decisions about expenditures, student charges, and academic programs. Alfred and Smydra present an analysis of the evolution of community college governance and the changing roles of key participants in the governance process. They then review six key issues that must be confronted in the decade ahead and conclude the chapter with a model for conceptualizing governance processes in the fifth generation.

S. V. Martorana and Eileen Kuhns trace the development of relations between community colleges and federal, state and local government in Chapter Ten. They discuss the impact of the dichotomy of ties to both the public school systems and to higher education, and they then analyze a number of current issues in relationships between community colleges and government agencies. The final section of the chapter proposes a new framework for viewing government and community college relationships—a framework that places community colleges within the context of a "communiversity."

James L. Wattenbarger begins Chapter Eleven with an analysis of the changes in community college finance that occurred in the first four generations. He then discusses the difficulties of relating philosophy and finance and presents a taxonomy of current models for financing community colleges. He concludes his analysis by proposing a set of guidelines that community college leaders and government representatives might consider as they develop plans for financing community colleges in the fifth generation.

In Chapter Twelve, Richard C. Richardson, Jr., and William R. Rhodes discuss the need for more effective planning as community college leaders confront the dual challenges of demands for increased quality and fiscal constraint. They then review major issues of leadership, including a number of impediments to change in educational institutions, and conclude that strategic planning is the most promising means of meeting the challenges of the fifth generation. The final section of the chapter presents an analysis of the differences between the management and leadership needs of community colleges and offers a conceptual framework and criteria to guide strategic planning in the decade ahead.

In Chapter Thirteen, William L. Deegan, Dale Tillery, and Rudy J. Melone propose an agenda of priority issues and actions that policy makers and managers can use as a focus for analysis, planning, and decision making. Together these chapters constitute a rich body of thinking about the fundamental tasks of governing, financing, and planning, and they present specific policy and program proposals for consideration as community college educators confront these issues in the fifth generation.

9

Richard L. Alfred
David F. Smydra

Reforming Governance: Resolving Challenges to Institutional Authority

As community colleges move toward the 1990s, many institutions will face serious new challenges to their status as self-governing organizations capable of making independent decisions about expenditures, student costs, and academic programs. These challenges will be present in the form of increasing pressure on college faculty and administrators to justify the utility of academic programs and services to local communities, states, and society as a whole. The source of pressure will be external factions including, but not limited to, state coordinating boards, state legislatures, higher education appropriation committees, business and industry, civic organizations, human service organizations, baccalaureate degree-granting institutions, accrediting associations, and federal agencies.

While questions concerning the governance and costs and benefits of community college education have constantly arisen, it has not been until recently that the decision authority of college boards, faculty, and administrators has been so vigorously and widely questioned. Compounding the problem is the fiscal stringency that is affecting most states and the fact that K–12 education and four-year colleges and universities have begun to commit large-scale resources to functions that have normally been the province of the community college. The evidence is considerable, for example, of high schools experiencing pressure to provide better basic education and four-year colleges attempting to inject career education into traditional baccalaureate degree programs. Both segments of education have for years operated extensive adult education programs and are now beginning to further their involvement in this area to replace declining numbers of high school-aged youth.

To the experienced community college administrator, one message would seem clear: Competition is on the increase among different institutions to meet the needs of a changing student population. Two-year colleges will require aggressive leadership and innovative governance (in other words, decision) strategies if they are to maintain or increase their share of the student market. Changes in social needs eventually lead to changes in social policy. If there are changes in the composition and interests of potential learners, then it is likely that there will be changes in the structure of relationships among higher education institutions. These changes will be designed to moderate the competition among institutions and to improve the delivery of educational services to new learners. The questions that must be faced by community college boards, faculty, and administrators are: To what extent will any changes or dislocations in the structure of postsecondary institutions affect governance in the two-year colleges? How will decision makers anticipate and react to these changes? Will the community colleges continue in their present form or will they extend beyond their current organization and deliver new services? Will they be selectively integrated with other sectors of education as pressures mount for coordination of educational services in a period of austerity?

Community College Governance: A Working Definition

Two recurring themes in the literature directed to governance guide its application in the community college: (1) a prevailing concern among institutional constituencies about the location of authority and power for decision making among different parties to the decision process and (2) the notion that one or more parties to the process can alter a decision depending on the nature and degree of influence they bring to bear on persons with authority. To illustrate, change in the finance patterns of community colleges to reflect increased dependence on state agencies has had the effect of adding new parties (state budget officials and coordinating board staff) to the decision process. State budget officials with authority to determine the volume and distribution of appropriations to community colleges may exercise power in the institutional budget process through the issuance of "budget guidelines" (technical instructions) that clearly specify the nature and scope of personnel decisions that can be made by the institution, allowable increases in costs to offset inflation, and enrollment levels that will be "supported" by the state. In effect, state budget officials have become a force for governance because they exercise power, authority, and influence in the development of decisions that determine the shape of the institutional budget. At the same time, these officials may alter the structure and outcomes of the decision process by adjusting the format and content of the budget guidelines. As new guidelines are developed and implemented, the number, type, and role perspectives of actors involved in institutional budget decisions can change. Planning and evaluation specialists can be added or subtracted from the process, information systems specialists can experience an expansion of role in the process, and budget officials at the state level can exert greater or lesser influence in budget decisions depending on the direction of change in the budgetary guidelines. Overall, the shape of governance would change as a function of change in the budget process.

For the purpose of contrast with governance models presented in the higher education literature, key elements in the conceptualization of governance in community colleges may be summarized as follows:

1. Community college governance is a process involving the location of authority, power, and influence for academic

decisions among a discernible set of actors within and outside of the institution.

2.   There is an established order for influence relationships among parties to the decision process in community colleges; this order will remain static unless one or more parties moves to change the outcome of a particular decision such that the new outcome is different from that which would be evident if the decision were made within the established order of influence relationships.

3.   The capacity of different individuals to influence or "shape" institutional decisions will vary in accord with the type of decision to be made, the formal authority ascribed to the individual(s) by virtue of statutes or position, and the degree of power accumulated by the individual(s) over time.

4   Decision-making behavior can be altered by the advent of new parties to the decision process or shifts in the distribution of power among existing parties.

5.   The nature and degree of influence carried by different individuals in the decision process will vary over time in accord with changing environmental conditions facing the college.

Governance, then, is a correlate of the decision process. It serves as a conduit for the exercise of influence by specific groups in relationship to specific issues. In addition, it performs an important function in adapting the institution to changing political realities in the external environment.

Governance in Historical Context: 1950–1984

Governance is complex under the best of circumstances. It can assume different shapes and forms encompassing, on the one hand, "all aspects of the control and direction of the college" (Monroe, 1972, p. 303) and limited to, on the other hand, "the process for locating authority, power, and influence for academic decisions among internal and external constituencies in the college" (Alfred, 1983, p. 1). Three stages in the evolution of governance in community colleges can be identified:

1950–1960	Search for legitimacy
1960–1975	Unregulated institutional growth
1975–1984	Selective growth and redefinition

Search for Legitimacy. In the early period of development, from 1950 to 1960, community colleges were engaged in a quest for legitimacy as a full partner in postsecondary education. Approximately 400 in number, locally controlled community colleges were governed in much the same way as other elements of the public schools. A locally elected board of trustees established policies for the college or colleges in the district under the laws enacted by the legislature and the regulations of a state education board. Administrators, responsible solely to the board of trustees, executed policy and administered all facets of institutional operations, seemingly with unlimited authority. Boards of trustees concerned themselves with decisions on how and what to teach, who should teach, how to organize a student personnel program, how to design facilities to meet pressing public needs, and how to finance growth. One of the greatest difficulties in the early period of development was locating and training faculty and staff whose image of themselves as staff members of a two-year college was in harmony with the distinctive purposes of this type of institution rather than with some other type. Yet as early as 1931, when Eells wrote *The Junior College,* problems related to the comprehensiveness and complexity of governance in two-year colleges had begun to surface. Although boards of trustees and administrators may have been able to govern without apparent conflict, issues of financing, staff morale, and conformity with state laws were present then just as they are today. Presidents often made decisions with a small group of administrators and depended upon the informal peer network to communicate the results of the decision process.

Unregulated Institutional Growth. A pyramidic structure for governance arose in the second period of development from 1960 to 1975, in which power flowed from the president at the top of the organization down through successive layers of staff—vice-presidents, deans, directors, department heads, and faculty. Community colleges were experiencing dramatic growth in enrollments, programs, staff, and facilities, and it became apparent that a division of labor and a specialized group of managers was necessary to make decisions appropriate to the condition of growth. The president and senior administrative staff became progressively removed from the faculty as their number grew and regulative procedures became necessary to coordinate workload. The primary functions of administration were to coordinate and balance diverse activities of the college and to give impetus to reform and change. Formal procedures for communicating decisions prohibited the effective use of the informal network to disseminate information. The allocation of resources in the institutional budget came to be the primary mechanism of control for many presidents in this period. Most, if not all decisions, were tied to resources, and rules and procedures were developed to guide personnel decisions.

The approach administrators took toward decision making in this period could best be described as authoritarian. A 1967 study conducted by the American Association of Higher Education found that, in a sample of two-year colleges, only 25 percent could be classified as shared-authority institutions. The other 75 percent were dominated by administrators with some evidence of increasing faculty consultation. Faculty maintained primary responsibility for decisions on courses, curricula, and matters that affected the teaching and learning environment, whereas administrators maintained responsibility for decisions related to the planning, coordination, and allocation of resources. The interests of students, faculty, administrators, and trustees were different, each holding unique goal sets and serving different constituencies. The result was the beginning of conflict between faculty and administrators regarding their roles in decision making. Issues were weighed in terms of their impact on group concerns, and the sheer mass of new staff in the institution made the availability of money the critical factor in decision making. Mistakes were tolerated because the pressures of growth permitted little opportunity for looking back to determine what had gone wrong. The result was a trial-and-error approach to management among a class of administrators who wielded considerable power and who became accustomed to autonomy.

Selective Growth and Redefinition. As the dual impacts of stabilizing enrollments and dwindling finances were felt, the conditions for governance in community colleges changed dramatically. In the third stage of development, from 1975 to 1984, the emphasis shifted from growth to stabilization and selective allocation of resources to achieve institutional goals. Institutions that had assigned a strong administrative role to the president in their developmental years found that authority for decision making had been extended to new actors—coordinating boards, legislative committees, legislators, and the executive branch of government. No issue generated more controversy in this period than that of the control of community colleges and who was to make the decisions on specific issues. During the past few years, a sharp increase in the proportion of financial support received from the state has been accompanied by state-level monitoring, auditing, and policies that affect the program and operations of the colleges.

The time span between identified need and programmatic response increased, and initiative and creativity were discouraged under the mounting weight of regulations. At the same time, as linkages with local organizations increased in importance, faculty and administrators found it imperative to spend more time in the state capital "protecting their interests." There was the added concern that the state might inappropriately have its hands in matters that could better be determined locally. Regardless of whether this charge was warranted, tension mounted between those responsible for the institution at the local and state levels.

A final development characterizing community college governance from 1975 to 1984 was the increased need for data to support long-range planning and resource allocation decisions. Every increase in federal- and state-level categorical programs led to an increased need for data to be provided to external agencies. Similarly, limitations on federal and state funds for community colleges made it imperative that information systems be devised to accommodate an era in which growth could be undertaken only in selected areas. State-wide coordination of information systems became increasingly common as many states developed student and management data systems using compatible software and working definitions for all institutions.

Governance in Transition: Context and Constituencies

Numerous issues will command attention as community colleges enter a new period of development. What elements of control should be maintained by state agencies? What should be reserved for local institutions? What new actors in governance will emerge in the future and what role will they play in shaping institutional programs and finances? What further changes in institutional management will result from the trend toward placing more control in the hands of external agencies? What is the effect of tightening resources on relationships within and between institutions? Can collegial relationships of faculty to faculty and faculty to administrators survive in a period of intense competition for resources and spiraling demands for quality and cost-efficiency? Is it possible for institutions to "age gracefully" in the face of changing conditions? Faculty and staff will grow older with mobility not as frequent between institutions, programs will age, equipment inventories will become dated, facilities will have been in existence for a decade or longer, and repairs or new construction will be necessary to replace dysfunctional structures. Growth in enrollment and resources will level off. Although institutional size will probably remain constant, it will vary among academic programs in accord with shifting economic conditions and labor market needs. Faculty and administrators increasingly comfortable with collective bargaining will form cooperative alliances on nonbargaining issues. These alliances will be strengthened by adverse financial conditions, challenges to the autonomy of institutions, and increasing competition for students and resources.

Many new parties will emerge in community college governance over the next ten years. A framework for examination of these parties and their role in governance is presented in Figure 1. "Environmental inputs" comprise the total set of factors in the external environment that will shape the flow of resources to the college. As changes occur in the locus of support for community college programs, such as increased dependence on state agencies and students for operating revenue, shifts will also take place in the degree of involvement of different constituencies in campus governance. To illustrate, it is reasonable to expect that

Figure 1. Parties to Governance 1969–1990.

Environmental Inputs

- Individual, group, agency motives, needs, and expectations
- Resources: physical and financial
- Information
- Influence attempts (demands/constraints)
- Legal constraints
- Interorganizational ties and networks

Parties to Governance

Decision Process
- Communication and information flows
- Power, control, and influence patterns
- Decision-making patterns
- Formal and Informal decisions

External
- Community agencies
- Institutional accreditation
- Program accreditation
- Civic interest groups
- Influential citizens
- Local government
- Business and industry
- Legislative committees and staff
- State Coordinating board
- State legislature
- Governor
- Federal government
- National education association

Internal
- Program committees
- Individual faculty advisor
- Administrators
- Classified staff
- Academic departments
- Board of Trustees
- Students
- Collective bargaining
- Faculty senates
- College committees

Outcomes

Products and services
  a. Volume
  b. Quality

Human capacity
  a. Turnover
  b. Morale and commitment
  c. Growth and satisfaction

External image
  a. Attractiveness
  b. External resource support
  c. Prestige

Efficiency and effeftiveness
  a. Goal achievement
  b. Resource utilization
  c. Conflict management

Long-term viability
  a. To innovate
  b. To respond to new inputs
  c. To control environment
  d. To plan for the future

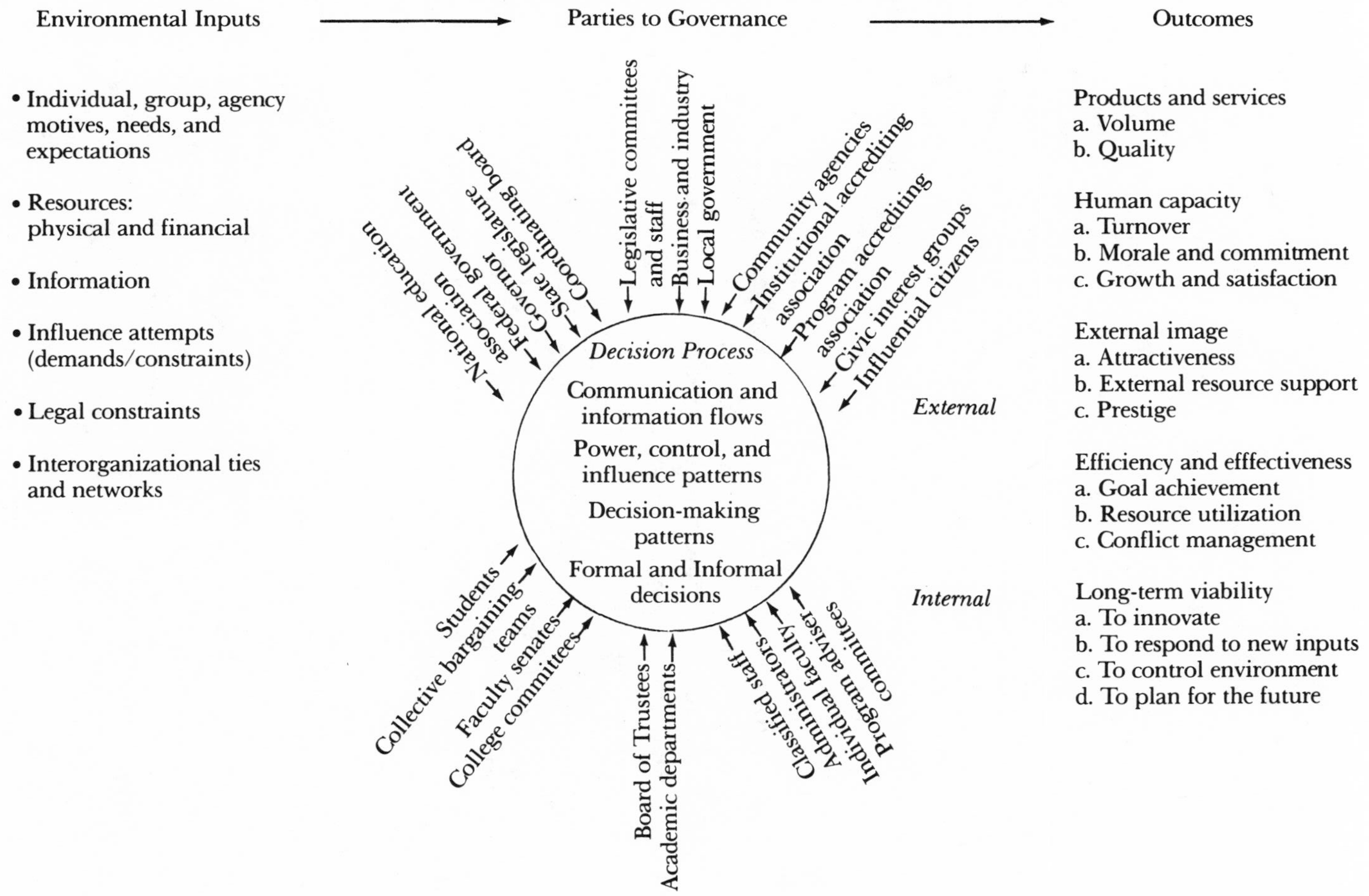

simultaneous trends of a decline in local tax as a percentage of the institutional revenue budget, higher student tuition charges, and increasing state support will expand the influence of students, state legislators, and coordinating board officials in institutional decisions and simultaneously limit the influence of local government agencies. The model presents four dimensions in the decision process: (1) communication and information flows, (2) power, control, and influence patterns, (3) decision-making patterns, and (4) formal and informal decisions. Extracampus constituencies will become more involved in each stage of the decision process, with increments in power for groups such as the executive branch of state government, state legislators, state budget officials, coordinating board officials, legislative staff, business and industry, organized community groups, political action committees, and influential citizens. Internal constituencies, such as the board of trustees, faculty senate, collective bargaining associations, and organized faculty and staff groups, will experience a decline in power in direct relationship to the degree of centralization of financial and programmatic decisions in state agencies. To the extent that community colleges begin to rely on private sector sources for operating revenue, business and industry and influential citizens will achieve a greater voice in decision making.

What alternatives are available for constituency involvement in community college governance in the mid 1980s to mid 1990s? The answer is selective involvement of constituencies based on their ability to shape the flow of resources to the college through determination of enrollment levels or direct operating dollars. Funds for community colleges pass through many decision levels before the campus gets them. The governor, the legislature, and the higher education coordinating board first assess prevailing economic conditions and apply different reasoning as to the resources available for community college education. At the same time, institutional boards of trustees, administrators, faculty, and budget committees determine the resource needs of the institution in accord with enrollment projections and spending priorities. State agencies have more freedom and more capability to shape enrollment levels, spending patterns, and tuition pricing in community colleges than do faculty and administrators. Assuming that governance can be examined in the context of resource decisions, internal and external constituencies might assume the following decision roles between 1985 and 1995.

Governor. As required by law, the governor must maintain a balanced budget for the state. The executive branch of government will maintain many options to shape programmatic and resource decisions. First, the governor will have the capability to propose modifications to funding formulas to alter revenue deployment in accord with changing economic conditions. Appropriations will be improved through selective utilization of reserve funds set aside to make up for faulty revenue estimates or transfer of funds from retirement accounts or reserves held for highways or human service agencies. Appropriations will be limited through executive orders reducing the amount of revenue available to community colleges or through working agreements with the legislature to hold taxes at a constant level or to appropriate new tax revenue to non-higher education spending priorities. The governor will also have the capacity to present a program to the legislature suggesting reductions or spending increments that should be made for community college education, taxes that should be raised or lowered, and programs that should be maintained at various levels of funding. Most states will have only about 40 percent of the state general revenue in services that can be funded on a discretionary basis through the regular appropriations process. These are the dozens of small state agencies, the courts, and law enforcement, corrections, mental health, and higher education agencies. On the basis of this broad range of possibilities for shaping the flow of resources to community colleges—general to the level of determining the total institutional allocation and specific to the level of determining resources for special program categories—the executive branch of state government will be a major force in community college governance in the decade ahead.

State Legislature. The legislature in different states currently holds differential powers in relation to community college governance and coordination. In a small number of states (Michigan, Missouri, and Oregon), the legislative appropriation of funds to community colleges represents the only act of coordination to which the colleges are subject. In other states (Illinois,

Connecticut, Texas, North Carolina, and Maryland), considerable coordination of programmatic and resource decisions in community colleges occurs outside of the legislature through the actions of state coordinating boards. The legislature is and will continue to be a powerful force in governance throughout the remainder of the decade. It will have the capacity to alter the resources available to community colleges through special or regular session. The governor's program of spending for higher education will become a major target for adjustments after legislative attention—all directed toward the goal of a balanced budget and satisfaction of important political interests. Taxes will be increased or decreased, programs will be funded at higher or lower levels than before, and college and university budgets will be funded differentially among the sectors. The legislature will encourage higher tuition by withholding some state funds to be made up from tuition sources. It will limit construction of new facilities, repair of existing facilities, and funds for new equipment to a fraction of that previously planned for community colleges. It may omit or heavily limit faculty salary increases (along with those for all state workers), and undoubtedly it will call for greater faculty productivity of student credit hours and improved academic standards reflected in stringent appropriations bills.

State Budget Office. An axiom related to coordination in higher education stipulates that increasing austerity brings on increasing centralization of decisions in colleges and universities. State budget offices will play a major role in developing demographic and economic projections over the next decade to guide resource decisions in community colleges. As states take on additional responsibility for the administration of federal programs, specialists will be hired to establish numerical data descriptive of population density and composition, anticipated tax revenue, labor market trends, mandatory state costs for retirement and social services, energy costs and availability, economic growth and development, natural resources, rates of unemployment, and manpower costs associated with different employment levels of the state work force. These data will be used to determine enrollment levels for two-year colleges, program offerings, expenditure patterns, faculty-student ratios, and capital construction needs.

Indeed, it is entirely possible that a new class of state-level bureaucrats will emerge to bring order, or at least an additional layer of complexity, to resource decisions. One unanswered question will be that of the linkage between state budget officers, coordinating board officials, and college administrators in budgetary decisions. Each party will bring a carefully prepared information portfolio to the decision process, and competition will be keen among various actors to gain acceptance of their portfolio as the basis for programmatic and finance decisions.

State Coordinating Board. The state coordinating board, and more particularly its director and staff, will play an influential role in relation to the governor and the legislature in community college governance. It will make recommendations on allocations for community colleges, determine enrollment levels and faculty/ student ratios, and perhaps even call for the elimination of specific programs that appear to be duplicative or the addition of new programs to meet emerging manpower needs. The recommendations will be based in part, if not wholly, on some conception of long-range education objectives previously adopted by the agency. The governor and the legislature will seriously consider agency recommendations in appropriations decisions, and while the final appropriation may be at substantial variance with the recommendations, agency influence will be significant. As may be true with the state budget office, coordinating boards will add staff with strong analytical skills in demographic projections, finance, and economic forecasting to develop the best possible case for college support.

Legislative Staff. Staff to legislators, particularly those serving on higher education appropriation committees, serve an important role in developing information for use by elected officials in voting on community college appropriations. This role is likely to expand in the future as lawmakers seek staff with established analytical skills to counter, or to function parallel with, budget office specialists and coordinating board staff. Legislators' knowledge of community college education may be limited to the analyses these staff provide. Analytical data will need to be accurate, referenced in the present and future, and capable of withstanding the scrutiny of skilled analysts. In cases in which legislative staff demonstrate strong political and analytical skills, their frame of reference on community college program and finance decisions will be adopted and reflected in the voting behavior of legislators.

Business and Industry. Private sector business and industrial executives will achieve recognition in the late 1980s as a major source of support for community college academic program development, faculty training and retraining, equipment acquisition, student support, and direct subsidization of career and technical programs. The price for such support will be a greater voice in program, staff, and financial decisions made by community college faculty and administrators. As administrators reach out to the private sector to supplement lagging state and local support for hard-pressed technical programs, business and industrial executives will begin to ask hard questions about the quality of programs and courses, the background and teaching skills of the faculty, the condition of instructional equipment and facilities, and the willingness of the institution to modify or eliminate weak programs. Program quality, which was once an issue in the decision to start-up or expand industry-sponsored employee development programs, will become more than rhetoric to business executives. These executives will push faculty and administrators to restructure the curriculum, identify weak faculty and seek to weed them out or get them into retraining programs, donate equipment to ensure that students receive up-to-date training, and call for faculty and program heads to create long-range plans and to develop quality standards for courses and staff to ensure that graduates can meet industry standards.

Political Action Groups. For political action groups, commitment to a purpose, a program, or an organization usually, although not inevitably, maintains the highest priority, and the substance of programs comes second. Increasingly, the goals and purposes of community colleges will be advanced to the forefront of public attention by political action groups comprised of trustees, citizen advocates, and political contacts. In difficult situations, these groups will function as an arm of the institution to improve institutional appropriations. These groups will not simply attempt to exert influence outside the college: They will insist on receiving information from college officials regarding budgetary needs and priorities, and they will provide analyses to college administrators of the political climate in the state capitol and of the current spending priorities of legislators and the executive branch of government. They will have some influence on the shape of community college governance through their role as a bridge between the institution and the legislature in financial matters.

Board of Trustees. Here substantial variation will be in effect among institutions depending on the age of the institution, state patterns of coordination, and the historical relationship between the president and trustees. Trustees will be an active force in governance in states with loosely federated community college systems and in institutions with an embedded pattern of trustee involvement in decision making. Trustees will choose to become more knowledgeable about institutional finance and long-range planning, and they will seek involvement in programmatic and financial decisions if for no other reason than to exercise the full extent of their fiduciary responsibility in the college. Trustees will leave routine operational decisions to faculty and administrators, choosing instead to focus on strategic decisions related to enrollments, programs, finances, and facilities. Needless to say, if board involvement in administrative decisions advances to a point that endangers the capacity of administrators to lead, long-range consequences could occur, such as gradual erosion in external support due to unclear authority lines in the institution. For the decade ahead, the participation of community college trustees in campus governance will be problematic if it is too limited, on the one hand, and too extensive on the other. Needed will be guidelines for trustee participation in governance based on involvement in decisions related to finance and programs where public- and private-sector contacts maintained by trustees will be of some value to the college.

College President. For community college presidents, a more reactive approach to decision making is likely in the decade ahead, especially if institutional dependence on state agencies for financial support becomes more pronounced. With the advent of information specialists at the state level charged with responsibility for establishing demographic and fiscal projections, presidents will turn to in-house specialists to develop internal data systems descriptive of institutional enrollment prospects, academic productivity, and financial needs. Decisions and political strategies will evolve from carefully prepared data bases, from extensive analyses applied to longer-range goals, and through negotiation with state officials employing similar data bases. Presidents will not respond to external pressures entirely in the reactive mode. They will forge linkages with organized lobbyists, private-sector executives, and influential citizens to build external support for institutional programs. Trendline data, carefully evaluated, will allow them to put forward documented assumptions about the future with funding sources. Computer simulations on student flows by program, by course, and by unit cost will provide a base for decision making from which institutional leaders and state agency administrators can develop negotiated solutions to complex issues. Political decisions will be much more rational than in previous years, and unreasonable decision alternatives will be quickly identified and eliminated. The premises for decisions will change, as will the decisions themselves.

Faculty. The faculty, and more particularly collective groups of faculty such as unions and academic senates, will play, in most community colleges, a more limited role in governance than was characteristic of their role in the 1970s. In the late 1980s, community college faculty increasingly will become a professional group in search of a collective identity. The search for identity will stem largely from the fact that age and curricular differences will introduce divisions among the faculty that will constrain cooperative working arrangements. Further, changing labor market conditions will exacerbate existing differences, making faculty in some programs more valuable than faculty in other programs and leading to variable conditions in workload, salaries, and bargaining power. Faculty in community colleges cannot hope to achieve a meaningful voice in institutional governance in the absence of a collective identity—an identity that will not be established until conditions of equity are in place between young and old instructors, liberal arts and technical faculty, and part-time and full-time instructional staff. Other issues facing faculty relate to quality and cost. What types of student learning outcomes is it reasonable to expect an institution to accomplish given a fixed level of costs and faculty who are divided along lines of age, sex, experience, and department status? It is axiomatic that faculty expect to exert a major voice in curriculum and course decisions. Increasing numbers of faculty, however, will use curriculum committees, academic senates, and collective bargaining associations to retard change. Some faculty will choose to maintain close ties with business and industry. Others will not. There will be burgeoning demands from external agencies for relevance in career and technical programs to emerging labor market needs. Because community colleges will experience increasing competition from four-year colleges and universities for students and resources, they will be forced to rely more heavily on private-sector support for improvement of programs and services. They will establish contractual relationships with business and industry, which will include industry involvement in curriculum and course decisions. Faculty will have no choice but to share authority with external constituencies if they want to maintain programs at a proper level of support.

The use of part-time faculty to make ends meet will have an important but little-noticed consequence for community colleges in the decade ahead. If part-time faculty can perform as well as full-time faculty at less than half the cost, then full-time faculty must be vastly overpaid for what they do. The logic of this argument will diminish the feeling of self-worth of full-time faculty and encourage them to seek satisfaction outside of the institutions in which they are employed. The result will be increasing neglect of students, since the full-time faculty will not only fail to pick up the responsibilities of part-time faculty who are not paid to be involved in the life of the college, but in addition will neglect their own responsibilities. Faculty will become the subject of increasing scrutiny by administrators and external agencies in terms of compensation and fringe benefits as questions arise with respect to parity in workload with part-time staff.

Academic Senates and Collective Bargaining Associations. Faculty participation in governance through the vehicle of collective association in academic senates and collective bargaining began with the advent of a fiscally restrictive environment. Academic senates, well established as the accepted mode for faculty involvement in decision making in most community colleges, began to dwindle in influence in the late 1970s as increasing numbers of faculty turned to the union to clarify issues of job protection, salary and benefits, and work conditions. Collective bargaining is time consuming and requires commitment from a large number of faculty to remain effective. That commitment must be expressed in a willingness to accept the results of the process as well as a willingness to support the structure. Faculty increasingly divided among lines of age, sex, experience, and changing market values associated with different disciplines will experience difficulty in achieving a collective voice in governance in the 1990s. Tensions will mount between small groups of faculty organized by department, academic rank, or special interest as resources become tighter and changing market conditions make some faculty more valuable than others. Add to this condition the burgeoning demands of external parties (business and industry officials, program accreditation boards, community interest groups, and so on) for involvement in academic decisions that affect the quality of courses and curricula, and the result will be erosion of group consensus as a technique for making academic decisions. In brief, unless faculty are willing to forego individual rewards associated with academic rank, experience, and department status in favor of collective benefits obtained through decision making in large groups, academic senates and collective bargaining associations will pale in significance as a force in governance in the 1990s. A major issue of concern to the faculty will become the absence of individuals interested in doing the work necessary to carry out union responsibilities and to staff the governance structure established in the agreement. A limited number of faculty will do most of the work.

Classified Staff. Classified staff comprised of secretarial support personnel, maintenance workers, security staff, and so on have traditionally maintained a very limited voice in community college governance. Drawing its members from the immediate geographical region in which the college is located, the classified staff reflect the economic, cultural, and ethnic interests of the area. Large in number in any single institution, this group theoretically should constitute an important force in governance. The movement toward statewide systems of community colleges and the resulting controls and bureaucratic red tape that go with such systems, however, have largely negated the utility of efforts undertaken by classified staff to expand their role in governance. In many cases, the state coordinating board and legislature bring more influence to bear on personnel and finance decisions than do the local college administrators and trustees. A second force is the significant advance of information processing and retrieval technology and the potential displacement of large numbers of classified staff. The combined influence of state coordinating board policies and procedures and advancing technology will serve to divert the attention of classified staff from involvement in decisions related to students, programs, and services to negotiations designed to protect jobs and improve working conditions.

Students. Student involvement in community college governance has been limited through time by situational factors such as commuting distance, part-time or full-time work, and home and community responsibilities. It does not appear that there will be a significant change in student interest or participation in the late 1980s. In general, the importance of student involvement in decision making will continue to be taken lightly by faculty and administrators, and little evidence exists to suggest that students object to this view. Students will continue their efforts toward involvement in decisions that affect college costs and financial aid, but they will also shun institutional attempts to broaden their participation in committee and task force structures. A new role for students in departmental curriculum committees and issues related to marketing of courses and curricula is likely in the decade ahead, although challenges could ensue from faculty regarding confidentiality and student competence. Students and faculty are likely to have opposing views about matters of academic policy, curriculum, academic standards and progression policies, and academic personnel. Although it is not clear how student participation in deliberations on these matters could be organized without conflict, student involvement in programmatic decisions could become a force in governance as community colleges move toward the 1990s.

Issues for the Fifth Generation

Critical in importance in the discussion of constituency roles in community college governance between 1985 and 1995 is the notion that power, authority, and influence in the decision process will shift from internal to external constituencies. The rising influence of external agencies will result in a governance structure that might best be described as a political-bureaucratic model devoted to regulation and control. An increasing number of colleges, especially those that are part of a state system, will be placed in a management mode rather than a governance context. Not only will the increasing complexity of governance demand a new breed of administrators to fill openings, but it will also demand that these administrators be individuals with far-reaching educational vision and that they be capable of interpreting community needs and expectations, committed to the types of students the institution serves, and adept at working with multiple constituencies, such as faculties, governing boards, state governments, and community groups, as well as with representatives of other segments of education. Pressing issues will need to be resolved by the new generation of leaders in the changing governance context of the 1990s. These issues include: (1) increasing complexity in the organizational structure, (2) aging facilities and equipment, (3) lack of discretionary income, (4) false security in terms of current economic conditions and enrollment demand, (5) squeeze between the secondary schools and four-year colleges in the delivery of educational programs, and (6) changing relationship between the states and the federal government.

To successfully address these issues, administrators will require sophisticated data about institutional characteristics and performance, as well as about changing environmental conditions. At the same time, state agencies will place increasing pressure on community colleges to furnish information about institutional performance—long- and short-term student outcomes, attrition and retention, graduation rates, and so on—to guide resource allocation decisions. Community colleges are not organized to provide such data. The institutional research function is fragmented among multiple offices, it lacks organizational identity, and it is not conducted in accord with a systematic plan. Needed is an approach to decision making that merges multiple "information systems" used by different groups into a single information system that can serve as a foundation for strategic decisions by policy makers both within and outside of the institution. This model for decision making is termed the "coordinated systems model," and it will become an important feature of community college governance between 1985 and 1995.

The 1990s will be a decade of rapid growth in information systems in community colleges, government agencies, and private-sector organizations. It will be a period in which decision makers will become comfortable with the new technology and employ sophisticated information systems in making decisions about programs, students, resources, staff, and facilities. The future shape of governance can best be described as one of "organizational dualism," in which multiple systems for decision making will be utilized consisting of four groups of decision makers: faculty, trustees and administrators, agencies of state and federal government, and private-sector organizations. In matters of academic affairs, organized faculty groups (through a representative senate, curriculum committee, or collective bargaining association), private-sector organizations (through program advisory committees, presidential advisory committees, and personal influence networks), and state government agencies (through program approval mechanisms and resource allocation procedures) will have considerable, if not final, authority regarding such questions as degree programs, degree requirements, curriculum structure, course offerings, faculty selection, admission standards, and the academic calendar. Administrative matters, such as fund raising, budgeting, public relations, institutional planning, student services, and academic support services, will tend to be resolved by trustees and administrators—but in direct relationship to the information networks and decision inputs of faculty, state agencies, and private-sector organizations. In short, it will be difficult for administrators to make major decisions—either academic or administrative—in isolation. The conjoined interest of internal and external constituencies and the increased capacity of these constituencies to shape institutional decisions through sophisticated information systems will be the driving force underlying new initiatives in governance. Governance in this context will differ from earlier depictions, because it will involve a much larger number of actors, many of whom are external to the institution. To illustrate, decisions about the development, design, modification, and discontinuation of academic programs have traditionally rested with internal constituencies, such as faculty and administrators. In the decade ahead, external constituencies will become more deeply involved in these decisions, as illustrated in Table 1.

Organizational dualism between internal and external constituencies concerned about academic and administrative decisions will intensify in the 1990s. Efforts will be made by campus administrators to develop sophisticated information systems to neutralize or counteract the information employed by external agencies in the decision process. Community colleges will adopt an approach to management built around the notion of internal subgroups of faculty and administrators responsible for the development and maintenance of specialized information subsystems. These systems will be capable of immediate application to specific decisions, and they will be coordinated by executive management—hence the derivation of the term *coordinated systems*.

Implementation of the coordinated systems model will involve establishment of participative decision systems keyed to the application of strategic information to ongoing institutional processes, such as budget development. Administrators responsible for planning, research, and business operations will work with academic department heads and cost center managers to collect, analyze, and input data into the decision spectrum at specific points in the budgetary process. For example, the task of executive administrators (presidents, vice-presidents, and deans) will be to assess economic, demographic, technological, and social conditions in the external environment as a prelude to establishment of written guidelines for development of the operating budget. Most likely, institutional research personnel and business officers will be involved in this assessment process through responsibility for collection of such data as future-year revenue projections for state and local tax districts, change in the size and distribution of the

Table 1. Involvement of External Constituencies
in Fifth-Generation Community Colleges.

External Constituency	Rationale for Involvement in Programmatic Decisions	Information Systems Utilized in Programmatic Decisions
Business and industry	Concern about the quality, skill training, and promotability of associate degree graduates entering the regional labor market	Private market forecasts for new and replacement positions by occupational title Data regarding anticipated change(s) in employee skill requirements by occupational title
State coordinating boards	Concern about program duplication and costs and benefits associated with career and technical programs offered by postsecondary institutions	Published forecast data for labor market needs by occupational title Student outcomes and cost data for comparable academic programs in different colleges
State legislature (Higher education appropriations committee)	Concern about appropriations to institution with duplicate, low-quality, or costly programs	Published forecast data for labor market needs by occupational title Student outcomes data Program cost data

regional population, college-going rates of high school seniors and adult learners, labor market forecasts, and public policy trends. These data will be used to develop parameters for academic department heads and nonacademic managers to guide judgments about resource requirements in specific cost centers.

Perhaps the most critical role in the application of the coordinated systems model to the budgetary process belongs to academic department heads and faculty. Department heads will be required to spend less time on day-to-day duties of organizing curricula and assigning faculty teaching loads and concentrate more on strategic goals that take into account the effective use of resources in today's austere and increasingly competitive postsecondary education market. In the coordinated systems model, department heads and faculty (on release time) will be required to collect data about program performance for use in documenting departmental budgetary requests. The following information will be needed to assess program requirements for financial resources:

- historical and current headcount and full-time equivalent enrollment
- projected student demand for programs
- labor market forecasts for job openings by curriculum specialization
- technological requirements for new equipment on a program-by-program basis
- job obtainment and performance of graduates
- transfer rates and academic performance of graduating and nongraduating students
- student attrition and graduation rates
- student performance on certification and licensure examinations
- student perceptions of courses, curricula, and faculty
- employer perceptions of student quality
- results of external program reviews and accreditation
- requisites for curriculum change in response to advancing technology
- requirements for faculty retraining to maintain program quality

- requirements for new and modernized facilities
- salary and benefit requirements to attract and hold quality faculty
- private-sector revenue available for direct support of academic programs

In the future, faculty and department heads will be responsible for generating such information for use in resource allocation decisions. They will also be responsible for bringing in a larger percentage of the resources needed to support departmental operations. Training for this role will come directly through participation in the budget development process. Academic departments lacking vital information in one or more of the preceding categories simply will not receive their full share of resources. As the administrators with the closest contact with faculty and classified staff, academic department heads and cost center managers can exert influence over staff performance and resource requirements without difficulty. The problem is that in today's community colleges the department head and cost center manager role is regarded as protective of a unit when, in fact, these are the individuals who will be called on in a total institutional context to make hard decisions about program and staff vitality based on information collected in the budgetary process.

The progression toward coordinated systems for governance is evolving at different rates in different states; but in almost all states, community college administrators will be expected to do more planning, develop new kinds of budget justifications based on sophisticated information systems, and develop more evaluative information about institutional programs and services. In states with a statewide board with major responsibility for planning and budgeting, two-year college administrators will be interacting primarily with the state higher education agency in developing and conducting new planning, program review, and budget review procedures. In other states, the primary initiative for planning and budgeting will come from the legislature or the state budget office. Regardless of the source, there will be an emphasis on more specific and realistic planning, more attention to effective management procedures, better control of information, and more accountability.

Budget formulas are also likely to be modified to put less emphasis on enrollment factors and more emphasis on reallocating limited resources. Using precepts presented by Folger (1980), the following sections will briefly review new management applications in community colleges that are likely to emerge in the 1990s as part of the coordinated systems approach to governance.

Program Review. Historically, program review has been primarily an institutional self-assessment for internal improvement. In the 1990s, however, new state and institutional interests will emerge for program review. The first will be reallocation of resources (faculty and dollars) among programs to enable community colleges to do more with available resources. Because faculty and administrators will have difficulty with academic resource reallocation, external agencies increasingly will need to assume a leadership role in the process. A second interest in program review will be the need to increase the quality of educational offerings and to eliminate substandard and marginal programs. Although the major faculty motivation for program review may be one of documentation of need for additional resources, this would logically be in opposition to external motivation to use program review as a basis for using existing resources more effectively. These differing motives will have the potential of creating a center of conflict for administrators, who will need to develop rational approaches to program modification while simultaneously maintaining an aura of collegiality. Administrators will experience great difficulty in satisfying both internal and external constituencies.

State Budgeting. The budget has always been the primary means of state influence on community college education. The state budget serves three principal purposes: It controls spending, it enables management of activities, and it determines objectives. Several changes in budget processes may occur in the next few years. Frequently mentioned will be the desire on the part of community colleges to change budget formulas and budget criteria so that less weight is given to enrollment in determining appropriations. Because a number of public colleges and universities will probably lose some enrollment in the next decade, they will want to cushion the revenue loss associated with the loss of enrollment.

There will be a similar state interest in reducing the fiscal pressure to compete for students at any cost, which may lower standards and lead to a proliferation of weak off-campus programs. States can use a number of adjustments to reduce the importance of enrollment. First, they can develop marginal-cost rather than average-cost funding formulas so that the addition or loss of a student only adds or subtracts part of the average cost per student. Second, states can appropriate funds for a particular enrollment level at each institution—for example, five thousand students. If the actual enrollment is within two hundred students plus or minus of the budgeted level, then no adjustment will be made in the institution's budget. This approach is called a "corridor" concept, and the corridor can be set at a percentage width or a numerical width. The corridor can be wide or small. Still another approach will be to use the average enrollment level for the last three years as the basis for funding. In this method, no adjustment will be made if the institution is under or over enrollment for the year; but the new enrollment figure is part of the next three-year average. These are only three examples of variations in funding criteria that can be used to deemphasize enrollment changes in the appropriations process. Administrators will need to understand the long- and short-term ramifications of each and to make adjustments in institutional policies for student admission and retention.

Statewide Planning. Statewide planning in community college education should provide the framework and sense of direction for program review and budgeting. A large majority of states have developed a state higher education plan, but the extent to which the plan is actually a guide for the development of community colleges and their financing varies widely from state to state. Some state plans emphasize broad goals and objectives; others focus on academic plans and role and mission statements for each public institution. Some plans embody most of the public policy objectives in community college education, including issues of opportunities for minorities, access for all citizens, quality improvement, fiscal policies, academic development, and institutional role and mission. Other plans are more limited in scope.

Despite the uneven experience with state educational planning during a period of growth, there will be increasing pressure on administrators to develop plans to deal with the conditions of stability and decline in the next decade. The consequences of every community college acting for its own short-run interest are predictably adverse during a period of fiscal austerity. Although there is an increased need for planning, the necessary political support for planning will be very difficult to maintain because budgetary reduction is politically unrewarding. In addition, there will likely be substantial fluctuations in enrollment and economic conditions during the next decade, which will result in periodic crises in funding and departures from plans and budget formulas by administrators in favor of across-the-board cuts and other crisis management techniques. Legislators, private-sector organizations, and state budget officers will be calling on the colleges to eliminate duplication and weak programs. In many states, community college administrators will move forward with planning on the ground that it is better to deal with the issues themselves than to have solutions handed to them by the legislature, often in response to a temporary crisis.

Conclusion

A potentially rewarding outcome of the emergence of a coordinated systems model of governance will be the proliferation of consensus among internal and external constituencies regarding undesirable solutions to complex problems. When duplicate information systems are brought to bear on a specific decision by state coordinating boards, business and industrial organizations, legislatures, and community college administrators, inappropriate decision alternatives will be quickly rejected from consideration. The coordinated systems model should lead to improvement of decisions, but it should also lead to a sharpened sense of understanding on the part of faculty and administrators as to the utility of accurate data in the decision process. Is it desirable for external agencies to be concerned about the quality of academic and administrative decisions and to utilize data to influence those decisions? The immediate response of faculty and administrators will be negative, even though multiple sources of information should sharpen academic decisions. Should resources allocated in the past on the basis of limited information be reallocated in different formats based on new sources of information? The immediate response of community college administrators—favored in past years by an information vacuum at the state level—will be to protect their turf at all costs. Similarly, should external agencies utilize student and cost/benefit data to identify marginal academic programs and encourage college faculty and administrators to eliminate these programs? And should agency officials retain authority to suspend or revoke authorization for programs identified as marginal in quality? The immediate administrative response will undoubtedly be hostile to either proposal. If community college faculty and administrators cannot adjust to the reality of increased external agency participation in campus governance in the 1990s, the consequence could be a loss of support for institutional programs and service.

In the future, external constituencies will perform a dual role in community college governance: providing resources for institutional programs and participating in the decision process. The role of external agencies in providing data for institutional decisions about programs, resources, and facilities will be more vital to the effective and efficient performance of two-year colleges than their role in providing financial support. If information generation and analysis is a management process that has an impact on decision making, the creative initiative lies with faculty and administrators who generate information about institutional performance. To expect faculty and administrators to retain exclusive control over academic and administrative decisions in a period of rising external influence over the flow of resources to the institution is unrealistic. Similarly, to expect state agencies and private-sector organizations to provide full support for college programs and services in the absence of data descriptive of program performance is also unrealistic.

In the decade ahead, community faculty, administrators, and external agency officials should be able to come together to improve decision making through coordinated information systems. It will be the task of administrators to present the recommended decision alternatives to the governing board. If the choice proves correct, all parties to the decision process will profit through the experience. If the choice proves incorrect, faculty and administrators will question the wisdom of engaging external constituencies in the decision process. The challenge to community college faculty and administrators is to achieve the first and avoid the second outcome.

References

Alfred, R. L. "Institutional Responses to Changing Sources of Revenue: Is the Community College Abandoning the Community Role?" Paper presented at the annual convention of the American Association of Community and Junior Colleges, New Orleans, Apr. 1983.

Eells, W. C. *The Junior College*. Boston: Houghton Mifflin, 1931.

Folger, J. K. "Implications of State Government Changes." In P. Jedamus, M. W. Peterson, and Associates, *Improving Academic Management: A Handbook of Planning and Institutional Research*. San Francisco: Jossey-Bass, 1980.

Monroe, C. R. *Profile of the Community College: A Handbook*. San Francisco: Jossey-Bass, 1972.

10

S. V. Martorana
Eileen Kuhns

Designing New Structures
for State and Local
Collaboration

As discussed in Chapter One, the first four generations of the community college have witnessed significant shifts in relationships with other institutions and dramatic shifts in political interactions with various levels of government. A most important interface for the fifth generation is likely to be a continuation and intensifying of relationships with government at local, state, regional, and federal levels. What have these relationships been? What forces work to change them? What are they likely to be in the year ahead? This chapter speaks to those questions.

Antecedents to Change in Government Relations

As discussed throughout this volume, there is good evidence that community colleges encounter difficulties as well as find strength from having their origins rooted in both the traditions of higher education and those of common school education. That organizational dualism permeated the struggle of community colleges for their own identity as institutions during their first four generations. The dualism influenced both the nature of the government bodies the community colleges had to deal with and how such relations were to be conducted, and it is operative still as community colleges continue to evolve into a fifth generation.

Debate over the issue of what forces gave greatest impetus to the American community college and contributed to its phenomenal growth and development dates back over half a century, but four directions of change gradually took hold and are particularly pertinent to a discussion of the future of community college-government relations. The four developments emerge clearly from the record describing the legal status of community colleges and trends in state legislation affecting community college education, which is provided by a series of longitudinal studies and reports on these subjects (Martorana, 1950, 1950–1963; Martorana and others, 1957–1964; Martorana and others, 1976–1983). These directions of change can be described as (1) the secession of community colleges from local school boards of education and local school districts, (2) the emergence of fiscally dependent local community college boards of control, (3) the drift of governance authority from local to state levels, and (4) the cooptation of community college control by state agencies responsible for other levels of postsecondary education. It should be noted that these shifts described the national scene, not the history of community colleges in a particular state. But enough states in the nation evolved along the lines of these four directions to cause significant changes in community college-government relations. The secession from local school systems characterizes what happened in such states as California, Illinois, Michigan, Texas, and Washington, among others. The appearance of fiscally dependent community college boards is a primarily Eastern occurrence dominating the states of New York, New Jersey, Maryland, and Pennsylvania. The third and fourth changes occurred throughout the nation.

Shift from Local School Boards to Separate Community College Boards. As a general rule, organizational reform does not take place by secession; most often pressures generated by threats of secession focus attention on needed reforms, which, when accomplished, remove the need for the threatened withdrawal. Therefore, few complex organizational entities can be identified that have experienced a secession comparable to that accomplished between 1940 and 1970 by the two-year colleges operating as parts of public school systems. At the start of that period, a majority of the public two-year colleges were associated with public school systems; at this writing, only a handful remain. As increasing numbers of two-year colleges severed their connections with public school systems, important changes also appeared in the relationships the colleges held with other organizations at all levels of government. At the local level, the move away from what Koos (1929) called the "associated" types of community colleges generated a new posture. In assuming this posture, the institutions sought two objectives. Like adolescent children feeling a new sense of freedom from familiar ties, the community colleges acted simultaneously in ways that (1) accentuated independence from local school systems and (2) wooed new associates, a practice which prior local school ties had either made difficult or prohibited completely. For example, as community colleges in California became independent operating institutions, use of the term *superintendent* to designate the chief executive officer of the system gradually was dropped in favor of the term *president* or, in the case of districts with multicampus operations, *chancellor*. Community college faculty in all of the states in which the secession movement took place also saw new opportunities to disassociate from their public school teacher colleagues and did so—for example, by forming chapters of the American Association of University Professors as opposed to being members of the National Education Association. Faculty rank, a university syndrome, also became more commonplace.

At the state level, new laws releasing community colleges from common school district administration brought gradual severance of relationships with state boards of education. Again, the separation was not a sudden happening. In California, public community colleges were authorized as separate districts under their own boards of control at the local level long before the California Board of Governors for Community Colleges was established to take over duties of coordination at the state level. During the interim, the function was centered in a separate division within the California State Department of Education under the State Superintendent of Public Instruction. This evolutionary pattern was also the one exhibited over the years in Illinois, Iowa, and Maryland, which also now have state boards for community colleges as well as separate boards of control for the local community college districts.

Emergence of Fiscally Dependent Local Community College Boards. While the secession movement described previously was shifting community college governmental relationships at local and state levels in states in which the community colleges had been rooted in the common schools, another national dvelopment was taking place with equally important organizational consequences. This second notable emergence occurred in the middle Atlantic states as they moved to become part of the nationwide expansion in community college education that took place between 1940 and 1970. In contrast to the states that provided settings for the secession movement, states in the middle Atlantic region contended with a different issue, with very different results. The issue was the presence of restrictions in the constitutions of the states making it difficult to create new governmental entities with authority to tax at the local level. This issue forced such states as New Jersey, New York, Maryland, and Pennsylvania to find other ways whereby the traditional division of responsibility for fiscal support between the state and local governments could be retained. That division placed the brunt of costs on the local community and the state, with student charges expected to be kept low and with reliance on other sources (principally the federal government and private gifts and grants) expected to serve marginal needs.

The solution found was ingenuous from a political science perspective, but it enormously complicated and inhibited community college freedom of organizational action from both the educational and fiscal perspectives. The key element in the solution is described by the words *sponsor* or *sponsorship*. It rests on the twofold proposition that: (1) governmental entities, which already possess authority to tax at the local level, will be enabled to finance public community colleges at the local level and will be made responsible for doing so; and (2) responsibility for educational policy direction and the general administration of the institutions will be vested in another local body without the power to tax.

Under this scheme, jurisdictions with power to raise local taxes and funds become heavily engaged in community college development and operations. The continuing evolution of effort to implement the concept of local sponsorship for fiscal purposes with a separate authority for educational policy is an interesting story with several chapters. During the 1960s, interest in sponsoring community colleges in New York, for example, came from virtually every type of local taxing authority—counties, cities, school districts. As a result, local community colleges sponsored by and fiscally dependent on each of these types of local jurisdictions were established and continue in the state. Combinations of sponsors within a class of sponsors (for example, two counties) were approved, but not combinations of types of sponsors. This pattern emerged in Pennsylvania and Maryland, but in New Jersey only county government can support the "county colleges," as the public two-year colleges are legally designated in that state.

It should be noted that while the concentration of fiscally dependent community college boards of contol is in the middle Atlantic region, illustrations of this structure also exist in other parts of the nation. The junior colleges in Mississippi, for example, depend on the counties for their local tax support. In such instances, the need of the colleges to relate in special ways to the local governmental body that provides fiscal support again became quickly apparent.

Community college relationships with local and state governments are quite different when local boards are fiscally independent of those that are not. When the community college local board has authority *and* control of general administrative policies and also the power to raise local funds to support the institutional operations, different procedures are followed for selection of board members. Members of fiscally independent boards typically are elected by the local constituency; those of fiscally dependent boards are generally appointed by local or state governmental officials (Martorana, 1981). While theoretically the relationships between executive and legislative offices of the local government and the community college board of control should exist and affect policies only in one operating realm (finances), that area is such a fundamental concern that it seems inevitably to foreshadow close, powerful, and frequently negative relationships and conflicts over policy direction in all other realms of operation. That this is in fact the case is well documented by the research reported by Phelon (1968).

Drift from Local to State Governance Authority. Another important thread in the warp and woof of community college governmental relations is the emergence of state-level governing boards. By the close of the 1970s, over a half dozen states had moved to place all governing authority for community colleges in a single board at the state level. This happened in several ways. Some states changed long-standing structures for governance authority from local to state levels; examples include Minnesota and Washington. Others, such as Alabama, Connecticut, Massachusetts, Virginia, and North Carolina, established a separate board for community college education opportunity available to citizens on a statewide basis.

When the locus of governance of institutions is at the state rather than the local level, the result typically is that relationships between the colleges and other locally based organizations become much more tenuous. Conversely, they are considerably stronger between the colleges and other organizations serving statewide functions and controlled at that level.

Cooptation of Community College Control by State Boards. Advocates of the community college are vocal in asserting that, while community colleges have roots in common with both the public schools and institutions of higher learning, these institutions now are not an integral part of either of these traditions. Rather, they claim, community college education in its own right is now an identifiable component of the country's total educational enterprise.

Whether or not community college advocates are correct in their efforts to find a separate identity for these institutions, there is ample evidence that at best they have only partially succeeded. While now virtually complete in their disassociation from the common schools, community colleges are by no means equally free of official administrative relationships with the general higher education establishment. And, since that establishment historically is heavily influenced, if not controlled, by interests based in the universities, it can be said that community colleges today relate more closely with institutions of higher learning. Because of this, relationships with state higher education agencies and institutions of higher learning are intensified; those with state agencies of public school systems are less emphasized.

Several trends in state legislation affecting community colleges moved these institutions into closer working relationships with other colleges and universities. One trend already described was the legislation encouraged by the wish of the community colleges to be separate from the structure of the public schools at both local and state levels. Another, found in several states, was the growth of interest in and action toward creating or designating a particular state agency for statewide planning and coordination of all postsecondary education. Contrary to Cohen and Brawer's (1982) suggestion that states were moved to this kind of action by the federal government's enactment of Section 1202 in the 1972 Amendments to the Higher Education Act, most states had already moved to locate statewide planning and coordinating responsibility in an agency at the state level. There is no question, however, that the cumulative effect of all such actions, whether inspired by the state or federal statutory initiatives, seemed to force community colleges to relate more closely with other higher education institutions and to find themselves constantly coopted by those interests.

Although in actual implementation of state practice these generalizations show a wide range of differences from state to state, the critical conclusion is that community colleges are by no means creatures of their own making. On the contrary, they struggle to shape their mission and character in a framework heavily dominated by state and university interests. To the extent that state statutes place community colleges under jurisdiction of such boards, they face a struggle for identity in a field in which the odds are often stacked against them. This is not to say that the responsible boards and their staffs are prejudiced in favor of university interests and against those of community colleges: The California Postsecondary Education Commission, the Illinois Board of Higher Education, the Minnesota Board of Higher Education, the Oklahoma Board of Regents, the Washington Board of Higher Education, and their counterparts in many other states would quite properly protest such a suggestion. It is simply to say that, in the politically charged arenas in which the drama of organizational interaction is played, interests that are university-based and typically statewide tend to prevail over those that are community college-based and more locally oriented. It is not surprising, therefore, to see the research findings report that community colleges are coming increasingly to be influenced more by state legislation directed to unversities or to the general operation of the total state government than by legislation specifically intended to apply directly to community colleges (Martorana and Smutz, 1980; Martorana and Broomall, 1982; Martorana and Corbett, 1983).

Enter the National and Federal Interest

Colleges and universities in America operated for more than one hundred and fifty years before they began to draw national attention from interests outside their own spheres of operation. That is a fact of considerable importance to the discussion in this chapter. Not until the first Morrill Act of 1862 did the larger national interest result in official federal governmental action to affect higher education. Public two-year colleges operated for some seventy years before anything like a major national recognition of their presence in the American educational enterprise took place. Historically, colleges and universities of all types, including the community colleges, were seen as serving only state or local educational purposes, and even at those levels they were often viewed as fulfilling narrowly defined functions for relatively well-defined clienteles. However, this emerging national purpose and the increasing impact of the postsecondary educational enterprise on the national welfare could not be denied. Following the pattern usually displayed in the growth of a meaningful movement, issues began in a national voluntary organization and emerged later in federal policy directives.

In retrospect, the initial action to create a national organization joining together institutions with a common "junior college" or "community college" sense of educational philosophy and mission must be described as intended to serve only internal rather than external purposes. The American Association of Junior Colleges, the forerunner of the American Association of Community and Junior Colleges (AACJC) was created in 1920 in St. Louis. The decision to form the organization was reached by the heads of a small number of junior colleges who gathered at a national conference in that city (Eells, 1931). With the growth and development of community colleges, the function of AACJC has dramatically changed over the years. Now the association is much less a support agency rendering services to individual institutions directed at their individual development, although as a membership organization it continues to do that kind of work. Rather, the national association is seen as the national voice and advocate of the philosophy and mission of community college education in those forums for organizational interaction in which interstate, regional, national, and even international interests of community colleges are to be represented.

In the more global arena, however, there is again strong evidence that community colleges are not sharply defined either as institutions or as the components of a clear-cut level within the larger educational enterprise in America. This becomes evident when the activities of other national organizations are examined and their inclusion of community college interests is observed. Good examples are found in the American Council on Education (ACE) and the American Vocational Association (AVA). Both of these organizations claim a role in representing types of organizational interests at the national level—the AVA for persons and organizations concerned with a special educational program and the ACE concerned with all institutions and organizations having a postsecondary educational purpose. Both the AVA and ACE see the AACJC and all of its member institutions as part of their scope of interest and responsibility for leadership at the national level. To some extent, the same observations can also be made about the Association of American Colleges (AAC).

Interorganizational relationships among voluntary associations at the national level go beyond those that bring together interests generated by the community college and those based in other types of institutions. Interorganizational relationships connecting different groups *within* those institutions need also to be recognized. The best illustration of this is found in the interplay between the AACJC, with its growing list of affiliated councils representing financial officers, community services personnel, and occupational faculty, along with others, and the Association of Community College Trustees (ACCT).

A proper discussion of community college governmental relationships requires distinction between national or nationwide and federal interests. They are not necessarily the same. Two forms of distinction are pertinent. First, there is a difference in geographic coverage. While a federal governmental interest generally appears to be a nationwide interest because it expresses a national concern, it may often become more regional than national in its presence. Thus, although elimination of racial segregation was clearly of federal and national concern, implementation of related federal policy stipulated by the laws, regulations, and court decisions carried considerably different impact in different regions of the country.

The second distinction is that many national concerns cannot be expressed as federal government concerns because of the restrictions placed on federal authority. Although recent interpretations by the courts of constitutional duties and powers of the federal government have greatly extended the scope of federal governmental power and influence on organizational operations in many realms, federal powers are still limited. Thus, for example, although student mobility and access to higher educational programs of students' choice can be viewed as a regional, interstate, or even national concern, it is not a matter of federal policy jurisdiction. Some analysts are beginning to argue that postsecondary education is operationally and functionally an interstate enterprise and, therefore, should operate under guidelines as mandated by the "commerce clause" of the United States Constitution. Since the enterprise has not yet been so defined, however, either by federal statute or court decision, the federal government cannot act on the matter.

In those areas in which national and federal interests coincided, such as in the matter of statewide planning to improve effectiveness of postsecondary education, a new page can be added to the history of community college governmental relations. The result is an interesting story of community college struggle for place and identity in the national scheme of things, with the focus on federal legislation. The struggle is reflected in particular programs, such as vocational education, which affect only a part of community college operations; it is also seen in efforts to develop legislation, such as policies on student financial aid, that would affect the entire institution.

The first of those two arenas is the long-standing battle-ground over federal funds provided to support vocational education. From the time of the first federal enactment of such legislation in the Smith-Hughes Act of 1917, postsecondary institutions offering occupational programs have insisted that they should be included. Since community and two-year technical colleges provide most such programs, they carried the brunt of the argument. Not until nearly fifty years later, however, in the 1965 Amendments to the Vocational Education Acts, did they succeed in gaining access to some federal vocational funds.

The push to authorize two-year college eligibility for federal vocational monies was only part of a larger effort made during the late 1950s and early 1960s. That effort saw a coalition of leadership from the AACJC, from state offices responsible for community college development, and from individual colleges throughout the country promoting a stronger national public policy in support of community college education and suggesting legislation to accomplish this (Martorana, 1966). Culmination of this effort came with enactments in the 1972 Amendments of the Higher Education Act. Two sections in particular showed the results of the new operating interfaces of individual colleges, state offices, and the AACJC, on the one hand, with the ACE, the AVA, and the United States Congress, on the other. One was Title X, the Community College Act, which marked the first mention of community college policy and advocacy in any federal law, and the other was Section 1202, which established state postsecondary education planning commissions. Statutory stipulation that these be "broadly representative of all postsecondary education" was a direct outcome of a community college lobbying effort to guarantee inclusion of their voice and interests in the vital statewide planning activities which at the time were sweeping over the land.

Where Has All the Power Gone?

Evolutionary Change. Throughout this volume, the theme sounded is that community colleges are vital, dynamic, changing organizations—four generations already can be described and a fifth is in the making. Consistent with that proposition, the period of rapid expansion of the 1950s and 1960s and the era of intensifying community-based operations of the 1970s must also be viewed as only transitional. We believe, furthermore, that three valid assumptions can be made that facilitate understanding the nature of interorganizational relations with agencies of government in the fifth generation of community colleges and how these new relationships can be managed.

First among the three assumptions is the simple one that change will be constant. It is impossible for community colleges to be static organizations, given their mission in the society and their dedication to serving specific and changing communities within the larger society. A second assumption basic to understanding the future is related to the first: It is that the forces now compelling change may well be different from those that will result in change during the rest of the 1980s and beyond, just as those forces now operative are not the same as those that shaped the 1930s and 1940s. We will build more on the importance of this statement later in this chapter. Our third and final assumption, therefore, is that conclusions about government relationships drawn on the basis of present forces must be considered as only tentative foundations for future definition of the community college.

Diffusion of Power and Spread of Influence. Differences in structure, mode of operation, and organizational relationships in which community colleges are involved are related to two major considerations. One consideration is the level at which control is to be placed. For most matters, control is at either local or state levels, but for some matters (for example, vocational education) it may be at one of three levels: local, state, or federal. The second consideration is the scope of responsibility of the educational enterprise which is to be given to the authoritative and controlling body. That is, responsibility may be specified as covering only elementary and secondary education or only community college education or combinations including other levels of higher education.

The pertinent questions raised by recognizing these two considerations are, then: Which of the two more strongly affects power or control over community college operations? And what related effects will appear in community college organizational relationships, particularly with governmental interests?

A basic premise of this chapter is that community colleges seek an organizational framework that gives them maximum control over their own destiny as organizations and the greatest possible freedom to interact with all other groups in order to fulfill their purpose. Given this premise, one must conclude from the record that at the local level community colleges won the power battle by seceding from local school systems. At that level, however, their victory was not an even achievement throughout the nation, for in some states they escaped the public school district structures only to become closely, and in some ways disadvantageously, entwined with other local government jurisdictional authorities, such as city councils or county commissions.

Another conclusion is that at the state and federal levels the community colleges nationwide seem to be losing (or now have already lost) the battle for a clear and separate identity. In very few states can community colleges act from a collective base at the state level to deal directly with the legislature, governor, executive offices, and other agencies of state government. Almost all states require the voice of community colleges to pass through or be joined with that of some other agency. This is not to say that these other agencies are always negatively inclined toward community colleges.

However, the structure puts special pressures on community college advocates to be diligent in protecting their interests within the structure. The period of the late 1960s and early 1970s in New York is illustrative. At that time, the rapidly expanding and burgeoning political power of the State University of New York threatened a complete takeover of the community colleges. This "crossroads" situation generated considerable public examination of the mission of the community colleges and their organizational structure, as well as political activity related to their financing. It also moved some leaders of the community colleges to challenge the board of regents and the trustees of the State University of New York to clarify their roles in relation to that of community colleges (Martorana, 1972).

Even at the national level, in matters not involving federal governmental relations, the operative voices of the community colleges reflect cooption of community college interests by others. Few issues see AACJC and ACCT leading in the pathway to change. On most issues, these organizations are joiners with other national voices for sectors and interests in education, for example, AVA and ACE. This is in contrast to the period during which ACE, the Association of American Universities (AAU), and other national organizations became involved in the 1202 Legislation Development Act not so much because it was their wish to do so but because the AACJC's case to the Congress was so compelling that they could not disregard it (Blocker, Bender, and Martorana, 1975.).

Governmental Relations Through a New Framework

No one can forecast the future of an institution like the American community college with assurance or confidence. Nor can even a specific aspect of its operation, such as the relationships it will likely have with governmental interests and agencies operating at local, state, regional, and national levels, be confidently projected. There are lessons to be learned from the past, however, which provide useful generalizations and which suggest a future course. The insights these lessons provide, moreover, seem to fit a theoretical approach to a better understanding of the future condition of community colleges. Among the generalizations possible is that the community colleges of the future will continue to be adaptive institutions. This suggests that, to understand how community colleges will relate to governments in the future, we should examine not so much the present pattern of those relationships as the forces that are likely to prevail in the future and that will have impact on the general mission of community colleges. Governmental interests are but one set, albeit one very powerful set, of external forces that will be at work. A large complex of others will be found as well. Thus, broad organizational goals and their interplay with forces internal and external to the organization are critical components of a proper understanding of change. We call this conceptualization the interactive forces theory (Martorana and Kuhns, 1975). We see the forces described throughout this volume generating changes that will produce a different framework within which community colleges will operate and which will have to be recognized as the fifth-generation community colleges relate to local, state, and federal governmental interests.

Cooperation and Competition in Postsecondary Education. We see the immediate future as one in which two competing scenarios will be played out and from which will emerge a new and broadly encompassing organizational form for the enterprise. Conditions that exist today and that likely will exist for some time argue for either an intensification of institutional "turfmanship" in postsecondary education or, in contrast, a new order of cooperation and interdependence. The first is characterized by intense competition for students, public support, and academic program superiority; it reflects concern over the three R's: "retrenchment, reduction, and reallocation" (Mortimer and Tierney, 1979). The second is evident in the development and growth of new consortia, increasing interest in regionalism as an approach to both intrastate and interstate planning and programming of postsecondary education, and emergence of other forms of linkages with noneducational organizations. This second scenario shows concern about both the effectiveness and the efficiency of educational operations—that is, the preservation of quality of academic programs and services without sacrifice of the goals of widespread access to postsecondary education, equality for all persons and groups served, and accountability to the public and private constituencies that provide the support needed (Martorana and Nespoli, 1980; Patterson, 1979).

From Community College to "Communiversity." Given the complex of new forces operating in the society of the future, we see a new dynamic developing between postsecondary education and the society it serves. The dynamic, while preserving the need for the classically recognized services of instruction, research, and public service as the essentials to be provided by postsecondary education, will call for a stronger commitment to help improve the quality of social and economic life in the community and will enable the structure of institutions to be different from that which now prevails. Gleazer sees the community college as "ideally suited to serving as the nexus" among agencies dedicated to community improvement (Gleazer, 1980, p. 10), but we see emergence of a new design by which the "nexus" function will be performed; this, we suggest, will be the "communiversity."

The communiversity, while loosely structured, nonetheless will need to include and provide for linking together much more than universities, colleges, and schools; it must include clearly identified centers for education and training in organizations whose missions are not primarily educational. The communiversity will also serve to help community colleges and other regularly recognized postsecondary institutions to accommodate, join forces with, connect with, and adopt a method of operation that encompasses interests having secondary educational effect in the society as opposed to only those that have education as their primary purpose.

The germ of this concept was first introduced by Martorana at a gathering of community college presidents in California in the mid 1960s (Martorana, 1965). The concept did not have a major impact at the time, but there was discussion of the idea. Since then, the concept has appeared in other places (Gould, 1970; Martorana and Kuhns, 1977) and is best expressed by Gould in his book, *Today's Academic Condition*, in which he includes a section called, "Enter the Communiversity." In it he says: "The university of the future, as I envision it, will be a loose federation of all the educational and cultural forces of a community—at every age level. It will be a coordinated educational entity serving a single, fairly large community, or a single, compact region if a group of communities is more appropriate. Whether it will have a single name or even be called a university any longer, is hard to say. Parts of it will undoubtedly have names similar to those they do now. But what we think of today as 'the college' or 'the university' will constitute only a portion of the future whole" (Gould, 1970, p. 90).

Although at present there are no fully developed complexes or collectives of community colleges, other postsecondary educational institutions, and other related community service cultural, economic, and social institutions, beginning forms of implementation of the communiversity concept are easy to see. They are evident, for example, in such concrete current developments in American postsecondary education as the community education councils advocated by the New York State Board of Regents to coordinate local and regional adult and continuing education; the Warren/Forest Higher Education Council, a private, nonprofit citizens' agency, which oversees the Warren/Forest Cooperative College Program and which links the offerings and related services of fourteen recognized colleges and universities, two area vocational schools, local public libraries, and business/industry training programs in a two-county area of Northwestern Pennsylvania; and a growing array of other similar voluntary consortia or official contractual arrangements across the land.

Emergence of the communiversity will cause changes in how community colleges, as part of the new construct, will relate to governments, as well as in how other aspects of their internal operations, such as planning and allocation of resources, will be conducted. Consequences of such a development for the way community colleges will relate to governments are easy to envision. A major one, for example, is that a community college will deal less often with local, state, and federal governmental interests and agencies on a one-on-one direct basis; these relations will more often be conducted in a collaborative manner jointly with other educational and related community service organizations and institutions in the locality.

We see the emergence of the communiversity as a development whose time has now arrived, a development that will profoundly affect community college relations with governments at all levels. It will not be a revolutionary development in terms of rapidity of change. Instead, it will be the result of gradual change, a kind of "organizational drift," which, amoeba-like, will slowly but powerfully touch and change the structure and operations of most postsecondary educational institutions. But the end result will be quite revolutionary in terms of impact on postsecondary education as now generally perceived, particularly among its many practitioners.

Effects of the Communiversity on Governmental Relations

How will the development of the communiversity change community college relationships with governments? We close with several predictions followed by a listing of suggested actions fifth-generation community college leaders should consider in adapting institutional policies and practices to the new conditions foreseen.

First, we see state governmental interests requiring a greater and a more effective level of interorganizational planning and action at local and regional levels. We do not see this as a means for government to control the methods of operation of community colleges and other components of the communiversity; rather, we see the requirement as a measure to ensure greater interorganizational communication, to facilitate joint planning, and to give greater assurance that resource sharing to better serve area and statewide needs will occur.

Second, we see a consequent emergence of the leadership center (however organized and made to function) as a new focal point for government interests at all levels. Community colleges of necessity will need to relate to this center, because questions about community college roles, programs, needed resources, responses to evaluations, and the like that are asked by local, state, and federal governments will be answered in a flow of communication passing through the communiversity.

Third, we see an increasingly important policy role for the area's citizens in coordinating an area's overall postsecondary education resources. Citizens currently serve on local boards of trustees, but here their attention is focused on the resources of only one institution—rather than on the resources of the diverse providers of postsecondary education throughout the community. In the communiversity model, the voice of area citizens becomes more active and influential, and, in fact, may take the form of the leadership center noted in the preceding paragraph. The citizens' role in interorganizational communication and planning can be important in setting the tone for cooperation rather than competition among the region's postsecondary institutions.

Because we see fifth-generation community colleges continuing to serve the fundamental educational wishes of individuals of widely divergent types as well as continuing to serve broader governmental purposes, we see no diminution of interface of fifth-generation community colleges with government. Indeed, governmental liaison will have to be a matter of expert attention by all concerned with the institution—student advocates, faculty, administration, boards of control, and taxpayers. In developing a capacity to give that attention expertly, all concerned will need to refine skills in a new political arena—in the communiversity of which they will be a part.

Given the expected new setting from which fifth-generation community colleges will be relating to local, state, and federal governments, we see several appropriate and needed actions. Specifically, we suggest that leadership of fifth-generation community colleges involved in communiversity collaborative operations should:

1. Develop new techniques and skill in forming effective coalitions with other components of the local or regional communiversity through which to relate to governmental interests and agencies at all levels (local, state, regional, national) and to promote the best interests of both the community college and the communiversity as a collective.
2. Recognize, as a corollary, that those governmental contacts will likely be made through mechanisms of joint action of the several components of the communiversity.
3. Adjust to there being a strong local or regional citizens' voice in determining broad general policies as well as more operational procedures for interrelating the communiversity component institutions; community colleges will face local citizen interests in new and different ways.
4. Assist in developing ways to ensure effective communication between and among components of the communiversity, on the one hand, and between the communiversity and representatives and agencies of governments, on the other.

5. Develop and adopt procedures to orient and educate personnel in their own institutions in the concept, structure, and method of operation of the communiversity and particularly in the ways that the communiversity can assist the community college in handling governmental relations, as well as other functions.

6. Recognize and find ways to lead rather than be led by the fact that, as the communiversity emerges in a locality or region, agencies of government will expect the broadened base for examining postsecondary education in the area (needs assessments, program and service coordination, plant and other resource utilization, and so on), which is provided by the communiversity, to actually be used for such purposes.

7. Cooperate with other communiversity components to convey to governmental interests at all levels that the communiversity both in concept and practice permits preservation of purposes and procedures of individual components while simultaneously creating a collection of means for serving the area that is greater than the sum of its parts.

8. Finally, since there is no escaping the expectation that governmental agencies will ultimately be drawn into the issue of how communiversity functioning is to be financed when the concept is translated to practice, adopt a statesmanship stance with other leaders of communiversity components to advance the effort to acquire the needed funds.

The communiversity may continue to be largely a construct, not an organizational entity—at least in the near future. The discrete organizations, however, will forge increasingly strong and apparent links. Eventually, the linkages may become strong enough to lead to an encompassing, larger, formal entity. This may never occur, but the absence of a strong formal entity is no measure of the importance of the concept and the process.

Thus, we conclude that the fifth-generation community college will reflect both stability and change in its relations to government. It will function in part as a substantially autonomous institution and will, therefore, have to relate to local, state, and federal governmental interests in much the way it does now. Increasingly, however, it will also have to relate to governments at all levels through its associations with other educational providers of the area as the concept of the communiversity evolves.

References

Blocker, C. E., Bender, L. W., and Martorana, S. V. *The Political Terrain of American Postsecondary Education.* Fort Lauderdale, Fla.: Nova University Press, 1975.

Cohen, A. M., and Brawer, F. B. *The American Community College.* San Francisco: Jossey-Bass, 1982.

Eells, W. C. *The Junior College.* Boston: Houghton Mifflin, 1931.

Gleazer, E. J., Jr. *The Community College: Values, Vision, and Vitality.* Washington, D.C.: American Association of Community and Junior Colleges, 1980.

Gould, S. B. *Today's Academic Condition.* New York: McGraw-Hill, 1970.

Koos, L. V. *The Junior College.* New York: Ginn, 1929.

Martorana, S. V. "Recent Legislation Affecting Junior Colleges," *Junior College Journal,* 1950, *20,* 241–252.

Martorana, S. V. "The Legal Status of American Public Junior Colleges." Chapters in *American Junior Colleges* (3rd ed., J. P. Bogue, ed., through 6th ed., E. J. Gleazer, Jr., ed.). Washington, D.C.: American Council on Education, 1950 through 1963.

Martorana, S. V. "The Expanding Responsibilities of Community Colleges." Paper presented at the Kellogg Community College leadership conference, Berkeley, Calif., June 15, 1965.

Martorana, S. V. "A Positive Community Junior College Policy for Lawmakers." Paper presented at the 46th annual convention of the American Association of Junior Colleges, St. Louis, Mo., Feb. 28–Mar. 4, 1966.

Martorana, S. V. "Community Colleges at the Crossroads." Paper presented at the annual convention of the Association of Boards and Councils of Two-Year Colleges, Lake Placid, N.Y., Oct. 7, 1972.

Martorana, S. V. *Methods of Selection of Boards of Control: The Special Case of the Community College.* Project report of the Association of Governing Boards Project on Board Member

Selection. Washington, D.C.: Association of Governing Boards, 1981.

Martorana, S. V., and Broomall, J. *State Legislation Affecting Community, Junior, and Two-Year Technical Colleges, 1981.* University Park: Center for the Study of Higher Education, Pennsylvania State University, 1982.

Martorana, S. V., and Corbett, P. C. *State Legislation Affecting Community, Junior, and Two-Year Technical Colleges, 1982.* University Park: Center for the Study of Higher Education, Pennsylvania State University, 1983.

Martorana, S. V., and Kuhns, E. *Managing Academic Change: Interactive Forces and Leadership in Higher Education.* San Francisco: Jossey-Bass, 1975.

Martorana, S. V., and Kuhns, E. "The Challenge of the Communiversity." *Change,* 1977, *9* (2), 54–55.

Martorana, S. V., and Nespoli, L. A. *Regionalism in American Postsecondary Education: Concept and Practice.* University Park: Center for the Study of Higher Education, Pennsylvania State University, 1980.

Martorana, S. V., and Smutz, W. D. *State Legislation Affecting Community, Junior, and Two-Year Technical Colleges, 1979.* University Park: Center for the Study of Higher Education, Pennsylvania State University, 1980.

Martorana, S. V., and others. *Survey of State Legislation Relating to Higher Education.* Washington, D.C.: United States Office of Education, 1957 through 1964. (OE-50008-57 through OE-50008-64.)

Martorana, S. V., and others. *State Legislation Affecting Community, Junior, and Two-Year Technical Colleges, 1975 through 1982.* University Park: Center for the Study of Higher Education, Pennsylvania State University, 1976 through 1983.

Mortimer, K. P., and Tierney, M. L. *The Three R's of the Eighties: Reduction, Reallocation, and Retrenchment.* Report no. 4. Washington, D.C.: Educational Resources Information Center/Association for the Study of Higher Education, 1979.

Patterson, L. D. *Benefits of Collegiate Cooperation.* Tuscaloosa: Council for Interinstitutional Leadership, University of Alabama, 1979.

Phelon, P. S. "A Study of the Impact of Local Sponsors on the Education and Operation of Selected Community Colleges in New York State." Unpublished doctoral dissertation, State University of New York at Albany, 1968.

11

James L. Wattenbarger

Dealing with New Competition for Public Funds: Guidelines for Financing Community Colleges

One cannot examine the problems of higher education in the United States without concluding that finance affects the potential solutions of almost all of them. This chapter provides an overview of the background for financing education as related to the current rivalry between community colleges and other elements of society needing public funds.

The news media are replete with features that list, analyze, and discuss the current problems of financial support for education in the United States. While community colleges have never been able to claim that they were generously supported, they had felt neither continued restrictions on their growth nor "caps" on their enrollments until recent years. These restrictions, however, now are limited to the community college sector of public education. Headlines in all parts of the country emphasize the "high budgets" of the public schools as well as the limited resources available to the state colleges and universities.

Competition for students has become a part of the relationships among institutions. Community colleges compete with the public school systems in providing vocational-technical education and the myriad of courses and activities labeled continuing education or community services. The community colleges compete with state colleges and universities for freshman enrollments, especially the high school graduates scoring high on standardized tests. These competitions are often viewed as a scramble for full-time equivalent enrollments (FTE), since most financial programs and formula allocations are based on numbers of students served.

Solutions to these problems are neither readily available nor easily found. The support for public education expressed by many officials is less than intense, and the traditional enthusiasm for higher education has been tempered by strong reactions to increasing costs. The effective use of income has been directly deferred by a fluctuating economy, persistent inflation, lessened respect for higher education, shifting priorities, and a declining interest in support for public services in general. Along with these problems have come decreases in the numbers of potential students brought on by reductions in the small population bases from traditional sources, such as the predicted cadre of eighteen-year-olds and the increase in the amounts that students are assessed for fees, causing financial dropouts. Each institution experiences these problems in different intensity and in different character. Some have reported enrollment declines; some have reported shifts in programs toward more costly education; some have noted rapidly increasing fixed costs; and some have noted all of these problems and more.

Competition for State Funds

The current problems in financing community colleges are a part of the total problem of financing public activities and are reflected in public budgets in general. Obviously, the competition for limited state funding is a shared and continuing concern.

Public Education. The search for the proper level of financial support for public education is a continuing one. Public education (defined herein as grades K–12) has traditionally been supported by local taxes, state appropriations, and some support from federal funds. The shift from local taxation, largely controlled by local boards, to tax appropriations controlled by state legislatures has increasingly forced school districts into more and more general competition with recipients of state tax dollars. Salary increases along with other significant costs of operation more often than not are seen as a state responsibility; school districts have become increasingly dependent on state support for meeting their mounting costs.

Higher Education. All of higher education has experienced the effects of increased costs of operations as well as increased accountability standards. The competition for dollars has been a major fact of life for state colleges and universities for years. The percentage of the total state budget allocated to institutions at this level, however, has not increased to any great extent, even though the numbers of colleges and universities, their geographical dispersion, and the diversity of programs has increased. Consequently, individual institutions now find themselves in an impossible position relative to their own unique problems of financial support. Now with limited funding, colleges have found that traditional concepts of faculty tenure and a free choice in new program development are not possible within current budget restrictions.

Community Colleges. The community colleges have also become increasingly dependent on state funds. Many community colleges were established as extensions of high schools and often were called junior colleges; these institutions were supported entirely by local taxes and student fees. Since the fees were usually very low, in most cases the major source of support was local property taxation. As programs increased in diversity and number, as enrollments included more part-time and nontraditional students, and as more institutions were established, the concept of local support for community colleges was modified through pressure for shifting to increased state support. This pressure reached a dramatic point in California when "Proposition 13" was approved and when similar measures were enacted in other states both before and after "13" through millage rollbacks and other limitations placed on local taxes. The shift to state support as a major source of community college funding has been documented repeatedly since the early 1960s. This shift presently exists in every state that supports public community colleges. As an indication of this change, some states established community colleges with state support as the sole public source of funding during the late 1960s and the 1970s. Examples of this are the development of the Virginia Community College System, the Tennessee Community College System, and the Alabama system.

Largely as a result of this change, community colleges, state colleges and universities, and the public school systems are all in competition for portions of the state dollar. As a result of this rivalry, the united front that is most productive in achieving legislative appropriations for education in general has often been difficult to construct and maintain. The continued growth of enrollment in community colleges, often coupled with decreases in public school and state college and university enrollments, has further complicated the problem. Some states, such as Florida, have provided increased support per student in grades K–12 and in the universities while making less support per student available in the community colleges.

Other State Agencies. Not only has the competition for state tax dollars been increasing within education as a whole, but it has also increased in relationship to other state agencies. Roads, health services, welfare services, rehabilitation services, provision for unemployment compensation, and governmental administration, among other services unique to particular states, have been in need of funding on an ever increasing spiral of established needs. Community college leadership has found itself facing more than one competitive and hostile agency in its attempt to obtain a larger share of available funds. This has been especially true of those agencies that have experienced increasing demands for services: welfare, unemployment, health services, prisons, and roads.

Factors Affecting Community College Budgets

Diversity and Support. Variations in the costs of programs have created a specific problem of support for the community colleges. In particular, studies have indicated a wide difference in costs between the diverse programs of occupational education. Most states, however, provide only one FTE formula for fund allocation to colleges. As a result, those colleges that have a majority of

students in low-cost courses are often overfunded, while those that
offer expensive occupational programs are at a disadvantage. This
creates a reluctance among colleges to move into expensive
programs even though the need is well established. So-called
glamorous programs, especially those with technology in the title,
achieve more acceptance in some instances because of the value of
public support.

Inflation and Reallocation of Funds. The effects of inflation
on community college budgets are particularly apparent in the
continuing and successful pressure to increase student fees. The
basic philosophical commitment to no or low tuition has come
under strong pressure, and most states and colleges have been forced
to increase fees as a way of maintaining their support level within
a productive operating range. The costs of energy have increased
through inflation, becoming more and more expensive. The major
problem is that, as a result of these rising costs, allocation of more
resources to colleges has not resulted in the changes that some feel
are needed. Colleges have no higher quality, provide no more
services, produce no more student credit hours, and are in reality no
better off as a result of allocating more resources to energy than
before. Inflation costs are in the same category; more money
expended yields no benefits, no improvements, no better quality.
But there seems to be little choice in the matter.

Some other examples of such nonproductive resource
allocations are: (1) more state and federal requirements for
reporting, with no additional support for preparation, (2) more
detailed information requiring computer support and thus an
upward spiraling of computer use, and (3) inflation as it affects
equipment replacement. Advanced technology results in improved
equipment but also increases costs. Allocations such as these
provide no specific improvements but do require increased funding.

Fixed Costs and Variable Costs. State support for community
colleges is generally based on FTE or other units that measure
numbers of students. The units are most often computed directly
and are unrelated to institutional size or relative cost factors.
However, the allocation of resources is always affected by cost
factors and is, indirectly at least, related to size. The last two or three
students who are added to a class of twenty students may cost very

little in actuality, but they enable one to spread the total cost more broadly in computing average FTE cost. There are fixed costs for the course that are not related to size and are only indirectly related to other factors—at least up to a specified limit imposed by facilities, for example. Some fixed costs will be present in any event, and there are variable costs that are increased through adding more students. Since the formulas do not usually consider these factors, some colleges may receive more support than the situation warrants while others receive inadequate support for similar courses. The increase in part-time student enrollments has an effect on these problems in particular. There are fixed costs in registering, counseling, and making arrangements for each student, full time or part time; there are also instructional costs related to the particular course in which he or she enrolls. The fixed costs are seldom supported adequately by part-time enrollment.

The View from the Top: State Directors, Presidents, and Researchers

State Directors. In a recent study conducted by the Institute of Higher Education at the University of Florida (Wattenbarger and Heck, 1983), state directors of community colleges listed their own evaluation of the problems that concern them. They mentioned the following:

The problems associated with small and rural colleges were described by several state directors as pervasive and multiple. Because of small enrollments, these colleges are expensive; furthermore, they cannot provide the full curricular offerings that are available in larger colleges. The net result of these problems is a financial dilemma: A higher level of support is needed for the rural colleges than for the larger suburban and urban institutions but is generally not available.

State directors also stress the increasing demands for educational services that are not financed directly by current formulas or procedures. Examples of such services are counseling services for part-time students, noncredit, community service types of offerings, the testing services that may be required for placement of students or that may be used for accountability measurements, and even, in some recent instances, regular credit courses in which enrollment is small. In addition, limitations often have been placed by the legislatures on developmental, remedial, and special services courses. The problems of financing the expected level of support of community college programs have been compounded through such funding limitations.

Another area identified by state directors is the inequities in funding that result from "flat" basic funding. Even though programs and/or courses actually cost different amounts of money, the majority of states allocate funds to institutions based on a single basic amount per FTE; only about ten states provide funds on the basis of cost differential funding formulas. Those states that have no cost-based funding find that the expensive occupational programs require greater financial support than is provided through the basic formula. This may mean that they receive more for some courses than is expended and less for others than is needed. The imbalance affects different institutions in different ways but is viewed as a major problem by state directors.

Community colleges have traditionally been supported by combinations of state and local funds. The state directors emphasize current limitations placed on local funds as another problem. These limits, both legal and operational, have increased the need for state funding and the attendant problems of competition for funds at that level. The ceilings on local funds have placed some colleges in a position of having no other source available for increasing support except increasing student tuition.

A problem related to this is the problem of limitations present in local districts that are too small. Several states report that enlarging local tax support through increasing the size of the district is a possible but very improbable solution to the local funding problem.

The inflationary increases in operating expenditures are viewed by state directors as another specific problem. They cite the factors of utility costs, equipment replacement, and automatic salary increases as the major influences on increased costs of operation. Almost all of the institutional budgets must be allocated for these purposes, leaving very little for such discretionary expenditures as meeting unanticipated financial exigencies or taking advantage of opportunities for new program development.

Institutional Viewpoints. Community college presidents regard financial problems as their major concern. Since, as was pointed out earlier, the portion of the budget that is discretionary is so small, an administrator is limited in his or her freedom to select alternatives. Also among the problems currently emphasized by college presidents are those caused by cutbacks in available funds imposed by state governments after budgets have been approved and funds allocated. These cuts, amounting in 1983 to 5 or even 10 percent of appropriated funds, constitute in many institutions the only area of discretion that remains in the budget.

College presidents report that state funding formulas are based on full-time students or full-time-equivalent students. The need for most student services is relatively the same, whether the student is full time or part time; currently the number of part-time students is even larger than the number of full-time students. The costs of providing services to these part-time students is much greater than the funds allocated to them through FTEs.

Another problem faced by presidents is the "one pie" problem. Legislative appropriations are not directly related to numbers of students being served; there has been a tendency to appropriate a single sum of money to be divided among the colleges via a basic formula that may be changed from time to time without good reason. This one pie approach means that colleges may have basic per student needs that cannot be met because funds are capped by legislative action. Colleges are thereby encouraged to increase their share of the pie by fair means or otherwise; thus, the various factors used in determining an institution's portion may be unrelated to the college mission. A larger share of the pie is controlled by the formula "in use this year."

One solution some college presidents advocate is to apportion funds on the basis of programs rather than numbers of students. This would be particularly important to colleges experiencing declines in enrollment. Suggestions for modifications that would yield equitable program allocations include "corridor" funding, in which no allocation can be decreased in an amount greater than 5 percent in any one year, and fixed program funding, which provides a fixed amount for a program without regard to size. No state, however, has adopted any plan other than differentiated cost center funding, and only a few have made limited use of the corridor concept. The problems have forced many institutions to seek funds from other sources. Many colleges have become very dependent on grants from federal programs in order to start new programs, to develop innovations, or even to consider reorganization and other institutional improvement activities. Community colleges have used the grant approach for all of these activities and have increased their attention as well to obtaining development funds for additional student support and other types of college improvement (Sharon, 1982).

Researchers' Viewpoints. Individuals studying the current problems of legislation and finance in community colleges and other institutions at the postsecondary level have discussed problems from a researcher's point of view. For example, Bowen (1980), whose "theory of costs" explains that the costs of higher education on a per student unit basis are determined by the revenues available for educational purposes, suggests that the problems of finance include the difficulty in achieving improvements in productivity through changes in technology, the effect of employee compensation on cost, the socially imposed costs that are uncontrollable by the institution, the continuing depreciation of physical assets, the deferred maintenance that has become common practice, the management decisions affecting operations, and the difficulty in identifying outcomes and effectiveness.

Johns, Morphet, and Alexander (1983), in their discussion of financing education, point out problems related to the sources of revenue for education, the apportionment of state funds to districts, the political strategies that have proved effective in enhancing financial support for education, the inequalities in opportunity and the redistribution effects of public education, the comparative procedures among the states, the options used in financing capital outlay, the influences of federal aid, and the management of resources. While their research focus is on public schools, their problem analysis is valid for higher education as well, and it is particularly applicable to the problems of the community college.

Hoy and Bernstein (1982) analyzed the financing of higher education, with special attention to the New England area. Their research searches for a public policy relative to support for higher education. In an area of the nation in which privately operated institutions constitute a large portion of the total, they identify problems related to levels of public support for higher education, commitment to public higher education, tax policy relative to individual income and exemptions, and federal relationships and support.

Public finance from a theoretical viewpoint (Musgrave and Musgrave, 1980) emphasizes the allocation function, the distribution function, and the stabilization function as policy objectives in relation to obtaining and using public tax support. The community colleges provide the social good of continued educational opportunity. This is available to all who qualify. The basic questions are not whether the community college should provide education but rather, "How much should there be?", and "At what level of support?". The distribution function is accomplished in community colleges through providing educational opportunity to individuals who in turn will contribute to the social welfare. The questions are, "Who should be served?", and "How many may be provided for within available resources?".

An additional question is suggested by the need to determine whether there is an individual benefit that needs to be paid for through tuition. The stabilization function is provided through the development of pools of manpower that meet fluctuating needs in society. The contribution of the community college is recognized in this regard. The problems of financing community colleges are in great measure related to problems of public finance as described, and most of the specific problems of financing community colleges might well be incorporated into more general theoretical descriptions. The basis for support of the community colleges lies in a sound theory of public finance.

Financing in the Four Generations

This discussion of financing community colleges may be organized in a format related to the four generations that were outlined earlier in this volume. Historically, the problems of community college finance have evolved parallel to the problems of financing public education in general, but as each generation successively enlarged the community college concept and delineated the increased responsibility of the community colleges, the problems of financing also broadened to encompass problems related to higher education, as well as to the public schools.

In Generation 1 (1900 to 1930), the junior colleges were largely supported by local school districts and student fees. The attempt to keep fees as low as possible was a major goal. Therefore, costs were kept as low as possible. The result was that junior colleges were often additions to existing high school districts and seldom achieved recognition as separate entities with financial independence. Local tax funds were the major source of revenue, and costs often were hidden within the total school budget.

During Generation 2 (1930 to 1950), the expansion of institutions came about in many states. Depression-level personal incomes were low, and the continued need to maintain low fees remained. However, state laws were passed approving the creation of local districts and, in some instances, establishing institutions as separate entities. Some attention was given to state support funds, but the main support pattern was still local taxation—sometimes specifically levied for junior college support but more often a part of the junior college support pattern as well. Local funds and student fees still constituted the major support sources, with those few instances of state support.

The rapid, expansive growth of community colleges occurred during Generation 3 (1950 to 1970). The conclusion of World War II and the social policy engendered by the GI Bill provided strong impetus for the establishment of hundreds of new community colleges. The change in name, suggested in part by President Truman's Commission on Higher Education (*Higher Education for American Democracy*, 1948), emphasized the major goal of these colleges to serve a particular community. However, the financial support pattern moved from a public school concept with heavy dependence on local taxes to a higher education concept with major emphasis on state-level support. While there were a number of factors that caused the shift from local to state support, including a similar shift in support for public schools, the main result was that competition for attention and for fiscal support moved away from local agencies to the more active arena of state-level agencies.

Federal support came into consideration during this generation through vocational education funds administered through state boards of vocational education and through the Higher Education Act. Here again, however, competition for these funds was with local school districts and vocational education departments at the state level, as well as with other colleges and universities. The point of contact was at the state level, and with the advent of increased state support came increased state concern for equity, efficiency, and opportunity. State planning became a major activity in those states that were serious about community college development. Financial support for a multiple location system had to consider coordination, equality of opportunity, formula funding, and common definitions as basic to expansion and development. As community colleges established governance and operational procedures separate from the lower grades, they also identified more completely with higher education; and as they identified more completely with colleges and universities, they incorporated financial procedures and controls into their structures that were more similar to those of higher education than to those of public schools. These procedures included institutional budgets, tenured faculty, departmental structures, degree programming, bureaucratic internal structures, and a never-ending relationship with the state legislature and the governor's office.

The fourth generation (1970 to 1980) continued the trends identified during the third generation: The shift from local to state support continued, the increased dependence on student fees was present in every state except California, the competition for state dollars intensified, federal funds were used for categorical aid, vocational funds were sought from state as well as federal sources, foundations were established to receive gifts and grants, student financial aid was emphasized, formulas were reexamined and modified, program priorities began to be discussed, linkages with business and industry were explored, improved management procedures were studied, and most, if not all, of the third-generation problems intensified.

The four generations reflect a somewhat broadened mission over their span of time. The mission change is reflected in the financial procedures and especially in the financial problems detailed in this chapter.

The university parallel curriculum was an extension of the academic high school of the early part of the century. The combination of student fees and local taxes reflected the extent of local concern for education beyond high school in this early junior college. It was a middle-class socioeconomic value that occasionally provided for the poor but capable young person with appropriate scholarships. This identification with higher education solidified the use of student fees, since that was the established pattern in American higher education.

The increased concern for occupational education brought in an interest from the state that directed, to a major extent, the vocational education development. This "terminal" education function and the pressure for more opportunity attracted students who ordinarily would not have considered college a goal or a possibility. The need for trained manpower wedded to a strong desire to extend education to everyone, like the earlier development of the high schools, brought about commission reports and long-range state plans envisioning at least half of the available young people in attendance. The financial support was more than local taxes could provide—the state and even the federal government were needed. The fees had to be kept low in order to accommodate the less-than-wealthy youth who were attending and were attracted to the community colleges.

After World War II, concern for building (or rebuilding) the human resources of American communities, extending education to nontraditional students, and recognizing that technology was moving so fast that lifelong education was a necessity, became major forces in the unbelievably rapid expansion of community colleges. Junior colleges became community colleges, at least in program and concept of mission, even though the name did not always change. Federal categorical aid was called for, state funds were sought, and local funds became less important. State plans for growth provided thoughtful state plans for financing—thoughtful in the sense that the plans recognized that support had to come from multiple sources with a price tag. The community college leaders were willing—even anxious—to pay the price, and the stage was set for the problems of the 1980s.

State Systems

A major development in Generation 3 was the emphasis on state planning and state systems (see Chapter Twelve). Even California, with an historical experience of junior college establishment dating back to 1907, did not develop a real state system until the late 1960s. The emphasis on planning and systematic development came about as a result of the pressure for more facilities, more colleges, and more students.

During the 1950s and 1960s, United States education emphasized universal opportunity for access to higher education. Returning war veterans received help from the federal GI Bills. These more mature students established new records of scholarship and accomplishment. Their experiences emphasized the social changes resulting from a changing work force and a changing economy. The need for technical skills and for a generally increased level of education was emphasized on all sides, and the community colleges began to develop by following these themes.

The state system planning procedures were exemplified in Florida, where a plan for twenty-eight institutions provided coverage for an entire state. Similar plans were implemented in Virginia, Illinois, Mississippi, Washington, Maryland, Massachusetts, and New Jersey. Existing planning schemes were incorporated into new planning procedures and organizations in California, Oregon, Connecticut, Pennsylvania, New York, and Colorado. New colleges were established and coordinating structures devised for Texas, Michigan, Ohio, Kansas, Missouri, and Alabama. State planning for establishing new colleges, state formulas for apportioning state funds, state coordination of institutional development, state leadership for building support—all of these were a part of community college development during this third generation.

Each of the fifty states is different. Among the most significant causes for these differences are the historical accidents that influenced the development of higher education in the various states. Previous developments in postsecondary education, the position of the state university, the extent of normal school development in the past, the balance between private and public colleges, the legal framework that evolved for establishing community colleges, the level of development of vocational education, the attitudes of the leadership in vocational/technical education, the existing patterns of financial support for public schools—these factors (among others) are unique to each state. The eventual form of community college development that emerged was largely dependent on them.

Also important are the demographic and socioeconomic characteristics of each state. Naturally, financial support procedures vary between states with largely urban populations and those that are primarily rural. The need for opportunity may be indicated through population profiles, age charts, race and sex percentages, median levels of education for persons twenty-five years of age or older, median family income levels, and similar data. The assessed value of property and retail sales data also provide information that influences the development of community colleges and underscores the need for support. Since localities within the states as well as the states themselves vary widely, it is not surprising that problems are also varied. Each state provides its own pattern of elements of support and of ways of providing support. The ratio among the various factors used to determine development and support needs is not the same from state to state.

In the literature there are fairly common philosophical positions relating to the community college mission. To read these would provide one with an impression that there is a clear understanding of and a well-accepted commitment to the community college philosophy. Even state laws and individual college catalogues use very similar language in describing the mission of the community college. However, the financial support programs do not necessarily provide resources to support these statements of mission.

For example, the majority of states allocate funds on the basis of an FTE student. An FTE is ordinarily defined in terms of semester (or quarter) hours registered. Credit is the basis for financial support. Even vocational and technical education is translated into credit hours. The result is that most community college funding is allocated on the basis of credit programs. The community services and other noncredit programs are often not included in the state funding program. When funds are provided for such programs or courses, limitations are placed on them. More often than not, such programs are expected to be self-sustaining. The developmental or remedial programs are most often supported in only a limited measure—usually barely adequate and often inadequate. Since these may not be considered college credit courses, they are placed in the same poorly supported category as the aforementioned noncredit courses and programs. In short, the mission of the college normally includes an open-door philosophy, an opportunity to correct previous gaps in education, a variety of university parallel courses leading to an associate degree, a well-considered occupational menu of offerings, and lifelong educational offerings to the residents of the area. The state financial program provides funds for the university parallel programs, the occupational program with some limitations, and the other programs with severe limitations. Local funding is often expected to fill in the gaps, but local tax support has been steadily decreasing. In all states, the result is that the financial plan for community colleges does not provide adequate funding for implementation of the mission as defined in that state.

The problems identified have their roots in the community college development patterns. Basically, these colleges began as local institutions receiving their major support from local property taxes. However, the limitations of local property taxes in supporting this level of education are apparent to anyone who has studied the American tax structure. The emphasis on state planning coupled with these taxing limitations provided a basis for broader support but, in times of stress, less commitment, perhaps, to the traditional values of community college education described in philosophical statements. Societal and economic influences placed further limitations but, at the same time, increased pressure for expansion of these institutions. Each state has experienced these factors in different forms and in different degrees of intensity. The origin of current problems lies in these past developments; state planning did not eliminate them.

Current Models

Major studies of higher education finance have attempted to deal with the dichotomous position that students should have the opportunity for free education through high school (at least free to the student and his parents except through their support in general taxation) but that they should share directly in the cost of their education after the twelfth grade. This position is generally accepted, and only a few even question it. The major question considered by most is, "How much should the students pay?", and not "Should they pay at all?". The major exceptions to this position have been the position of the state of California and the traditional philosophical commitment of the community colleges. The latter commitment usually resulted, however, in a "low-tuition" policy rather than a "no-tuition" policy in most states.

Although most studies of the financing of higher education have involved private as well as public institutions, the problems related to public institutions are given major attention in this chapter, since the community college is generally defined as a public institution. Research in the area of higher education finance has examined the sources of support and has conjectured about what those sources should be. To move from what is to what should be constitutes a major activity. In an analysis of higher education finance, the economic aspects were summarized by Bolton (Stark, 1969) as having three facets: the public interest (the distinction between private benefits and external benefits), investment in human capital (education as a capital good), and difficulties of loan finance (financing investment by borrowing). These three facets raise serious doubts as to whether reliance on private financing is an appropriate avenue of support for public institutions and to some extent even for private institutions. Schultz (Orwig, 1971) further explores these concepts by concluding that investment in education is an investment in human capital. Bowen, in several sources, outlines the complexities of the problem and the benefits of sound solutions (see Orwig, 1971; Bowen, 1977, 1980). The National Commission on the Financing of Postsecondary Education (1973) summarized the concerns of higher education finance as centered on student access, student choice, student opportunity, educational diversity and flexibility, institutional excellence, institutional independence, institutional accountability, and adequate financial support.

Problems of finance and economics relating to higher education have been researched under the concepts of equity, efficiency, access, tuition pricing, external benefits, private benefits, capital enhancement, and economies of scale. While all of these affect the financing of community colleges, several of them deserve and have received special attention. Wattenbarger and his colleagues at the Institute of Higher Education at the University of Florida have provided recent analyses of state-level financial patterns of support. Guidelines and criteria useful for analyzing state financial plans were developed by Martorana and Wattenbarger (1978, p. 8). These emphasized:

1. Consistency with the characteristic educational and philosophical goals of community colleges: (a) open access, (b) comprehensive programs, and (c) local voice in governance to ensure responsiveness to local area needs.
2. Reservation to the administration of the college, including the body responsible for the local voice in governance, of the authority and duty to set academic policy for the institution.
3. Objectivity in determining the magnitude (or weight) of value to be assigned the factors used in the financial plan, including the availability, reliability, and validity of data for evaluating support formulas.
4. Protection of a minimum foundation level of quality of programs and services provided.
5. Nonpreemption of policy prerogatives of local authority to administer the budget once approved, flexibility in administration and management, and use of the fiscal support provided for the college.

6. Equity among local tax jurisdictions sponsoring and supporting community colleges.
7. Accountability to the supporting agencies and to the public at large.

Hyde (1982) explored the problems of access and concluded that, while access has been improved as a result of the development of community colleges, the access problem has not been solved, especially for nontraditional students. The level of public concern for lifelong educational opportunity, the state policies that affect student enrollment, and the institutional management decisions that encourage attendance are all instrumental in affecting access to the community college. Some of these are directly influenced by financial support and others are not.

Breneman and Nelson (1981) provided a research perspective on the economics of community college financial programs. Their analysis described in some detail the concepts of efficiency and equity, and they applied these to the data they assembled relating to the community colleges. Using these data, they developed a list of eight questions that could be used in developing or modifying a plan for financing community colleges:

1. Should the plan be simple or complex?
2. Should it involve public funding from the state only or should there be state and local sharing?
3. If there is sharing, should the state ignore or attempt to offset differences in revenue-raising ability among local jurisdictions?
4. Should program cost differences be considered or ignored?
5. Should tuition cover a specific portion of costs or be set on some other basis?
6. Should budgets be negotiated or follow a statutory formula?
7. Should only courses for credit be financed, or should support be provided for some or all noncredit courses?
8. Should the level of state support be linked to that provided to other public institutions of higher education, or should community colleges be treated in isolation?

In addition, there are several administrative and technical choices that influence the allocation of funds:

1. Should there be strict line-item control or local discretion to shift funds among classes of expenditure?
2. Should average cost or some form of incremental costs be used?
3. Should cost parameters be based on systemwide averages (or medians), or should standard costs be used?
4. Should differences in college size (and hence in unit costs) be considered or ignored?
5. Should the formula be based on average daily attendance, weekly contact hours, or some other work load measure?

Taxonomy of Financial Plans

There are four basic approaches to state plans for financing community colleges. These have been described in more detail by Wattenbarger and Cage (1974) who work at the Institute of Higher Education at the University of Florida. As pointed out earlier, each of the fifty states has developed programs and procedures that are different and are related to its history and other factors. Some states have provided each college an opportunity to negotiate an operating budget with the state legislature. These negotiated budgets may be analyzed in terms of some common criteria, but they are not necessarily based, in the final analysis, on any formula or other objective basis. These states may be classified as *negotiated budget states*.

The community colleges in a second group of states receive their funds for operation as a portion of the total amount appropriated for community colleges. These portions are determined by FTE, which is calculated for each college. Common definition of FTE is of prime importance, and the amount per FTE may change from year to year. This method may be described as a *unit rate formula*.

The colleges in a third group of states receive their funds on the basis of an established amount of money for each FTE or for each student credit hour. There may be different rates for different sizes of colleges or for different types of courses. These states allocate on a *foundation program formula base.*

The final category includes those states that allocate on a *cost center basis.* This may be considered a further refinement of the unit rate formula and the foundation program formula. Using this strategy, costs are computed periodically for each of several defined categories, and funds are allocated to colleges based on the number of students enrolled in each of the cost centers.

The four categories used in classifying the various states are, thus, negotiated budget, unit rate formula, foundation program formula, and cost center program funding. There are, of course, a great many variations and modifications making the assignment of a state to any one of these categories a matter of judgment. In all instances, additional funds are received from other sources: Student fees provide a part of this support, local taxes are a part in some states but not in others, and federal funds are used to a greater or lesser degree in various states.

A recent study conducted by the Institute of Higher Education (Wattenbarger and Heck, 1983) reported a range of state support from as low as 19 percent of the operating funds to as high as 91 percent; student fees ranged from 0 to 69 percent; local support ranged from 0 to 51 percent; and federal funds reached as high as 16 percent in one state, although most states reported only 1 or 2 percent.

An ideal formula for state support would provide funds for all programs in a format related to the program costs as well as to the number of students served in each program. The data base for these statistics would be the most recent available, with flexibility for accommodating special unanticipated problems.

Guidelines

The following guidelines may be used to describe an acceptable financial program.

1. The plan should recognize the community colleges as the primary provider of publicly supported postsecondary education at this level by designating the state as the agent

responsible for developing a plan for the total financial
support of these institutions.

2. The plan should recognize the responsibility of the state for
    providing equal educational opportunity for all citizens by
    requiring an open-door policy for admissions and by
    providing funds for the full cost of all instruction, regardless
    of level.

3. The plan should provide for primary support from state-level
    sources supplemented by other funding sources; student fees,
    therefore, should be kept as low as possible.

4. The plan should recognize the importance of maintaining
    maximum sensitivity to local community needs in the
    planning, programming, and operation of each institution by
    delegating both the responsibility and the authority for
    institutional operation to local boards of trustees.

5. The plan should provide the advantages and benefits of a
    long-range, coordinated approach to education at this level by
    providing for a statewide coordinating agency that has only
    one responsibility—to coordinate these institutions at the state
    level. This agency may be responsible to another state-level
    planning agency that has concerns for all of education.

6. The plan should recognize responsibility for supporting with
    equal emphasis all programs and activities designed to carry
    out the mission of the community college by distributing
    funds on the basis of objective formulas: (a) assessment,
    counseling, and placement, (b) general education, (c)
    occupational education, (d) university parallel education, (e)
    lifelong education and community services.

7. The plan should be directly related to program cost factors
    and should use the most recent data available. There should
    be provisions for fixed costs common to all institutions,
    semivariable costs that will be somewhat different for each
    institution, and variable costs related to factors of numbers,
    institution size, and similar data.

8. The plan should include parameters related to the differenti-
    ation of funding for each institution. These parameters
    should include at least the following: (a) number of students
    enrolled, (b) geographical location of the campus, (c) status of

the campus or center, (d) cost of programs or course, and (e) cost of function.

9. The plan should provide the state coordinating agency with discretionary authority to alleviate emergency situations (a) by establishing a contingency fund to act as a buffer in times of fluctuating enrollments and (b) by devising a policy on making special grants to colleges that enable an institution to start new programs to develop models for improving college management or to carry out new untried or experimental programs.

10. The plan should provide a management information system used by all institutions and should establish a common format for accountability.

11. The plan should provide for ways of rewarding efficiency, good management, and improved service.

12. The plan should establish a three-step process model in allocating funds to each institution: (a) conduct an annual cost analysis of expenditures in each college and summarize as a basis for establishing values for the subsequent year, (b) compute the total appropriation request and forward with supporting data to the legislature, and (c) compute for each college the allocation of funds for that institution.

An essential part of the concept of this financial plan is that each institution administers its own budget by allocating funds within its allotment without line item supervision from the state agency. By providing incentives for good management practices, the cost basis for a subsequent year may be affected in a positive way, thereby forcing other institutions to avoid the trap of the status quo.

The annual cost analysis should be effected by the state agency to guarantee uniformity in treating the data. The format and the determination of cost centers must also be a statewide decision. When data are assembled and analyzed, there is need for immediate feedback to the institutions, with a total system emphasis on improved management.

Current Trends

In examining the current procedures in the various states, one may observe that few states approach the guidelines outlined here. There has been a continued trend toward acceptance of the state's responsibility for providing the major support for community college education. Only a few states do not provide the major part of per student support from state funds appropriated by the legislature. However, these funds are not provided for all programs. While state funds are provided for FTE credit enrollments, in most states a limit is placed by the legislature either by designating caps on enrollment or through other defined limitations. Noncredit courses more often than not are placed in a self-sustaining category. Limits are also placed on the developmental or remedial courses. In other words, the trends have not been in the direction of implementing this guideline.

There has been a universal trend toward increasing fees. Even in California, where student fees have been a major concern since the passage of Proposition 13, there is increasing emphasis on and now acceptance of the establishment of a fee structure. Several states have modified or otherwise limited the local control provisions in their law. In a few states, after unsuccessful referendums to consider establishing new community college districts, the state took action by establishing a state-operated institution. In several other states, there is now little or no local funding; the result is state plans with little or no flexibility.

One cannot ignore the legislative interest in the so-called "superboard" approach to coordination. While only one or two states have actually established such boards for operation or coordination, many states have developed such boards for planning. These planning boards are usually not in conflict with the guidelines.

Not very much progress has been made in developing formula funding based on cost factors. Most states seem to prefer a system of calculated support based on a simple FTE figure. It is not uncommon for the states to divide a predetermined appropriation among the institutions based on a proportional share of the total FTE.

Management information as established by the state has become universal, and all states have improved their data-gathering capabilities, at least to some extent. However, there are still no universal definitions for FTE, academic year, credit hour, faculty load, and similar terms.

In summary, the current trends in financing community colleges do not implement the guidelines outlined above. While a number of states made considerable progress during Generation 3, as described in this volume, and to some extent during the early part of Generation 4, the present situation is one of a static description-status quo.

Recent Experiences

Since funds for support of public community colleges can come from only a few sources—federal taxes, state taxes, local taxes, student fees, gifts and grants, and auxiliary income—there can be only limited magic formulas. The most recent battles for funds have been centered at the state level. Attempts to increase state appropriations have been carried out in most states through various political procedures. The emergence of a powerful senator or house member who is favorable to community colleges often results in attempts to increase basic state appropriations. These involve increasing per student support by an inflation factor and/or providing categorical support for special programs, such as developmental education and vocational/technical programs serving business or industrial development. Arguments for maintaining equity with university appropriations are often used. In some cases, the need to maintain equity with public schools support is also effective.

Local taxes usually require local referendums, but in some instances local taxes may be assessed up to a statutory limit by a local board of trustees. Increases are always difficult and are always achieved only when excellent preparation on the part of the college is carried out. Voters have authorized increases in some cases and boards have levied up to their limits—in both cases, however, amid much protest and heavy criticism from community representatives.

The latter is often so strong that further increases must overcome even greater reluctance.

Student fees have become a major target and have been increased in most states. While a solid analysis of the amount of increases has not been carried out as of this date, a valid estimate ranging from 20 percent to 100 percent increases over the past ten years would not be far off the actual fact.

The auxiliary sources provide little or no increased revenues. Most colleges are pleased to break even in their auxiliary activities. For instance, there has been a crisis in dormitory support in many of the few community colleges that have dormitories.

A major focus of attention has been placed on gifts and grants, especially the gift part of the development function. Several community colleges have had excellent success, while many are still not sure "how to do it." A carefully planned organization is essential. Knowledgeable professional leadership is necessary. Constant followthrough is required. Examples of success stories do not always tell the full story, and there is no generally acceptable model for all to follow.

Internal changes involving improved marketing, reduced dropout rates, and sensitive curriculum developments have been positive results of community college concerns over income. Those should result in a better program for students in any case. Overall, however, the current change attempts have been patchwork approaches to a continuing problem.

Looking to the Future

The recent study from the Brookings Institute (Breneman and Nelson, 1981) on financing community colleges concluded with a chapter on predictions and implications for the future. The "optimistic" and "pessimistic" scenarios of the study outline contrasting futures for community college development, and the authors conclude that economic predictions as foreseen would tilt the community colleges toward their pessimistic scenario. The factors that are specifically related to financial planning would include: increased dependence on student fees in the support plan, increased emphasis on local support above and beyond the state funds, an increased emphasis on "user fees" for programs in lifelong learning and community services, and increased emphasis on the traditional university parallel and limited occupational programs with a real reluctance to provide for remedial and developmental education.

Hyde (1982) has indicated that there should be increased attention to access for nontraditional students. He would obviously point to the need for a financial plan that would incorporate that concept. Others, including state directors and college presidents, have noted that the current trends lead to a disaster: a constant battle to maintain faculty salaries and to meet the effects of increasing utility costs. Presidents note that after a year of holdbacks in their operating budgets there are no discretionary decisions left to be made. The budget is allocated by previous commitments and expenditures.

A discussion of the future of community college financing is not based solely on a desire to implement the philosophy of the community college, although that would be a happy approach. Nor is it based solely on the economic and political factors that may be traced by those who are knowledgeable in those fields. It is not based solely on the desire of many members of the state legislatures to curtail or at least contain expenditures as much as possible. It should be based on a judicious mixture of all these, tempered, in this case at least, by an optimistic outlook and a concern for the welfare of the citizens of the various states.

The need for the educational opportunity provided by the community college will obviously increase. The "megatrends" described by Naisbitt (1982), as well as by other futurists, will require the education provided by the community colleges. The community colleges are in place in most states and are in a position to serve these educational needs.

In order to accomplish this assignment, the following will be required:

1. Each state will need to formulate and adopt a plan for the community college development in that state.
2. This plan will need to be built on existing status but will need to unify responsibility for this level of education.

3. The financial plan will need to recognize existing procedures and to modify them in keeping with the guidelines described earlier herein. Several specific concerns will need special attention: a) a formula should be developed that recognizes fixed costs, variable costs, and semivariable costs; (b) every attempt should be made to provide for the total mission of the community college, but should this not be politically feasible, a priority system should be developed that permits individual institutions to establish their own local priorities; (c) the state agency responsible for coordinating or operating the community colleges should establish a management information system and should calculate the cost-analysis data.

The financing of community colleges will require the best use of available resources in a none-too-perfect political milieu. While each state will have its own variety of problems, just as each has its own system of education, attention to the guidelines and models presented in this chapter can provide a useful focus for analyses as states and colleges determine the financing of community colleges in the fifth generation.

References

Arney, L. H. *State Patterns of Financial Support for Community Colleges.* Gainesville: Institute of Higher Education, University of Florida, 1970.

Bender, L. *Federal Regulation and Higher Education.* Washington, D.C.: American Association for Higher Education, 1977.

Benson, C. S. *The Economics of Public Education.* (2nd ed.) Boston: Houghton Mifflin, 1968.

Bowen, H. R. *Investment in Learning: The Individual and Social Value of American Higher Education.* San Francisco: Jossey-Bass, 1977.

Bowen, H. R. *The Costs of Higher Education: How Much Do Colleges and Universities Spend Per Student and How Much Should They Spend?* San Francisco: Jossey-Bass, 1980.

Breneman, D. W., and Finn, C. *Public Policy and Private Higher Education.* Washington, D.C.: Brookings Institution, 1978.

Breneman, D. W., and Nelson, S. C. *Financing Community Colleges: An Economic Perspective.* Washington, D.C.: Brookings Institution, 1981.

Caffrey, J., and Isaacs, H. *Estimating the Impact of a College or University on the Local Economy.* Washington, D.C.: American Council on Education, 1972.

Carnegie Commission on Higher Education. *Capitol and the Campus: State Responsibility for Postsecondary Education.* New York: McGraw-Hill, 1971.

Carnegie Commission on Higher Education. *The More Effective Use of Resources.* New York: McGraw-Hill, 1972.

Carnegie Commission on Higher Education. *Higher Education: Who Pays? Who benefits? Who Should Pay?* New York: McGraw-Hill, 1973a.

Carnegie Commission on Higher Education. *Toward a Learning Society: Alternative Channels to Life, Work, and Service.* New York: McGraw-Hill, 1973b.

Carnegie Council on Policy Studies in Higher Education. *The Federal Role in Postsecondary Education: Unfinished Business 1975–1980.* San Francisco: Jossey-Bass, 1975.

Carnegie Council on Policy Studies in Higher Education. *Next Steps for the 1980s in Student Financial Aid: A Fourth Alternative.* San Francisco: Jossey-Bass, 1979.

Chambers, M. M. *Higher Education: Who Pays? Who Gains?* Danville, Ill.: Interstate, 1968.

Cheit, E. *The New Depression in Higher Education: A Study of Financial Conditions at 41 Colleges and Universities.* New York: McGraw-Hill, 1971.

Cosand, J. P. *Perspective: Community Colleges in the 1980s.* Washington, D.C.: American Association of Community and Junior Colleges, 1979.

El-Khawas, E. *Public and Private Higher Education: Differences in Role, Character, and Clientele.* Washington, D.C.: American Council on Education, 1976.

Eulau, H., and Quinley, H. *State Officials and Higher Education.* New York: McGraw-Hill, 1970.

Folger, J. "Prospects for Higher Education Finance in the Next Decade." *Journal of Education Finance,* 1977, *3*, 187–198.

Garms, W. L. *Financing Community Colleges.* New York: Teachers College Press, Columbia University, 1972.

Halstead, D. K. *Higher Education Planning: A Bibliographic Handbook.* Washington, D.C.: U.S. Government Printing Office, 1974.

Hansen, W. L., and Weisbrod, B. *Benefits, Costs and Finance of Public Higher Education.* Chicago: Markham, 1969.

Higher Education for American Democracy: A Report of the President's Commission on Higher Education. New York: Harper & Row, 1948.

Hoy, J., and Bernstein, H. H. (eds.). *Financing Higher Education: The Public Investment.* Boston: Autumn House, 1982.

Hyde, W. *A New Look at Community College Access.* Report no. F82-3. Denver, Colo.: Education Commission of the States, 1982.

Jensen, E. "Student Financial Aid and Persistence in College." *Journal of Higher Education,* 1981, *52,* 280–293.

Johns, R., Morphet, E., and Alexander, K. *The Economics and Financing of Education.* (4th ed.) Englewood Cliffs, N.J.: Prentice-Hall, 1983.

Joint Economic Committee, Congress of the United States. *The Economics and Financing of Higher Education in the United States: A Compendium of Papers Submitted to the Joint Economic Committee, Congress of the United States.* Washington, D.C.: U.S. Government Printing Office, 1969.

Leslie, L. "The Financial Prospects for Higher Education in the 1980s." *Journal of Higher Education,* 1980, *51,* 1–17.

Leslie, L., and Otto, H. L. (eds.). *Financing and Budgeting Postsecondary Education in the 1980s.* Tucson: Center for the Study of Higher Education, University of Arizona, 1980.

Lombardi, J. *The Financial Crisis in the Community College.* Topical Paper no. 29. Los Angeles: ERIC Clearinghouse for Junior Colleges, 1972. (ED 058 873)

Lombardi, J. *Managing Finances in Community Colleges.* San Francisco: Jossey-Bass, 1973.

McCoy, M., and Halstead, D. K. *Higher Education Financing in the Fifty States: Interstate Comparison-Fiscal Year 1976.* Washington, D.C.: U.S. Government Printing Office, 1979.

McMahon, W. *Investment in Higher Education.* Lexington, Mass.: Lexington Books, 1974.

Martorana, S. V., and Wattenbarger, J. L. *Principles, Practices, and Alternatives in State Methods of Financing Community Colleges and an Approach to their Evaluation, with Pennsylvania a Case State.* Report no. 32. University Park: Center for the Study of Higher Education, University of Pennsylvania, 1978.

Martorana, S. V., Wattenbarger, J. L., and Smutz, W. D. *Dollars and Directions: Issues and Problems Related to Financial Support and Legal Authorization of Community Colleges.* Washington, D.C.: American Association of Community and Junior Colleges, 1978.

Minter, W. J., and Bowen, H. *Independent Higher Education: Fourth Annual Report on Financial and Educational Trends in the Independent Sector of American Higher Education.* Washington, D.C.: National Association of Independent Colleges and Universities, 1978.

Musgrave, R. A., and Musgrave, P. B. *Public Finance in Theory and Practice.* (3rd ed.) New York: McGraw-Hill, 1980.

Naisbitt, J. *Megatrends: Ten New Directions Transforming Our Lives.* New York: Warner Books, 1982.

National Commission on the Financing of Postsecondary Education. *Financing Postsecondary Education in the United States.* Washington, D.C.: U.S. Government Printing Office, 1973.

Orwig, M. D. (ed.). *Financing Higher Education: Alternatives for the Federal Government.* Iowa City, Iowa: American College Testing Program, 1971.

Pattillo, M., and MacKenzie, D. *Church-Sponsored Higher Education in the United States.* Washington, D.C.: American Council on Education, 1966.

Richardson, R. C., Jr., and Leslie, L. L. *The Impossible Dream? Financing Community Colleges' Evolving Missions.* Washington, D.C.: American Association of Community and Junior Colleges, 1980.

Schultz, T. W. *Investing in People: The Economics of Population Quality.* Berkeley: University of California Press, 1981.

Sharon, W. H., Jr. (ed.). *The Community Foundation.* Washington, D.C.: National Council for Resource Development, American Association of Community and Junior Colleges, 1982.

Stark, J. R. (ed.). *The Economics and Financing of Higher Education in the United States.* Washington, D.C.: U.S. Government Printing Office, 1969.

Wattenbarger, J. L. *Financial Support for Community Colleges.* Gainesville: Institute of Higher Education, University of Florida, 1974.

Wattenbarger, J. L. *Financial Support Patterns for Community Colleges 1976.* Gainesville: Institute of Higher Education, University of Florida, 1976.

Wattenbarger, J. L., and Bibby, P. *Financing Community Colleges 1981.* Gainesville: Institute of Higher Education, University of Florida, 1981.

Wattenbarger, J. L., and Cage, B. *More Money for More Opportunity: Financial Support of Community College Systems.* San Francisco: Jossey-Bass, 1974.

Wattenbarger, J. L., and Heck, J. *Financing Community Colleges 1983.* Gainesville: Institute of Higher Education, University of Florida, 1983.

Wattenbarger, J. L., and Starnes, P. M. *State Funding Formulae for Public Two-Year Colleges.* Gainesville: Institute of Higher Education, University of Florida, 1973.

Wattenbarger, J. L., and Stepp, W. *Financing Community Colleges 1978.* Gainesville: Institute of Higher Education, University of Florida, 1978.

Wilson, R. A. (ed.). *Responses to Fiscal Stress in Higher Education.* Tucson: Center for the Study of Higher Education, University of Arizona, 1982.

Wolk, R. A. *Alternative Methods of Federal Funding for Higher Education.* Berkeley, Calif.: Carnegie Commission on the Future of Higher Education, 1968.

Young, K. E. *Exploring the Case for Low Tuition in Public Higher Education.* Iowa City, Iowa: American Association of Community and Junior Colleges, American Association of State Colleges and Universities, National Association of State Universities and Land-Grant Colleges, and the American College Testing Program, 1974.

Richard C. Richardson, Jr.
William R. Rhodes

12

Effective Strategic Planning: Balancing Demands for Quality and Fiscal Realities

Community colleges have entered a fifth generation under two unprecedented and seemingly conflicting conditions—fiscal constraint and a demand for quality. These conditions are likely to prevail for the remainder of this century. In response, there will be increased effort to address three central issues: Who should be served? What services can be offered? Who will pay for those services?

During the growth era of Generation 3, public policy emphasized "quantity" education as a response to the need for promoting access. Community colleges were ideally suited for the emphasis on numbers of students and attempts to serve every member of the community. As a result, it appears that "community college planning has been anchored in the assumption that there are no real limits on the kinds of students they should serve or the programs they might develop" (Knoell, 1980, pp. 555–556). Legislative attempts to impose planning priorities through differential funding formulas were largely frustrated by administrative actions designed to make all courses look like those that received maximum funding (Breneman and Nelson, 1981). In the

284

fifth generation, a public policy emphasis on quality will require different strategies and different funding approaches from those that proved so effective during the "quantity years."

The movement in which community colleges became community-based learning centers largely resulted from two fundamental assumptions that are no longer valid. It was assumed that funding formulas guaranteed that more students meant more income, that there were unlimited resources for doing good. The second assumption was that more students would translate into more political support for enriching those funding formulas. Both assumptions now appear incorrect. Legislators are placing enrollment caps and/or funding caps on many public institutions, including community colleges, and it appears that those served represent an uncertain basis of support for reversing these policy decisions. Student-initiated attempts to influence policymakers have been made on issues related to the imposition of tuition or the severe curtailment of critical services, such as English as a second language programs. However, in a recent survey, part-time community college students in Arizona did not favor continued tax support for many of the courses in which they were currently enrolled. On the average, they were more negative than were state legislators who responded on the same issue (Richardson, Doucette, and Armenta, 1982).

Keller (1983, p. 72) summarized the demands that the new climate will place on all institutions of higher education: "Institutions are being pressed to inquire, what business are we really in? What is most central to us? How shall we proceed?" These are tough questions for any institution. For the community college, they will undoubtedly result in both heated and emotional debate— one reason they have been avoided in the past. Yet the debate seems unavoidable. It is likely to result in dramatic changes in many of the policies that guided the actions of fourth-generation leaders.

New Directions for the Fifth Generation

The alternative to serving everyone at some minimal level is to provide more extensive services to a more limited clientele. The judicious selection of services to be terminated, reduced, or enhanced will depend in part on what legislators are willing to fund; but, more importantly, such action should result from a realistic assessment of what the institution can do best with the resources at hand, including a heavily tenured faculty that is relatively specialized and inflexible. A desirable outcome would emphasize those services that can be provided most effectively by the institution along with those that are most desired by the community.

Achieving this outcome requires reexamining the meaning of open access. At the extreme, this philosophical commitment has been interpreted to mean admission of anyone eighteen years of age or older, regardless of demonstrated ability or commitment. When this interpretation has been accompanied by course advisory placement for full-time students only and an absence of placement for part-time students, college-level classes have been overrun with underprepared students. To prevent discouragement, take advantage of funding formulas, and ensure eligibility for financial aid, many remedial courses have been offered for college credit.

The results of open access defined as the opportunity to attempt all but the limited-seat, high-cost, technical programs have affected every community college student. Qualified students who wish to earn legitimate college and occupational credentials are handicapped by college-level courses that are taught at less-demanding levels in order to accommodate underqualified students. The result of including students with serious deficiencies seems to be less, rather than more, opportunity (Richardon, Fisk, and Okun, 1983).

Community colleges exist because the communities see them as a means of improving access to better occupations, higher salaries, more responsibility, and improved citizenship. A community college certificate or degree should improve access and social mobility for its holder, but evidence for this outcome is far from conclusive. The open-door policy allows many students to attend community colleges that would not have the same opportunity elsewhere, but attempts to meet everyone's needs have impaired the ability to help those who could benefit most from the services offered.

The alternative to providing everyone with some minimal level of service is to redefine the open door and require a high school diploma or a recognized equivalent for admission to college-level courses and programs. Minimal admissions standards would relieve part of the burden of underqualified and uncommitted students. Such standards would not preclude enrollments in precollegiate remedial or high school equivalency programs offered as distinct and separate services of the community college or by some other community agency.

More stringent requirements for admission to college-level classes and programs and for classroom performance and progress in both colleges and precollegiate courses would have the initial effect of reducing access and increasing attrition. But there is evidence that the longer-term effect of higher standards combined with efforts to reduce attrition could be very positive. McCabe and Skidmore (1983) report that graduation rates dropped during the early stages of Miami-Dade Community College's highly publicized five-year reform, but current graduation rates are significantly higher than prior to the 1978 changes.

The strategic changes required of fifth-generation community colleges to cope with the dual issues of access and achievement will not come easily. On the surface, they appear to attack deeply held beliefs in the community college as an institution devoted to meeting the needs of the community. At the same time, emphasis on achievement rather than course enrollments runs counter to existing funding formulas. But if community colleges do not act to emphasize high quality and student achievement, they will by default be deciding in favor of low quality and limited student achievement. When resources are constrained, some will not be served. Community colleges can engage in strategic planning to focus their efforts on target populations who receive "opportunity with excellence." Alternatively, they can watch dwindling dollars produce diminished quality across the board in their continuing pursuit of the "all things to all people" philosophy.

Leadership Issues

The impediments to change in educational institutions are well known—the traditions, power structures, values, and personnel, especially faculty. But one major impediment we often fail to recognize involves the quality of leadership provided by the president. Planning, the key strategy for achieving change, is only as effective as the skill of those who lead the effort. The most crucial and difficult issue in successful planning, whatever its form, is leadership. The question for the fifth generation is whether chief administrators can learn and practice the skills that will be necessary to alter priorities from quantity to quality education.

The last decade might be described as the era of the manager. We have witnessed attempts to adopt strategies and programs that were primarily aimed at improving employee productivity. Management by objectives and organizational development are two examples of methods that have been widely adopted, often with little result. New organizational structures have been imposed on colleges only to result in one more layer of administrative bureaucracy. Management-oriented administrators have pursued a form of operation that Mintzberg (1979) defined as "administrative adhocracy." The emphasis has been on unceasing change in response to targets of opportunity in the external environment. In the face of formidable resistance from faculty, sustained change was accomplished through increasing reliance on support staff and part-time faculty. Full-time faculty were isolated from the mainstream of institutional decision making and left to the drudgery of maintaining established programs while administrators moved on to the novel. The observation that faculty, left to their own devices, have not done well at sustaining the transfer program lies at the heart of current concerns about quality.

Administrative adhocracies are ideally suited to dynamic environments in which changes occur through the addition of new resources. But, according to Mintzberg (1979), they are inherently unstable organizations that are particularly susceptible to adversity, partly because they are not competent to do ordinary things. Under the best of circumstances, they are pulled toward the professional bureaucracy, a model that describes very well their change-resistant university colleagues.

Attempting to preserve the rate of change that was so exhilarating in the sixties and seventies under circumstances in which most of the changes are likely to have unfavorable consequences for at least some organizational members produces what Casey (1982, p. 15) has described as the "cycle of disbelief, annoyance, frustration, anger, fear, and cannibalism." The way to change this sequence is to change what has resembled a disorderly route into a strategic withdrawal.

Selznick's (1957) distinction between managers and leaders suggests one way to accomplish this transition. Managers know that their organizations are headed in appropriate directions: their central focus is efficiency. In contrast, leaders are concerned about where their organizations should be going: their central focus is effectiveness. Selznick described the responsible leader as one who avoids both opportunism and utopianism. Opportunism, defined as the pursuit of immediate advantages without regard for longer-range consequences, has characterized much of the development of community colleges during the past two decades. Opportunism combined with utopianism, the overgeneralization of institutional purpose, has been largely responsible for the change and diffusion of the original mission of the community college. Institutions that once emphasized access and educational opportunity through college transfer and occupational programs have become community-based learning centers for which no task appears too difficult or too trivial. Selznick suggested that opportunism and utopianism result in attentuation and confusion. Organizational purpose becomes vague and abstract: "The formulation of institutional goals is an afterthought, a way of rationalizing activities actually resulting from opportunistic decisions" (Selznick, 1957, p. 145). Organizations with this type of leadership are unable to mobilize the support of their staffs and will not be responsive to changing external forces.

One of the most serious problems faced during a period of contraction is managerial preoccupation with efficiency in accomplishing existing activities. One result may be inadequate attention to evaluating the relevance of existing activities to a changing external environment. While administrators cannot avoid dealing on a day-to-day basis with the efficiency issues that characterized the fourth-generation era of quantity higher education, the key issue of the fifth generation will be the effectiveness or quality issue.

In *Three Thousand Futures,* the Carnegie Council on Policy Studies in Higher Education (1980) reflected on the conditions facing educational leaders: "The effective 'management of decline' is extraordinarily difficult. Our tendency is to preserve the status quo in the short run, thus sometimes encouraging even further decline in the long run. . . . higher education has been better at addition than subtraction" (p. 102), and "a period such as that ahead does not readily attract the ablest leadership—the tasks are grinding ones, the victories too often take the form of greater losses avoided, the internal constituencies are more likely to be united around doing nothing than doing something" (p. 108). Hesburgh (1983), who quotes the latter statement, sees its direct relevance to his own office of president, in which the conditions of the future will demand "a tighter ship, and only the faculty can rig it. But it will require vision and perceptiveness, strength and decision that have not always been present in more expansive and more affluent days" (p. 17).

A fifth generation of community college leaders will need to find ways of reengaging an often alienated faculty in the serious study of institutional priorities. Twenty-five years of unceasing change have set the stage for a period of reflection and consolidation. From among the many tasks undertaken, community colleges must select those representing the most pressing need. At the same time, the tasks chosen must be done well and within the scope of available resources. We turn now to a discussion of strategic planning as the most promising means for accomplishing these requirements.

Strategic Planning: A Conceptual Framework

We have previously suggested that current priorities and activities of many community college leaders focus on access or quantity education. To alter practices and pursue quality education within an open-access framework will require significant changes in both attitudes and behaviors. The most promising candidate for an institutional strategy designed to achieve necessary changes without causing unmanageable levels of conflict is planning. Before developing criteria for planning processes likely to prove effective in helping community colleges meet fifth-generation challenges, it will be useful to review planning concepts.

Everyone plans, and almost every organization engages in some form of planning. Such efforts enable persons and organizations to anticipate and prepare for events and conditions in the near or distant future. Planning may be the result of coordinated or uncoordinated efforts of a single individual, a group, or many groups with formal or informal authority and structure. It may be internally or externally oriented, continuous or discontinuous, concerned with internal or external conditions, oriented to the immediate or distant 'future, and focused on goals, tasks, or the planning process itself. Planning may have the purpose of promoting change, organizational improvement, or maintenance in a stressful environment.

The tension between planning as a rational search for the most efficient means of employing scarce resources and planning as a political means of reconciling conflict is at the heart of most discussions about the philosophy and structure that planning should take. Keller (1983) recognizes two major schools of thought or approaches to planning as seen in educational institutions. The first has its roots in management science. Such scientific planning relies heavily on a rational decision-making process that is supported by quantitative information and sophisticated modeling and forecasting techniques. During the seventies, colleges and universities attempted to adopt scientific approaches to management and planning. But as Keller points out, the scientific approach has failed to take root because of skepticism over "the dismal record of forecasting, on which management science stands" (p. 111), and the deep adherence of institutional managers to the second approach—incrementalism (Lindblom, 1959). Both Lindblom and Wildavsky (1974) see this political approach as the rational means of coping with powerful interest groups both inside and outside the organization. But incrementalism has also suffered from its inherent tendency toward nearsightedness and the perception of power brokering and political maneuvering that offends the value of many academics.

Alone, neither scientific planning nor incrementalism has been notably successful, but the value of the two approaches cannot be discarded. A third approach to planning, strategic planning, has emerged as a synthesis of "the best wisdom of both approaches" (Keller, 1983, p. 108). Peterson (1980, p. 140) defined strategic planning as a form of planning in which "the primary purpose is to foster adaptation by assuring congruence with the external environment." Such planning involves assessment and master plan creation.

Shirley's (1980–81) "strategic analysis paradigm" illustrates the potential scope of a comprehensive strategic planning effort that addresses the following risks: (1) assessment of what the institution might and cannot do given environmental opportunities and constraints, (2) clarification of what the institution can and cannot do based on assessment of internal strengths and weaknesses, (3) identification of what the constituents of the institutions want it to do through assessment of collective personal values, and (4) development of recommendations for specific strategic decisions through a matching process that resolves conflicts and inconsistencies among all of the above. To these we would add that the planning process must be a commitment-building process, resulting in behavioral and attitudinal support from both internal and external constituencies. This process would provide the foundation for campus-wide tactical and procedural planning.

Ideally, a strategic planning process should be responsive to pressures from the community and from government agencies, as well as sensitive to the values, needs, and skills of students and faculty. It should be a process that results in a distinct institutional identity and vision of the future. A well-managed planning process can allow the institution to lead as well as to be led. It can result in changed attitudes and behavior from those who are outside as well as those who are inside the institution.

Few institutions will find the need or have the luxury or resources to engage in the comprehensive effort that is sometimes suggested by discussions of strategic planning. Each institution can develop its own strategic planning process tailored to local needs and capabilities. In the following section, we discuss design parameters and suggest guidelines for structuring a planning process so that it becomes the means for reconciling conflicting pressures for efficiency and effectiveness without becoming an end in itself.

Defining a Planning Process

There is no single design for a planning process. Peterson's (1980) effort to describe systematically the approaches, elements, and dimensions of planning suggests an unlimited variety of approaches and designs for planning. But there is need for caution. It is important to understand that although the range of choices will allow for development of a planning process that can suit the unique needs of almost any institution, it is naive to assume that any planning process will do the job. This discussion, while not a comprehensive treatment of planning or a prescription for planning in the community college, is intended to identify and suggest useful criteria for designing a strategic planning process.

Institutional Fit. A planning philosophy and structure should be adopted to fit the institution's particular set of expectations for decision making. It seems reasonable to incorporate rather than replace planning structures that are currently in place. For example, many institutions have engaged in some form of master planning, and almost all utilize at least short-term planning in the budgetary process. The challenge in defining a strategic planning process will be to achieve an appropriate balance between the perception that strategic planning will be "more of the same" and creating concerns among senates, bargaining units, or other existing governance structures about a potential change in ground rules and players.

Short-Term Results. Planning is an activity that is future oriented. As a means of changing behavior, planning can lead to an emphasis on process for its own sake. Planning that stops with an institutional master plan or wish list has nothing tangible to justify the time and resources absorbed. As Peterson (1980, p. 159) warns: "Planning to effect institutional change needs to produce short-range results in order to maintain the commitment of executive officers and the involvement of participants." Too much emphasis on process over outcomes results in high attrition among frustrated participants amid circular discussions.

Purpose. Planning is an appropriate response to external pressures as well as a means of meeting critical institutional needs, clarifying the problems that face an institution, increasing the perception of being well managed, and improving communication within the institution (Richardson and Gardner, 1983). Functional needs that can be met include adaptation to the external environment, improving flow of information and resources, improving institutional management, and improving faculty and staff morale, commitment, and performance. Keller (1983) suggests that planning will be necessary to establish institutional identity and direction. Planning should not be undertaken as a way to impose administrative values on faculty or to share the blame for an unpopular action that cannot be avoided (for example, reduction in force).

Scope. Palola and Padgett (1971) define scope as the amount that will be planned. The obvious extremes are nothing and everything, but almost every institution finds its scope of planning in the middle range. For those who adopt strategic planning, the temptation is likely to be toward planning comprehensively. But there are good reasons to limit the scope of the process. One of the most important is cost. Planning is demanding of the time and energy of those who participate. Since "new money" to fund and staff the process is unlikely, planning will compete for available resources with other activities. Under such circumstances, the probability of achieving substantive change is inversely related to the number of changes attempted. Alternatively, we need not plan for anything that will happen in a more or less satisfactory form without planning. The single-minded pursuit of a limited number of priorities emphasizing quality and student achievement offers the best hope of moving away from the quantity orientation of the past.

Participation. If planning is to change behavior as well as to identify strategic and tactical adjustments, it would seem best to involve as many key personnel as possible. Cosand (1980, p. 165) suggests, "those who are involved in planning must anticipate that any plan imposed upon others without their understanding will probably be doomed to failure." In the colleges, faculty acceptance, support, and adjustment will be the key to change without added resources. Conditions that seem to point to the desirability of more faculty involvement include: (1) probable need to reduce or terminate programs (as distinct from imminent requirement), (2) need to change behavior and attitudes in instructional programs, such as adapting new instructional technology, increasing advisement activity, or adapting existing courses to more effectively support an objective such as writing across the curriculum, and (3) the desire to prevent or moderate conflict where this priority is more important than achieving specific goals.

Resources. Resources include funds, released time, facilities, offices, technical support, and information/data base support. Tying resource allocation to strategic planning gives the process legitimacy. The difference between goals or objectives that simply serve as pronouncements of what the institution would like to do and those that become operational will result from institutional willingness to channel funds, facilities, and staff into implementing decisions of the planning group.

Leadership. The most crucial issue in successful planning will be leadership. The individual who has responsibility for the planning process and the chairs of planning committees are indeed key personnel, but the major contributor to the success or failure of institutional planning will be the chief administrator, whose visible participation in the planning process will serve as a barometer through which other organizational members evaluate the importance attached by the organization to strategic planning.

Through the sixties and most of the seventies, each year brought new resources to undertake new ventures or to correct past mistakes. Under such circumstances, there was little incentive for chief administrators to share responsibilities for planning, for by doing so they were accepting unnecessary constraints on their freedom of action as well as undesired delays in implementing new programs and services. In the late seventies and early eighties, fiscal crises hit state after state, resulting in salary freezes and reductions in force. Under these latter circumstances, chief executives were eager to establish participative planning procedures as a means for diffusing responsibility for unpopular actions over which they had very little control. There were few takers among the faculty, however. Most preferred to rely on union security agreements or, in the absence of collective bargaining, on contracts and board benevolence.

Broad-based planning activities were not a welcome guest during good times, so they could not be relied on when the going got rough. From this experience, it is fair to assume that planning may not be the strategy of choice in either the best or the worst of times. But leaders of the fifth-generation community college seem more likely to face a future of varying shades of gray than the extremes of the past two decades. Times may get a little better but not good enough to permit a return to the unrestrained growth of the recent past. Times may get a little worse but not bad enough to justify major administrative decisions in a crisis environment.

Administrators in the fifth-generation community college will turn to strategic planning because there will be no reasonable alternative for accomplishing the needed change in emphasis from access to achievement. Faculty who participate in making decisions about institutional priorities cannot remain aloof from the constituencies they serve or the changing needs in their communities. The administrative adhocracy of the fourth-generation college will be replaced by a professional bureaucracy in which at least partial ownership of the educational program will return to the faculty as their reasonable reward for their renewed commitment to purposes they and administrative leaders have mutually redefined.

Making program changes will require more time of the professional bureaucracy, and some changes desired by administrators may not occur at all. The difficulties in making program changes through strategic planning as distinct from ad hoc administrative decisions will be tolerated because the tasks of the next two decades will focus on achieving quality and stability rather than growth and change.

Strategic Planning in Practice

We have suggested a central theme for a fifth-generation community college: Quantity education focused on increasing access must give way to quality education concerned with student achievement. This fundamental change in direction can be attained without sacrificing historical philosophical commitments only through the use of a process that encourages community college leaders to determine appropriate priorities and to pursue them effectively. In times of great change, it is not enough simply to pursue old priorities with increased efficiency. Instead, the relevancy of existing priorities must be examined in the light of changing preferences among both internal and external constituencies. Among the alternatives available to guide this process, none shows greater promise than the concept of strategic planning.

Strategic planning involves reconciling the conflicting demands of the political process and our knowledge of management science. While much has been written about strategic planning, we still know more about what it is not than about what it is. With Keller (1983), we believe that strategic planning is neither the production of a master plan or a set of platitudes nor a personal vision of the chief administrator. It is not a compilation of departmental plans, a form of surrender to external conditions, or something done at an annual retreat. Yet many of these elements may be incorporated into a strategic planning process which, while future oriented, remains responsive to the needs of the present. Strategic planning must be externally oriented without sacrificing internal strength and vitality. The process needs to be participatory, involving those who will be expected to carry out its mandates. Strategic planning has its own structure, is tailored to each institution in which it occurs, and is tied to resource allocation. Strategic planning does aim at cost-effective outcomes while avoiding excessive formality, inappropriate rules, and process for the sake of process.

There is a temptation to look for successful models of strategic planning, and models do exist. (For case examples of strategic planning in practice, see Keller, 1983, and Office of the Chancellor, California Community Colleges, 1983.) While studies of models and theory can inform and guide practice, there is no single approach to strategic planning. Rather, as the analysis of case studies conducted by the Office of the Chancellor of the California Community Colleges concluded: "The four cases in strategic planning argue persuasively for the fit between this mode of planning and the unique characteristics of individual community colleges. Like their peer institutions elsewhere in the country, the districts are different in their histories, organization and leadership patterns, and their responses to local communities. Consequently, the four colleges have used common elements of strategic planning in quite different ways. In doing so, they have affirmed a fundamental premise of this new approach to planning: The process of planning must fit the individual characteristics of institutions and their people. There is no single nor ideal way to begin, conduct, and use the outcomes of strategic planning. So it is not surprising that each of the community college districts views its planning as a "home-grown" project, even though the participants are familiar with the theory and practices of strategic planning" (p. 58).

Despite the uniqueness of each approach to strategic planning, there were some common values, components, and cycles of behavior that emerged in the case studies. These were:

Leadership and Support are Essential. The chief executive officer of each district personally affirmed this aspect of strategic planning, and it was reinforced by institutional teams. Strong leadership is essential in moving from incrementalism to strategic planning.

A Continuing Process Is Crucial. Each of the institutions committed itself to a continuing process rather than to a plan to be written and filed away. This is a compelling premise for each college. It was communicated in different ways but always represented a move away from past experience.

Planning Is Active. A common theme in the cases was a sense of being "on the move" and of being results oriented. It is important to demonstrate the fruits of the planning effort, particularly in making sure that the planning process "drives the budget."

Those Who Use the System Should Design It. Wide participation is universal in strategic planning, but each case illustrated different techniques for gaining and sustaining wide participation. It seems likely that these differences reflect differences in intradistrict relationships, as well as in leadership styles. Whether the decision was to go slowly with a low profile or to create a large-scale, complex project at the very beginning, there was a common goal of broad understanding, participation, and ownership by the several constituency groups of the institution.

Planning Has Multiple Uses. The cases were not those of single-purpose planning. Rather, each institution saw the planning process as part of management and accountability. In different ways, the four teams envisioned the use of planning in budgeting and program review. Some were quite explicit about the uses of strategic planning in preparing the accreditation self-study. The cycling of these several activities to maximize efficiency and to enhance quality are implicit in the case reports.

Information Is Power in Planning. It is apparent from each of the cases that the colleges undertook major new efforts to gather reliable and usable information. These efforts included various kinds of forecasting and development of techniques for managing information in the planning process. Teams sought a balance of "hard" normative as well as "soft" qualitative information. All the colleges sought ways to reduce large amounts of information into assumptions, goals, appraisal items, and institutional themes.

Conclusion

To achieve the agenda for a fifth generation, administrative leaders must demonstrate their confidence in strategic planning through their willingness to participate and through being honest with participants. Their personal agendas must be subordinate to the collective wisdom of those chosen to participate in planning, and this willingness to subordinate personal preferences must be as evident in resource allocation as in the generation of priorities. The standard scenario in which the president routinely overrules the outcomes of participative decision making, either overtly through directive or covertly through withholding necessary resources, has been a primary source of faculty and administrative criticisms of planning as a strategy for change. In the fourth generation with its expanding resources, such criticism was more of an inconvenience than a barrier. In the fifth generation, the inability to use existing staff resources to achieve new objectives will frustrate efforts to define and achieve the new agenda unless a planning process capable of achieving consensus is implemented.

The use of strategic planning in tandem with emerging forms of leadership will permit fifth-generation community colleges to strive for quality in an environment of scarcity without relinquishing their historic commitment to open access. Community colleges will cease trying to be all things to all people by defining what they do well and what they cannot or should not attempt. The decision to achieve defined levels of quality in priority activities will assist community colleges in strengthening their own sense of identity and in communicating that identity to those on whom they depend for resources.

In pursuing new directions through planning, community colleges will redefine the behaviors expected from key leaders. Keller (1983) suggests that the management requirements for leaders in the next decade have yet to be defined. Hesburgh (1983) adds that when such requirements are made known, we may discover that the job is no longer attractive to those with the necessary competencies. It will not be easy to solve a dilemma in which the emerging demands for leadership run strongly counter to the beliefs and preferences of those currently in positions of leadership. The one lesson history teaches with certainty, however, is that a new generation of leaders will rise to tackle the issues of a fifth-generation community college.

References

Breneman, D. W., and Nelson, S. C. *Financing Community Colleges: An Economic Perspective.* Washington, D.C.: Brookings Institution, 1981.

Carnegie Council on Policy Studies in Higher Education, *Three Thousand Futures: The Next Twenty Years for Higher Education.* San Francisco: Jossey-Bass, 1980.

Casey, J. W. "Managing Contraction." Unpublished paper, Seattle Community College District, 1982.

Cosand, J. P. "Developing an Institutional Master Plan." In P. Jedamus, M. W. Peterson, and Associates, *Improving Academic Management: A Handbook of Planning and Institutional Research.* San Francisco: Jossey-Bass, 1980.

Hesburgh, T. M. "Preparing for the Millennium: Finding an Identity and a Future." *Change*, 1983, *15* (7), 14–17.

Keller, G. *Academic Strategy: The Management Revolution in American Higher Education.* Baltimore, Md.: Johns Hopkins University Press, 1983.

Kieft, R. N., Armizo, F., and Bucklew, N. S. *A Handbook for Institutional Academic and Program Planning: From Idea to Implementation.* Boulder, Colo.: National Center for Higher Education Management Systems, 1978.

Knoell, D. M. "Planning in Community Colleges." In P. Jedamus, M. W. Peterson, and Associates, *Improving Academic Management: A Handbook of Planning and Institutional Research.* San Francisco: Jossey-Bass, 1980.

Lindblom, C. E. "The Science of Muddling Through." *Public Administration Review*, 1959, *19*, 79–88.

McCabe, R. H., and Skidmore, S. B. "Miami-Dade Results Justify Reforms." *Community and Junior College Journal*, 1983, *54* (1), 26–29.

Mintzberg, H. *The Structuring of Organizations.* Englewood Cliffs, N.J.: Prentice-Hall, 1979.

Office of the Chancellor, California Community Colleges. *Models of Strategic Planning in Community Colleges.* Sacramento: Office of the Chancellor, California Community Colleges, 1983.

Palola, E. C., and Padgett, W. *Planning for Institutional Renewal.* Berkeley: Center for Research and Development in Higher Education, University of California, 1971.

Peterson, M. W. "Analyzing Alternative Approaches to Planning." In P. Jedamus, M. W. Peterson, and Associates, *Improving Academic Management: A Handbook of Planning and Institutional Research.* San Francisco: Jossey-Bass, 1980.

Richardson, R. C., Jr., Doucette, D. S., and Armenta, R. R. *Missions of Arizona Community Colleges: A Research Description.* Tempe: Arizona State University, 1982. (ED 215 716)

Richardson, R. C., Jr., Fisk, E. C., and Okun, M. A. *Literacy in the Open-Access College.* San Francisco: Jossey-Bass, 1983.

Richardson, R. C., Jr., and Gardner, D. E. "Avoiding Extremes on the Planning Continuum." *Journal of Higher Education*, 1983, *54* (2), 180–192.

Selznick, P. *Leadership in Administration.* New York: Harper & Row, 1957.

Shirley, R. *Workshop Materials for NCHEMS-Sponsored Seminar on Strategic Planning in Higher Education.* Boulder, Colo.: National Center for Higher Education Management Systems, 1980–81.

Wildavsky, A. *The Politics of the Budgetary Process.* (2nd ed.) Boston: Little, Brown, 1974.

Wildavsky, A. *Speaking Truth to Power: The Art and Craft of Policy Analysis.* Boston: Little, Brown, 1979.

13

William L. Deegan
Dale Tillery
Rudy J. Melone

The Process of Renewal: An Agenda for Action

The preceding chapters have examined the development of the American community college through the framework of four generations of evolution and have offered scenarios or alternative scenarios that can serve as a focus for analysis by policymakers and managers in the fifth generation. The objective of this chapter is to propose an agenda of priority issues for action that, viewed in consort with the policy and program proposals made in each chapter, can serve as a stimulus to policymakers as they consider funding, research, and program changes. The issues are presented as questions and may be confronted in a variety of ways: some may lead to pilot or experimental programs; some require research at campus, state, or national levels; some may lead to policy, program, or structural changes. There is no one way to respond to the issues, but there is a need to confront them if community colleges are to successfully progress in the fifth generation. As discussed throughout this book, community colleges are in a period of intense debate about their future. To some, the emergence of the fully comprehensive community college, with its role as a democratizing institution in state systems of higher education and its responsiveness to local needs, has made it one of America's most successful educational contributions. To others, the community college is seen as having promoted itself as a social panacea, promised results it cannot ensure, and failed to provide real opportunities to large numbers of students.

The debate about the mission and contributions of community colleges heightened as we progressed through the fourth generation with its attending fiscal, social, and political pressures. The community college educational paradigm that has emerged has five philosophical bases: (1) a commitment to democracy—implemented through open-access and low-cost programs, (2) program comprehensiveness—implemented through a wide range of programs and services, (3) a dedication to lifelong learning—implemented through an emphasis on programs and services in adult education and continuing education, (4) a community-centered focus—implemented through its struggle to retain local control and its responsiveness to local community needs, and (5) adaptability—implemented through responsiveness to changing needs in society and the ever evolving purposes and programs that have culminated in the comprehensive mission of transfer, occupational, remedial, and community services, and continuing education. These bases now need to be reexamined and perhaps reconceptualized for the fifth generation of community college education.

Each of the previous four generations of community college education was guided by a predominant theme that in turn strongly influenced or shifted the educational paradigm of that generation (see Chapter One). Now, in the mid 1980s, the dominant themes of quality and productivity will set the climate for the foreseeable future and will strongly influence any new paradigm that emerges. And these twin themes will offer a climate and opportunity much more conducive to careful self-examination and action than either the unevaluated period of rapid growth of the 1960s or the endless "rhetorical" accountability reports of the 1970s.

While individual colleges will vary in their emphases on mission and philosophy, and while we are not advocating any single paradigm for the over 1,000 public community colleges, we do want to draw the insights of the book together by offering a specific agenda of issues for action. We believe the agenda will serve as a stimulus to national, state, and campus policymakers as they attempt to resolve the serious questions of philosophy, mission, and policy that currently confront them. Too often, at all levels of education, we see little of the kind of useful experimentation, development, and evaluation necessary to assess the results of new or traditional programs and to guide decisions. We recognize the past efforts that many community college leaders have made and the complexity of the community college. However, if we are to improve and to plan more effectively for the future, we must be more rigorous in assessing the outcomes of our efforts and in reconsidering the fundamental questions about our educational paradigm.

The community colleges were the prime agents of democratization in higher education through their first four generations. The access mission has been achieved. The emphasis for the fifth generation must now shift to one of assessing and resolving the fundamental questions before us. While this will be done state by state and campus by campus, we recommend the following agenda of issues for action as a focal point for discussion to aid policymakers in their deliberations.

Issues of Mission

Community colleges must resolve misunderstandings and conflicts over their comprehensive mission. The calls for a reassessment of mission have been adequately sounded by a number of authors, and K. Patricia Cross adeptly sums up the choices in Chapter Two of this volume. We now need to go beyond exhortations and begin to critically examine the *responses* of community colleges to the serious issues of mission confronting them. Specific questions that can serve as a focus for analysis for national, state, and campus leaders include the following:

1. What changes in mission are taking place? Is a fundamental reassessment of mission and program balance really occurring at community colleges across the country? What changes should take place?

2. In systems and colleges in which changes took place, how did the changes occur? What role did institutional research and/or strategic planning play in the change process? What were the financial implications of changes in mission or changes in mission priorities?
3. What values and criteria have guided the change process? For example, have changes been based on fundamental value shifts, changing clientele, expedient responses to fiscal crises or opportunities, or other criteria?
4. What intended and unintended consequences have resulted in state systems and institutions at which reassessment of mission has been attempted?
5. What major policy questions arise in the process of mission reassessment and/or change, and how are they resolved?

The mission dilemma of community colleges is a fundamental issue that must be confronted by community college leaders. What is most important is to overcome the conflicts and misunderstandings about mission that often inhibit community colleges from improving instruction and services. While there is no single universally acceptable response to this issue, the questions proposed should provide a focus for analysis by community college leaders and a stimulus to change that considers issues of both process and substance concerning this critical topic.

Issues of Educational Outcome and Theory

There is a need to consolidate and integrate knowledge about the outcomes of education in order to refine concepts and theories that are appropriate for community college students. This concern is dominated by two issues.

Developmental Education. The first issue concerns the need to consolidate knowledge and to move toward more generalizable and comprehensive theories of developmental education. Recent reports by the California Postsecondary Education Commission (1983) and the Southern Regional Education Board (1983) have called for more sophisticated and effective evaluation of the outcomes of developmental efforts. As one report put it: "The lack of evaluation found in remedial programs across all three segments is not limited to California but appears in institutions across the country . . . no one knows if remediation is really working or if one segment or one approach is more effective than another" (California Postsecondary Education Commission, 1983, pp. 109–110).

Many community colleges have made substantial efforts in program design, and a few community college specialists in university programs have been leaders in the developmental education movement in this country. However, as Donovan (in Chapter Five) describes the situation: "For the most part, developmental educators in the 1970s were sailing uncharted waters. Without many role models and without much of a literature to draw upon, faculty improvised and learned while they taught."

Given the tremendous importance of developmental education at all levels of higher education and the rapidly increasing costs of these efforts, there is a pressing need to consolidate findings, to evaluate successful models, to go beyond the many pieces of the developmental puzzle, and to move ahead toward more generalizable models and useful theories about developmental education. To aid in that effort, the proposals made in Chapter Five and the following questions should help guide institutional studies, planning, and decision making: (1) What are the outcomes of the major developmental efforts in community colleges? What works for whom and at what cost? (2) Should there be an "academic floor" of achievement below which students should not be admitted for college-level study? If yes, how and by whom should that floor be established? (3) What are the advantages and disadvantages of the various developmental efforts for different student groups? (4) What cooperative arrangements have community colleges established with other agencies or institutions to coordinate developmental efforts? What have been the results of these arrangements? (5) What consolidation of research can take place in developmental education? The public two-year colleges began with efforts to remedy learning deficiencies, and the past two decades have seen intense and massive experiences in developmental education. We recognize the complexity of the challenge, the achievements that have been made, and the difficulties of both instruction and assessment of undereducated students. We believe, however, that collaborative efforts must be made to consolidate existing knowledge and to build more generalizable models and theories about developmental curriculum, instruction, and evaluation. Community college leaders should give equal attention to the costs and benefits of developmental education in the fifth generation.

Learning Outcomes. A second priority is the need to experiment with measuring the outcomes of learning while students are in college and after they leave. The use of such findings in review and strategic planning has great implications for the renewal of curriculum, teaching, and counseling. A number of authors have analyzed the need for and the difficulty of assessing learner outcomes in improving the quality of education and meeting the expectations of public accountability. Critics of community colleges, using traditional academic criteria, cite the high attrition rates and the failure of many community college students to earn degrees. Yet for many students, as Cohen and Brawer (1982, p. 211) concluded, "Program completion is an institutional artifact." Proponents of community college education have long countered critics by asserting that attrition rates are misleading measures of institutional success. Student needs are often met in a short time, and they thus leave community colleges having achieved their immediate goals.

The issue is further complicated by both the difficulty in assessing changes in achievement—let alone assessing the broad personal and social consequences of a community college experience—and by faculty reluctance to engage in the assessment of short- and long-term outcomes of education. Yet, as Warren writes in Chapter Three, participation in community colleges in the fifth generation is likely to be dominated by older, part-time, and recurrent students. The focus on the consequences of education holds significant potential for helping community college educators to meet the needs of these students more effectively and to make a better case for the achievements of community colleges in educating these often high-risk groups of students.

Major questions about the assessment of learner outcomes are: (1) What are the findings of efforts to assess short- and long-term outcomes of participation in community college programs? (2) What strategies and instruments have been used to measure outcomes of different groups of students? (3) What implications for instruction, curriculum, and counseling can be drawn from current findings? (4) How can university and community college educators collaborate to conceptualize this complex challenge, to design instruments, and to develop a relevant methodology for the future?

The problems of relying solely on traditional academic measures to assess the outcomes of community college students have been well documented. Having acknowledged the variety and complexity of purposes for which students attend community colleges, we now need to develop assessment techniques to assist us more effectively in gauging the success of community colleges in helping students meet their own needs. The use of learner outcomes assessment has the potential to do that in ways unknown in earlier generations.

Issues of Governance

More coherent governance structures and practices for community colleges must be achieved at state and local levels. The way educational institutions and systems of institutions are governed determines who gets educated and how. This view of how and by whom decisions are made in community college affairs suggests a major challenge to community colleges in the fifth generation. There are dramatically different models of governance, particularly among state systems of community colleges, but all are under stress, and none seems appropriate for the future. These models vary from highly centralized state governance structures, as in Virginia, to university control, as in Hawaii, to widely decentralized governance, as in California. The strengths and weaknesses of these various approaches are discussed in several chapters of this book.

Systemwide Governance. There is no eminently successful model of system governance for community colleges. Earlier criteria set forth in Generation 3 have largely been ignored as a result of the near-universal shift to predominantly state funding and the strengthening of state agencies. Since we assume that institutional diversity in response to community differences is essential to community college education, centralization of authority is a source of serious challenge to community colleges. On the one hand, the highly centralized systems of governance threaten to homogenize the role and programs of colleges that purport to serve the educational needs of quite different communities and people. On the other hand, in those states, such as California, in which there is serious conflict between local institutions and state agencies, there is pressing need for rational delineation of responsibilities in governance.

Across the states, there are needs for governance studies and strategic decisions. Major issues for analysis and action include the following:

1. How do differences in decentralization/centralization in system governance affect the ability of community colleges to respond to community differences? Are there ameliorative structures and policies in state-local relations that protect the *community* college concept?
2. What is the evidence that control follows the dollar in the governance of community colleges? Are there concepts and models of state financial support that are not tied to extensive compliance requirements or to line item budgeting?
3. What efforts are being made, and with what results, to delineate responsibilities for achieving mission clarification, educational quality, and productivity among state agencies, local governing boards, and nongovernmental accrediting agencies?
4. Does the political behavior of organized constituency groups (faculty, trustees, administrators, students, among others) help resolve or exacerbate conflicts in system governance? How might new concepts and theories about the political model of academic governance contribute to effective system governance for community colleges?

Local Institutional Governance.

1. How has the concept and practice of trusteeship changed? Are differences in trustee values related to governance processes? How can we better prepare trustees for their role?
2. What changes are taking place in the role, selection, and behavior of the community college chief executive officer as a result of fiscal constraint, collective bargaining, and trends toward centralization of state authority? How have these changes affected leadership in community colleges?
3. To what extent is the union contract a governance document? How has collective bargaining affected the role of faculty in campus academic affairs?
4. What are the major trends and patterns of governance in multi-unit community college districts? How does district governance affect program balance on the campus and response to local community needs?
5. Are there effective options used by local institutions to supplement state funding in order to enhance programs and services to their communities?

Internally, many individual community colleges seem to have found reasonably collegial and effective ways of resolving conflicts. However, the increased complexity of multi-unit institutions has resulted in new problems and exacerbated old ones. Furthermore, the continuing centralization and politicizing of governance arrangements in the states pose fundamental governance issues for community colleges. The proposed agenda for analysis, viewed in tandem with the proposals contained in Chapters Nine and Ten, can contribute needed knowledge about these issues and should lead to suggested strategies for improving governance processes at all levels in the fifth generation.

Issues of Organizational and Staff Development

Community colleges must develop more effective programs of organizational and staff development in the fifth generation. The literature of higher education has become increasingly filled with proposals, models, and exhortations for community colleges to make more concerted efforts at organizational and staff development. Many colleges have responded, and some states have set aside funding for development programs. Too often, however, development programs are cosmetic, piecemeal, and unrelated to institutional, professional, or individual development needs. The essential question confronting community college leaders is not whether to engage in developmental programs; the needs are clear. The essential question is what we have learned about the *impact* of the major models for development tried in the fourth generation and how we can use that knowledge to better integrate efforts to respond to the serious problems currently confronting community colleges. For example, a number of authors have done an excellent job of documenting the major processes and forms of faculty development. We now need to go beyond those kinds of contributions to an analysis of the impact of those forms and processes and the relationship between organizational and staff development efforts. Major issues include the following:

1. What are the major models for organizational and staff development and what is the impact of each for:
   - *institutional development*—moving the college as a whole toward stated goals and a coherent organizational culture?
   - *professional development*—helping faculty and staff remain current in their disciplines?
   - *individual development*—helping staff grow as individuals and cope with problems of burnout and stress?
2. Who participates in developmental programs and why? Who does not participate and why? How can nonparticipants be induced to take part in development programs?
3. Are there successful collaborations for organizational and staff development between community colleges and universities or businesses? If yes, by what criteria are these programs judged successful?
4. Are there major models for using new delivery systems, such as self-paced learning, distance learning, learning contracts, or the new technology for staff and organizational development?

If yes, what are the impacts, the advantages, and the disadvantages of these models?

5. What major issues of policy, program, and morale have arisen where institutions have made major efforts at organizational and staff development? How were these issues resolved? What intended and unintended consequences have resulted from these efforts?

A related issue, and a growing cause of concern, is the use and development of part-time faculty in community colleges. Statistics compiled by the American Association of Community and Junior Colleges show that in 1971 adjuncts accounted for 40 percent of all faculty in community colleges. By 1981, the percentage of adjuncts in the nation's community colleges had increased to 56 percent (Cohen and Brawer, 1982). Given the current fiscal constraints and enrollment fluctuations experienced by many community colleges, as well as the need to constantly change program offerings to reflect the new technology, community college administrators and boards of trustees are likely to continue their preference for part-time hirings, thereby avoiding long-term, locked-in commitments to full-time, tenured faculty.

This state of affairs suggests an urgency for quantitative and qualitative analysis of the use of part-time faculty in community colleges. This analysis needs to focus on several central questions: (1) How are part-time faculty used in community colleges? Specifically, to what extent are part-time faculty used in college credit course instruction, noncredit instruction, curriculum design, academic advisement, career counseling, and college governance? (2) What is the nature of their involvement in these areas? (3) What are the major factors that currently determine the extent to which part-time faculty are used in credit course instruction? What other factors should be taken into consideration in making those decisions? (4) What is the impact of using large numbers of part-time faculty on the institution? On the full-time faculty? On the students? (5) To what extent do programs for the integration and development of part-time faculty exist in community colleges, and what is the nature of these programs? Where are the most successful models for the development of part-time faculty?

The challenges to mission, the developments in technology, the needs for developmental education, the problems of a largely "tenured in" and immobile faculty and staff, and the changing needs of American society will all be powerful forces for institutional and individual adaptation. The need for organizational and staff development to help cope with these needs will be a more critical imperative in the coming decade than at any time in the history of community colleges. Present efforts to move beyond models and processes to a period of assessment of the impact of models and processes will pay rich dividends for community colleges in the fifth generation.

Issues of Curriculum

Effective planning, evaluation, and coordination of the community college curriculum are essential for achieving quality and productivity in the fifth generation. Curriculum is not addressed as a separate chapter in this volume, but aspects and issues of curriculum are addressed in almost every chapter of the book, and most especially in Chapters One, Two, Five, Seven, Eight, and Twelve. However, several key issues of curriculum demand examination as community colleges seek to more effectively plan and coordinate curriculum efforts.

As stressed throughout this book, the fifth generation will be a period of major change for community colleges. Retrenchment, as a result of financial constraints, will cause reexamination of organization, mission, and accountability of programs and courses. Although the mission may remain fundamentally intact, many "jugular vein" decisions (Baldridge, 1981) will have to be made under adverse pressures that may cause some institutions to ignore the integrity of their curricula. While courses have been dropped from schedules at many institutions in order to maintain fiscal balance, other colleges have aborted whole programs. These latter decisions may have merit as missions are reconsidered. However, decisions made impetuously may cause a decline in the integrity and appropriateness of programs and services that is unlikely to be regained. This will be especially true if administrators and faculty have not joined in thoughtful program review and a consideration of ways of protecting both program balance and solvency.

A second major issue concerns the search for a value base for curriculum planning. One of the distinguishing hallmarks of an organization striving for excellence is that it is value driven (Peters and Waterman, 1982). Such organizations have a value base that guides the behavior of all its personnel, regardless of role and rank. Values, however, appear to be in a state of disarray in our society as we emerge from the turmoil of the late sixties and seventies. The events of those years have also had a strong impact on community colleges. For a variety of reasons, it appears that board members, faculty, and administrators lack accord on values that must shape the mission and goals of their colleges. Further, there is often little agreement regarding the role of the colleges in helping students shape their own values. It is important for community colleges to state their institutional values in an orderly and explicit fashion. By being systematic and explicit, colleges can build a value base for decision making, be it for setting long-range goals or for making immediate decisions.

A third major issue concerns the integration and coherence of curricula so that students develop the skills necessary to successfully cope with the challenges of our society. Students must be given the basic tools by which to learn. Many must be trained to manipulate the increasingly complex tools of a technical society. But *all* students need to develop the mental tools necessary to survive in a democratic, but increasingly complex, society. They must be able to adapt and participate in the creation of the change that will surely dominate the fifth generation. Beyond the "basics," there are the "big" skills—those that broaden the vistas of individuals and enlarge their concern for and ability to manage the environment in which they live, play, and work. These skills include such tools as critical thinking; problem definition, analysis, and solution; synthesis of existing knowledge; and development of creativity.

While these three issues may provide an overall context for curriculum decisions, there are several specific questions that can serve as a focus for analysis and decisions concerning curriculum needs and changes. These include:

1. What is the value base of the curriculum? Is there a coherent relationship between patterns of educational requirements and the carefully determined values colleges want students to confront?

2. How will concerns about development of skills in using the "new technology" be accommodated in the curriculum? Will two cultures—the sciences and the humanities—go separate ways? How can these two cultures be more effectively integrated?

3. Should general education courses and requirements be organized as a separate unit? Would such a separate organization facilitate integration of the curriculum or lead to further fragmentation?

4. What are the most effective ways of monitoring and coordinating the curriculum with the changing programs of high schools and the four-year institutions?

5. What impact has the increased role and power of state agencies had on curriculum and program review? Are existing procedures for program review adequate? If not, what changes are necessary at the state level? At the college-wide level? At the division or department level?

In looking back over the past four generations, it appears that the community colleges have performed their curriculum mission well. They have created a special educational institution that is well suited to a democratic society. The colleges have been inventive—indeed, daring on occasion—in their curriculum designs, content, and methods of delivery. Some of this adaptiveness has made them vulnerable to public dissatisfaction and to loss of resources. The fifth generation provides an opportunity to move on from a mostly successful past. College leaders need to address the issues suggested, to continue to take risks, and to constantly seek to improve what they teach, how they teach, and how they motivate students to value the quality and continuity of learning.

Issues of Student Services

Major changes are needed in the conceptualization, management, and roles of student service professionals. Student service professionals in community colleges have been wrenched in a number of directions in their history, but most especially in the fourth generation. They had to meet the demands of tremendous growth in the 1960s and early 1970s, they had to deal with the serious challenges of student protest during the Vietnam War era, and they have had to cope with increasingly diverse student populations at a time when fiscal resources are becoming increasingly difficult to maintain. This increasing diversity has been further magnified by changing attendance patterns and fundamental changes in student interests and needs.

As discussed in Chapter Six, there have been a number of proposals for changes in both the programs and the management strategies of student affairs professionals. Program proposals range from defense of the status quo to divestiture of certain programs; management proposals range from decentralization of support services to departments via matrix organization to experimentation with concepts such as job rotation, cultural audits, quality circles, and complex computer-based information systems (Deegan, 1982; Deegan, Steele, and Thielen, 1985; McCabe and Skidmore, 1983). Despite these proposals, Ames and Elsner (1983) summed up the current dilemma of student affairs programs in community colleges as follows: "No genuine consensus exists about the nature of, need for, or direction of community college student service programs. A model for change seems to elude most leaders. Leaders of community colleges and student service staffs agree on one point: Student services need to be redesigned. The student service function needs an infusion of new ideas, new approaches, and a new reason for being." (p. 139).

In view of the need for a reexamination of the student service function, consideration of the following issues, in conjunction with the proposals made in Chapter Six, seems most vital to providing the needed perspectives and empirical base to help improve student services in community colleges in the fifth generation:

1. What have been the program and management responses of
    student service professionals to the dual challenges of changing
    student needs and fiscal austerity?
2. What are the current major models for providing student
    services? What impact does each of these various models have
    and how is that impact assessed?
3. What organizational models have led to effective integration of
    student service programs into the mainstream as a complement
    to academic programs?
4. Where there are successful adaptations of student affairs to
    changing student populations and fiscal problems, what policy
    or program issues did administrators and faculty confront in
    making those successful adaptations?
5. What training and development programs should be provided
    for student service professionals to help them cope with the
    dual challenges of increasing student diversity and fiscal
    austerity projected for the decade ahead?

Student service programs were in a period of crisis and rapid
change almost throughout the fourth generation. Aside from
proposals, models, or small-scale studies, there has not been a major
national assessment of student service programs in community
colleges since Raines' study in the mid 1960s (Collins, 1967). There
is a need for a broad-based national assessment of the major
responses of student service professionals to the significant
challenges currently confronting them. Answers to the questions
suggested could provide a sorely lacking empirical base for what
could emerge as a whole new conceptualization of what student
services should become in the fifth generation.

Issues of Linkages

*New and improved linkages between the community colleges
and other educational providers will be essential in the fifth
generation.* The increased emphasis by community colleges on
linkages with other organizations and institutions was traced
through its evolution (Chapter One) and discussed in terms of
community services (Chapter Seven) and the general theme of

linking (Chapter Eight). Three issues now seem to predominate as major themes for the fifth generation.

Linking with Businesses. The first issue has to do with the growing emphasis on the relationships between community colleges and businesses. The emphasis on these relationships emerged as a major force of the community colleges in the fourth generation. The American Association of Community and Junior Colleges has made these linkages a priority, and colleges throughout the country have aggressively followed that lead.

A special dimension of linkages with businesses is contract training. Preliminary data from a study of the management of contract training programs underway at the Center for Community Colleges at Teachers College, Columbia University, found that almost 70 percent of the community colleges responding to a national survey had established contract training programs (Deegan and Drisko, 1985). At their best, contract training programs may be a natural part of the community service and continuing education functions. At their worst, these programs can distort the educational mission to one of providing low-cost training, which may not be in the best interest of the college or the taxpayers. There is a need to step back from these linkages with businesses and to assess their impact on the fundamental values and mission of community colleges. Consideration of the following issues would provide important insights about the costs and benefits of these efforts:

1. How have contract programs affected the priorities of community colleges? Specifically, how do these programs influence educational policies and programs? What is their impact on staff? On finance?

2. Where is the locus of control for decision making about these programs: Do corporations specify programs, do community colleges offer choices, or are programs negotiated? What is the faculty role in these decisions?

3. What conditions lead to successful contract training programs? What conditions lead to problems? By what criteria are programs judged successful?

4. What impact are contract training programs having on state education policies? What public monies are provided, in what form, and for what activities?

5. What benefits accrue from increased linkages and contracts with businesses—do staff exchanges, equipment sharing, or other benefits for the college result from contracts?

6. What are the likely future issues in contract training, and how might they affect the fundamental values and missions of community colleges?

Linkages with High Schools. A second major issue of linkages in the fifth generation concerns relations between community colleges and high schools. In Generations 3 and 4, the focus was on relations between community colleges and four-year colleges and universities. Although articulation with senior institutions began to break down in the 1970s, there are both traditions and structures for renewing these relations. High schools and community colleges do not have a modern tradition of good communication; thus, linkages between the two institutions emerge as challenges of major importance and opportunity in the fifth generation. The widely publicized report of the National Commission on Excellence in Education, *A Nation at Risk* (1983) documents the serious problems facing our schools and colleges: an illiteracy rate of 23 million, sharply decreasing scores in standard achievement tests, and the growing problem of remedial education. We would add the shocking drop in high school completion rates, particularly among minority ethnic groups.

Boyer (1983), in his report on secondary education in America, also identifies the problems of our schools and the need for improving linkages between schools and colleges. Many forms of collaboration are underway, ranging from variations in the scheduling of programs and services, to faculty exchanges, to special programs for students, parents, and even faculty. We need a better understanding of the potentials, problems, and outcomes of new linkages between the high schools and community colleges. Answers to the following questions will help improve the articulation between school and college: (1) What are the major forms of linkages between high schools and community colleges?

(2) What impact have these connections had on improving co-operative relations? What impact have they had on the staff of both institutions? On student achievement in school and college? By what criteria should these efforts be judged successful? (3) How is articulation between high school and community colleges managed? How are priorities and projects determined? What role do faculty play in articulation? (4) What assessments of students and programs have been made in the articulation process? How have these assessments been used in program development? (5) What are the most effective ways of providing feedback to high schools concerning student achievement in community colleges? How do high schools use such information? (6) What are the most important areas for experimentation in linking high schools and community colleges?

Linkages Within Higher Education. The fifth generation began with a recognition that articulation between community colleges and other institutions of higher education had been increasingly neglected. The factors contributing to such neglect have included scarcity of resources, movement into leadership positions of new professionals with local orientations, competition for students, and centralization of authority. Much of the mission crises of community colleges has resulted from a deterioration in the close working relationship between colleges and public universities. Community college faculty and administrators have lost touch with the expectations of the senior institutions in the preparation of students for transfer. In turn, their peers in higher education have failed to note the changing student population in community colleges and have false expectations about realistic transfer rates from community colleges. Fortunately, the mutual discontent has resulted in improved transfer studies, reestablishment of working relationships between administrators and faculties, and state-wide studies of higher education master plans.

Several major questions should guide studies and the improvement of articulation between institutions of higher education: (1) What are precise and appropriate definitions of groups of community college students who are likely to transfer to senior institutions? What are the most effective ways of providing program advisement and counseling in order to achieve improved transfer rates of interested and qualified students? (2) What are the most effective structures and strategies to promote good working relationships among professionals in higher education? (3) Is there agreement on the most effective locus of leadership and management of the articulation process? (4) What roles do and should state coordinating agencies play in ensuring effective articulation in higher education? (5) What kind of information systems are needed for making decisions and establishing procedures for articulation? Who should manage such information systems? Who should have access to information about the movement of students within systems?

Equal access to higher education is not possible if students do not have the opportunity and preparation to move within state systems of higher education over time, place, and purpose. This is the central objective of coordinated systems of public higher education and of articulation. The community colleges of the fifth generation should both contribute to and benefit from improved relations with other segments of higher education.

Linkages with high schools, businesses, and four-year institutions are emerging as central themes for the fifth generation of community colleges. The colleges have some experience with all of these endeavors. The need now is to assess the impact of these linkages on programs, policies, and the fundamental values that have evolved through the first four generations of the community college. That community colleges should be engaged in a variety of linkages seems a natural part of their mission. How to link, who controls these links, and at what cost to students, taxpayers, and the institutions is the issue in need of more careful examination than has occurred to date.

Conclusion

As the institutions that enroll almost half of the students in higher education in America, community colleges have been the subject of relatively little research and policy analysis. Community colleges have also been subject to broad misunderstandings about their mission, their quality, and even their evolution.

The four generations of community college history discussed in this book were periods of achieving identity, evolving mission, and growth. The fifth generation and beyond will usher in potentially significant changes in mission, delivery systems, and student needs and attendance patterns. The major needs in the fifth generation are for a reexamination of the community college paradigm that has evolved, a consolidation of knowledge about the community college, and perhaps a reconceptualization of what community colleges should become if they are to meet the challenges and changes on the horizon. We need to know better what works and what does not, under what conditions, and at what cost. Community colleges also need to critically examine the fundamental values that have guided decisions through the first four generations and decide if those values should be modified for the future. These are critical issues, and they will require financial support and a commitment to assessment and development.

In closing, we hope that the framework of four generations from the past will provide a useful perspective on the evolution and the complexity of community colleges. We hope that the analyses and alternatives provided in each chapter will be a stimulus to critical review of the issues examined. And we hope that the agenda of issues for action will provide a useful focus for community college leaders as they confront the challenges and opportunities facing community colleges in the fifth generation.

References

Ames, W. C., and Elsner, P. A. "Redirecting Student Services." In G. B. Vaughan and Associates, *Issues for Community College Leaders in a New Era*. San Francisco: Jossey-Bass, 1983.

Baldridge, J. V. "Higher Education's 'Jugular Vein Decisions.'" *American Association of Higher Education Bulletin*, 1981, *33* (10), 6 and 11–12.

Boyer, E. L. *High School—A Report on Secondary Education in America*. New York: Harper & Row, 1983.

California Postsecondary Education Commission. *Promises to Keep*. Sacramento: California Postsecondary Education Commission, 1983.

Cohen, A. M., and Brawer, F. B. *The American Community College.* San Francisco: Jossey-Bass, 1982.

Collins, C. C. *Junior College Student Personnel Programs—What They Are and What They Should Be.* Washington, D.C.: American Association of Junior Colleges, 1967.

Cross, K. P. "Community Colleges on the Plateau." *Journal of Higher Education,* 1981, *52* (2), 113–123.

Deegan, W. L. *The Management of Student Affairs Programs in Community Colleges: Revamping Processes and Structures.* Washington, D.C.: American Association of Community and Junior Colleges/ERIC Clearinghouse for Junior Colleges, 1982.

Deegan, W. L., and Drisko, R. "Contract Training in Community Colleges." *Community and Junior College Journal,* 1985, *55* (6), 14–17.

Deegan, W. L., Steele, B., and Thielen, T. *Translating Theory Into Practice: Implications of Japanese Management Theory for Student Personnel Administration.* Monograph series no. 3. Columbus, Ohio: National Association of Student Personnel Administrators, 1985.

McCabe, R. H., and Skidmore, S. B. "Miami-Dade: Results Justify Reforms." *Community and Junior College Journal,* 1983, *54* (1), 26–29.

National Commission on Excellence in Education. *A Nation at Risk: The Imperative for Educational Reform.* Washington, D.C.: National Commission on Excellence in Education, 1983.

Peters, T. J., and Waterman, R. H., Jr. *In Search of Excellence: Lessons from America's Best-Run Companies.* New York: Harper & Row, 1982.

Southern Regional Education Board. *Remedial Education in College: The Problem of Underprepared Students.* Atlanta, Ga.: Southern Regional Education Board, 1983.

Index

❖❖❖❖❖❖❖❖❖❖❖❖❖❖❖❖❖❖❖❖❖❖❖❖❖❖